In Peace
Let Us Pray to
the Lord

IN PEACE LET US PRAY TO THE LORD

An Orthodox Interpretation of the Gifts of the Spirit

Fr. Alexis (Trader)
Monastery of Karakallou
Mount Athos, Greece

ISBN 1-928653-06-5

Cover Photo: "Pentecost" Byzantine Icon, twelfth century. St. Catherine's Monastery, Sinai. Used by permission.

Regina Orthodox Press
P.O. Box 5288
Salisbury, MA 01952
1-800-636-2470
FAX: 978-462-5079

www.reginaorthodoxpress.com

Table of Contents

CONTENTS

PART II
The Pentecostal Churches

CONTENTS

CONTENTS

About the Author

Fr. Alexis (1965-) was raised in a fervent Methodist household in which he was exposed to Protestantism in its liberal, ecumenical, evangelical, and pentecostal manifestations. He also received instruction in Roman Catholicism while attending a parochial high school. In his early teens, he asked his Sunday school teacher some questions about the Truth in his denomination that remained unanswered. From that time onwards, he began to search for Christ and His Church. In reading Dostoyevsky's *The Brothers Karamazov*, he encountered a strange yet beautiful Christianity that seemed so very humble and true that he decided to find that church in America.

After receiving a B.A. in chemistry at Franklin and Marshall College in Lancaster, PA (1987) and later an M.A. in divinity at the University of Chicago (1988), he entered the Orthodox Church at St. Tikhon's monastery in South Canaan, PA (1989). There, he received a M.Div. in Orthodox theology (1994), was tonsured a monk of the lesser schema, and taught in the adjacent seminary as a lecturer in patristics, offering courses in spirituality and the ascetic tradition.

To further his education, he was sent to Greece to study modern Greek (1995). While studying in Thessalonica, he spent much time on the Holy Mountain and came to the decision, with the blessing of his spiritual father, that the Garden of the Mother of

God was the place in which he was to work out his salvation. Since 1996, he has remained in the Monastery of Karakallou on the Holy Mountain happily preparing vegetables in the monastery kitchen.

Prologue

This present study was written in order to answer some sincere yet pointed questions of a close relative who has been involved in the charismatic movement and Pentecostal Churches for the past thirty years. "What is wrong with tongues," she would ask, "since Saint Paul spoke in tongues more than all the rest?" "Why do the Orthodox resist speaking in tongues?" "How do the Orthodox understand Saint Paul's description of tongues in *First Corinthians* and Saint Luke's description in *Acts?* "

These were not the idle questions of someone disinterested in the Truth. This relative of mine was quite open to Holy Orthodoxy and would willing read the writings and lives of Orthodox Saints and marvel at the wisdom contained therein. Being unsatisfied with any current treatises written on the subject, I began to comb the writings of the Holy Fathers in order to find an illumined response to my relative's specific questions and to help her to evaluate Pentecostalism as a whole. Realizing that there are others who may have similar questions, I offer this labor of love to them as well.

At this time, I should express my gratitude to Father Damaskinos of the Cell of the Forerunner at Karakallou Monastery for his helpful suggestions for this manuscript in its earliest form. I should also like to thank Father Sergios Black and Father Seraphim Bell for their encouragement. And above all, I must thank Archimandrite Philotheos, Abbot of the Monastery of Karakallou on the Holy Mountain, for without his blessing, his support, and his prayers, none of this would have been possible.

For all inadequacies of thought or expression that the kind reader will encounter, I am fully responsible and ask his indulgence and forgiveness.

fr. alexis (trader)
The Feast of the Holy Apostles Peter and Paul, 2000
The Holy Monastery of Karakallou, the Holy Mountain of Athos

Introduction

1. The Orthodox Church and the Gift of Tongues

Following our Lord's Holy Resurrection, He Himself told His divine Apostles that "they shall speak with new tongues (languages)" as a sign following belief in Him. And indeed, the Apostles did speak "in new languages" and with renewed tongues. On the day of Holy Pentecost, by the Grace of the Holy Spirit, they proclaimed the Gospel of Christ before those foreigners present at Jerusalem who in turn heard the apostolic proclamation in their native tongue as the foreigners themselves bore witness: "we do hear them speak in our languages the wonderful works of God."[1] Before tyrants and rulers, they spoke the words of "the new language" of Grace inspired by the self-same Spirit. "For I," Christ told His disciples, "will give you a mouth and wisdom, which all your adversaries shall not be able to gainsay nor resist."[2] Finally with "psalms and spiritual songs," they spoke "the new language" of prayer in their hearts through the Grace of the Divine Spirit following the Apostle Paul's exhortation: "teaching and admonishing one another in psalms and hymns and spiritual songs, singing with grace in your hearts to the Lord."[3]

---

[1] *Acts* 2:11.
[2] *Luke* 21:15.
[3] *I Colossians* 3:16.

In Christ's Holy Church, these "new languages" have always been present. One need only turn to the lives of the Martyrs and Confessors to see Christians speaking a new language, full of wisdom and strength that no philosopher or clever sage could overturn. One need only look to the Great Ecumenical Teachers and Fathers of the Church to find that "new language" that is able to formulate the saving Truth of Christ that purifies the heart, illumines the soul, and unites man with God. One need only read the lives of the God-bearing fathers, "of whom the world was not worthy," who lived "in deserts, and in mountains, and in dens and caves of the earth,"[4] to encounter a "new language" sanctified by fasting and tears, the pure, yet silent, tongue of the prayer of the heart.

At the same time, it is clear that "speaking in tongues," when interpreted (or misinterpreted) *literally* as the gift of "speaking in foreign languages" is by no means the *sine qua non* of sanctity encountered in the life of every saint. In every generation there are those who are given the grace to heal the sick in soul and body. There are those who through the grace of the Holy Spirit are intimately united with God in prayer. There are those who can see deep into the hearts of men. There are those who can see the future as though it were the present.[5] Yet, it seems

---

[4] *Hebrews* 11:38.

[5] Cf., Saint Paul's list of the gifts of the Spirit: "For to one is given by the Spirit the word of wisdom; to another the word of knowledge by the same Spirit; to another faith by the same Spirit; to another the gifts of healing by the same Spirit; to an-

that only a few literally speak "foreign languages" by the grace of the Holy Spirit. Modern Pentecostals, Charismatics and non-denominational, born-again Christians clearly see this as a "deficiency." Saint John Chrysostom himself in fact bewailed the difference between the presence of the gifts (and above all virtue) in the first days of the Church and his own time, but he did not seek to acquire a gift that was God's to give, but sought to acquire virtue and holiness, those fruits of the synergy between the human and divine will, fruits which in turn through the grace of God have the power to unite God with man.[6] The Orthodox Christian's broad vision of the meaning of salvation (man's restoration to spiritual health), with the aid of his spiritual father, gives him the perspective necessary to perceive what he in fact lacks. Furthermore, he understands from experience that everything that takes place in his own life and that of the Church at large is governed by the Wisdom of God. Gifts are given not at random, but according to the will of God to those good and faithful servants who have been faithful with a little. And these God-given gifts are precisely what are needed for the salvation of the believer and those around him. It is no deficiency for a heart surgeon to be lacking a plumber's wrench.

Thus, the Holy Orthodox Church was never subjected to a "Protestant Reformation" because, un-

other the working of miracles; to another prophecy; to another discerning of spirits; to another divers kinds of tongues; to another the interpretation of tongues." (*1 Corinthians* 12:8-10).

[6] Cf., the commentary on *First Corinthians*.

16

like the Roman Catholic Church, the Orthodox Church never ceased to pursue Her Apostolic mission of healing the souls of those who turned to Her in faith.[7] In other words, She never fell into heresy, which spreads spiritual sickness rather than healing it. Likewise, She was never in need of "a Charismatic renewal" in order for Her children to experience the life of the Holy Spirit. To assert such is to assert that the Church is not the Church, to utter "a blasphemy against the Holy Spirit."[8] Father J. Romanides notes, "we literally cannot speak about renewal of the life of the Church since:

> 1). The Church is the Body of Christ in Whom the believers abide and with Whom the members of the Church are filled from Pentecost.
>
> 2). The life of the Church is the glory of the Holy Trinity in the human nature of the Word; it is the house of God and the faithful.

Thus, neither the Church nor Her life are renewed. Only Her members are renewed."[9]

---

[7] Even the most superficial study of the Medieval Papacy indicates a radical shift in the Papacy's understanding of its mission after the eighth century. For an enlightening interpretation of the cause of this change, please see J. Romanides *Franks, Romans, and Feudalism.*

[8] *Matthew* 12:31.

[9] Father John Romanides, "Test for the Application of Theology," pages 474-475 (in Greek).

IN PEACE LET US PRAY TO THE LORD

In the Holy Orthodox Church, the grace of the Holy Spirit is tangibly present in all the aspects of Her life. The believer experiences Divine Grace through the Holy Mysteries, through the Divine Services, through the Holy Icons, through the Holy Relics, through the divine writings (scriptural and patristic), through those perfected members of the Church (the Saints in both the Church militant and triumphant), through obedience to his spiritual father, and his own labors at prayer. For this reason, the believer is not in need of some "movement" outside of the Church to supply him with that which the Church so naturally possesses in abundance. He is aware of his spiritual sickness and the Church places the means for his recovery at his disposal.

2. Intuitions and Convictions

Those outside of the Holy Orthodox Church, however, find themselves in a radically different and most difficult situation. The sincere among them feel the presence of a sickness within themselves in particular and within the institutions to which they belong in general, but are lacking the diagnostic tools to determine its causes with precision and to apply the appropriate remedy with certainty. They are aware that their "church" is not providing them with the fullness of life that they recognize in the Gospels, but again they are not in a position (i.e., a state of spiritual health) to determine what is lacking or to "form a church" that will be "the fullness of Him that

18

filleth all in all."[10] They sense the lack of grace in the sterile forms of Protestant worship. They recognize the truth of Savior's affirmation that "God is a Spirit: and they that worship Him must worship Him in spirit and in truth."[11] But again, who left to his own devices can chart a path from the sterility of Protestant worship to that worship in spirit and in truth?

Nevertheless, in the early part of the twentieth century, a new movement in Christianity began at the Bethel Bible College in Topeka, Kansas through the spiritual experimentation of Charles Parham. This new movement, known initially as the Pentecostal movement and later infiltrating Protestantism and Catholicism as the Charismatic movement, was for many Christians an answer to the dryness of their more conventional forms of worship. Those Christians who were initiated into this new form of worship that culminated in what was identified as "speaking in tongues" entered a new realm of spiritual pleasure and power. Few, however, would question precisely what world they had entered, perhaps fearing that such would be "a blasphemy against the Holy Spirit."

The basically correct initial intuitions of the modern Pentecostals or Charismatics[12] concerning

---

[10] *Ephesians* 1:23.

[11] *John* 4:24.

[12] Unless specified otherwise, when we employ the term "Pentecostal," we also include the Charismatics and the Christians of the Third Wave, for despite the understandable protests that these latter groups differ from the original Pentecostals,

19

much of Protestantism would, in turn, give them the strong inward conviction that their participation in the Pentecostalism is also quite correct, especially since their worship is certainly more "alive" than what they encountered in the "dead" Protestant worship services. Being convinced by "real experiences," they find it quite difficult to accept another interpretation, nor are they inclined to examine the subject more carefully, especially since there is a lack of sound teaching on the dangers of spiritual deception and the importance of humility, self-reproach, and not believing one's thoughts (*logismoi*). Their logic is rather straightforward. "I believe in Christ. I am sincerely seeking the Holy Spirit. The experience I have *must* be of the Holy Spirit. My experience *must* correspond to the experience of the Apostles at Pentecost and that of those in the Church of Corinth."

What most convinces the Pentecostal about the propriety of his participation in the Pentecostal worship, however, is not cool logic, but warm emotion, a certain spiritual pleasure that he experiences in Pentecostal meetings. The precept of modern man—"if it feels good, do it"—can be applied not only to the carnal sphere, but also to the subtlety of the spiritual realm. Again the absence of teaching on the subtle workings of grace and deception as well as the enormity of the problematic of pleasure and pain in the life of man after the Fall prevents the Pentecostal from questioning the source of the spiritual pleasure

their understanding of Pentecost and tongues is essentially the same.

he feels and from distinguishing it from genuine spiritual sweetness.

A third factor that strengthens the Pentecostal's certainty is the feeling that to reject this seemingly central part of his understanding about Christianity would be equivalent to the rejection of everything he has learned about Christ. He knows in his heart that it is right to love Christ, that it is right to try to live in accord with His commandments, and that it is good to read Holy Scripture. As he mixes his "Pentecostal experiences" together with the above entirely honorable positions, he finds it difficult to reject his experiences without calling into question the entirety of his Christian beliefs that rest upon the foundation of pentecostal experiences.

Finally, the Pentecostal Christian believes that he is being faithful to Holy Scripture precisely as Martin Luther *thought* he was being faithful to Holy Scripture. And as Luther based his new Protestant Christianity on his own interpretation of *Romans,* in particular justification by faith, to the exclusion of other parts of Scripture, in like manner the modern day Pentecostal bases his new Pentecostal Christianity on his own interpretation of *Acts* and *First Corinthians* (especially chapters 12-14). Since Scripture is true, seeking to follow the life portrayed in Scripture *as he understands it* must also be true.

With this being said, it is understandable how difficult it is for the modern Pentecostal to question his experience, above all, because he has given his innermost self, his very soul, over to a method of prayer that for him defines his identity as a Christian. It is so personal that to reject it may seem to be for him a rejection of his innermost self. Thus, it requires a great deal of courage, self-denial, and an ardent desire for the Truth for him to make a closer and more objective examination of Pentecostalism. If he does so, however, he has nothing to lose and everything to gain.

During the past two decades, a large group of Evangelical Protestants began to ask themselves *how* they can be assured that their interpretation of Holy Scripture is correct. Their search led them to the conclusion that they needed to investigate how those who lived closest to the time of the Apostles interpreted Scripture. Their search led them to the Holy Orthodox Church. If contemporary Pentecostals would dare to ask a similar question, *how* they can be assured that their experience of the Holy Spirit is genuine, they would no doubt follow their former Evangelical brethren to the same haven. Even as those former Evangelicals found a Church far more scriptural than anything they formerly imagined, so Pentecostals would find a church much more laden with the gifts and especially the fruits of the Holy Spirit than anything they could possibly conceive.

There are already several admirable studies available that offer an Orthodox response to the Charismatic movement or Pentecostal churches. Father Seraphim Rose situates the movement within the modern religious consciousness and finds startling parallels with non-Christian phenomena. Father John Morris examines the movement in the context of Church history and doctrine. The Abbot

George refers to the movement in terms of the goal of the Christian life. These studies, however, seem to be oriented primarily to Orthodox Christians that might be curious about Pentecostalism and do not always prove to be so helpful with Charismatics who are still involved in the Charismatic movement or Pentecostals in the Pentecostal churches. Furthermore, the aforementioned studies neither provide a sufficiently detailed examination of the relevant chapters of *Acts* and *First Corinthians,* nor make use of Father John Romanides' masterful exegesis of these same passages.

When Saint Gregory the Theologian was speaking about the Holy Spirit on the feast of Pentecost, there were present at that time those who believed that the Holy Spirit was God, those who vehemently denied the divinity of the Holy Spirit, and finally those who did not accept the divinity of the Holy Spirit, but were willing to listen and desired to discover the Truth. With respect to this third group with open hearts, but unclear minds, he said, "It is necessary to lead them forward step by step, slowly elevating them to higher things, granting them light by light, and guiding them to the one Truth by smaller truths."[13] This present little study is devoted precisely to that third group of sincere seekers of Christ who desire the Truth above all else,

[13] Saint Gregory the Theologian, "Discourse 41 on Pentecost" *The Complete Works of Gregory the Theologian, Discourses 5,* Greek Fathers of the Church text, trans. (into modern Greek), and comments by Panagiotos Christos, (Gregory Palamas Patristic Publications, Thessalonika, 1977) page 126 (in Greek).

being mindful that the Truth sets us all free. The words of Saint Silouan to a young Orthodox missionary among other confessions will serve as a guide,

> Father Archimandrite, people feel in their souls when they are doing the proper thing, believing in Jesus Christ, revering the Mother of God and the Saints, whom they call upon in prayer, so if you condemn their faith they will not listen to you. But if you were to confirm that they were doing well to believe in God and honor the Mother of God and the Saints; that they are right to go to church, and say their prayers at home, and read the Divine word, and so on: and then gently point out their mistakes and show them what they ought to amend, then they would listen to you, the Lord would rejoice over them. And this way by God's mercy we shall all find salvation. God is love and therefore the preaching of His word must always proceed from love. Then both preacher and listener will profit.[14]

With such in mind, the following study is offered to help contemporary Pentecostals to properly evaluate their own experiences and the movement as

---

[14] Archimandrite Sophrony (Sakharov), *Saint Silouan the Athonite,* trans. by Rosemary Edmonds (Stavropegic Monastery of Saint John the Baptist: Essex, 1991), pages 64-67.

a whole. As they base their Pentecostal experience on their reading of *Acts* and *First Corinthians*, it seems wise to examine the interpretation which the spirit-bearing and truly charismatic Fathers of the Church provide for these scriptural passages relating to Pentecost and the gift of speaking in tongues. As their own personal experience is so crucial for them, we will also sketch out the characteristics of experiences of grace and experiences of deception, together with the proper place of experience in the Christian life as a whole. Only with such a framework in place, can we then examine together and appraise the history, teaching, and practice of the Pentecostal movements. As the experience of others is also important to them, it seems worthwhile also to include as an appendix some significant excerpts from the Lives of the Saints past and present in which by the grace of God, communication between those who spoke different languages took place.

Such an examination, however, by no means pretends to be a full answer to the Pentecostal seeker. For while Pentecostal Christianity justifies itself on the basis of its understanding of Saint Paul's *First Epistle to the Corinthians* and certain passages in *the Acts of the Apostles*, the Orthodox Church is not based on any given Scriptural passage, nor selection of passages, nor Scripture in its entirety, nor even on the wealth of Patristic writings, but on Christ and communion with Him to which the Prophets, Apostles and Saints bear witness in written and oral form (Scripture and Tradition).[15] Thus, this small study hopes but to offer a preliminary answer, and an invitation to a more thorough examination of the fruits of intimate communion with Christ (the patristic writings) and above all to that communion with Christ that the Holy Orthodox Church opens to all.

[15] Fr. John Romanides, *Dogmatic and Symbolic Theology of the Orthodox Catholic Church,* (Pournara: Thessalonica, 1983) page 109 (in Greek).

PART ONE

THE CHURCH OF PENTECOST:
THE HOLY ORTHODOX CHURCH

Quotations on "Tongues" and the Prayer of the Heart

And *they were all filled with the Holy Ghost,* and *began to speak with other tongues.*

— Saint Luke,
The Acts of the Apostles 2:4

When the Holy Spirit dwells in a man, as the Apostle says, *he never ceases to pray,* since the Spirit Himself prays within him. Then, whether he sleeps or wakes, prayer is never separated from his soul. If he eats, drinks, or lies down, or does something, or even in deep slumber, the sweet fragrance of prayer effortlessly exhale in his heart.[1]

— Saint Isaac the Syrian,
The Ascetic Homilies, 37

I will pray with the spirit, and I will pray with the mind also: I will sing with the spirit, and I will sing with the mind also.

— Saint Paul,
The First Epistle to the Corinthians 14:15

Movements produced in the soul by the Divine Spirit as a result of efforts make the heart quiet *and urge it to call out constantly:* '*Abba Father!*' This is not accompanied by any imaginings but is

---

[1] *The Ascetic Homilies of Saint Isaac the Syrian* trans. by. Holy Transfiguration Monastery (Holy Transfiguration Monastery, Boston: 1984) page 182.

devoid of all images. But we ourselves become than transformed by the dawning of Divine Light, which endows us with an image in keeping with the burning of the Divine Spirit. More than that, it changes and alters us by Divine power. How -- He alone knows.[2]

— Saint Kallistos, "Texts on Prayer."

[2] *Writings from the Philokalia on Prayer of the Heart,* trans. by E. Kadloubovsky and G.E. Palmer (London, Faber and Faber: 1992) page 272.

Interpretive Choices in *Acts* and *First Corinthians* on Tongues and Spiritual Gifts

1. Inspiration, Revelation, and Interpretation

"That which we have seen and heard declare we unto you, that ye also may have fellowship with us: and truly our fellowship is with the Father, and with his Son Jesus Christ. And these things write we unto you, that your joy may be full."
— *1 John* 1:3-4

Before we examine the patristic interpretation of the scriptural passages that seem most relevant to Pentecostalism, it is necessary to be clear about the nature and purpose of all inspired writings (scriptural and patristic) and the proper Orthodox approach to them. Only by coming to terms with what is divine inspiration can we in turn choose the appropriate method for interpretation. Only by being precise about what is revelation and why the Fathers wrote their writings can we in turn judge what can be learned and what can not be learned from a brief examination of patristic commentaries.

Every Christian confession can agree that the Old Testament and New Testament are inspired as well as certain interpretations of these scriptures.[1] All agree that the very words of the Old Testament and New Testament are inspired, but there is a vast chasm separating the Orthodox and non-Orthodox understanding of what the Prophet, Apostle, or Saint "hears" and what he "writes down."

Protestants and Roman Catholics have long identified Revelation with the Bible, making no real distinction between the written word and the experience that is the source of that written word. The "traditional Augustinian" Western view is that the Prophet, Apostle, or Saint simply "writes down" what he hears. The Holy Spirit dictates, and the Prophet transcribes word for word. No special attention is placed upon the purity of the Prophet's heart, nor the grace that enables his spiritual eyes to see and his spiritual ears to hear. In fact, the experience of the Prophet or Apostle, outside of what he himself relates, remains utterly unknown. Hence, the "conservative" maintain a doctrine of inerrancy of divine inspiration in which the Prophets and Apostles wrote what they heard much like the Muslims suppose that Mohammed wrote the Koran. The "liberal" more "progressive" wing, on the other hand, insert an "(undeified) human element" that is self-destructive

---

[1] For the Orthodox, the trusted interpretations are the Patristic Writings of the god-bearing fathers. For those other Confessions, the founders' interpretations are seen as God-inspired whereas the interpretation of their opponents as inspired by the devil (e.g., the famous debate between Luther and Zwingli over the words of institution). Father John Romanides, "Test for the Application of Theology," pages 482-483.

to their very understanding of inspiration, for if this human element results in an inability to transcribe accurately the words of the Spirit, but results in a mixture of human reflections and those of the Spirit, than what is written is by necessity no longer entirely inspired. Both "liberal" and "conservative" alike, however, readily turn to linguistic or cultural studies in order to interpret the inspired text, because the written word is the only "given" with which they can work.[2]

In the Orthodox Church, the experience of the Prophet, Apostle, or Saint is not some unknown phenomenon, but is the vision beyond sight of the uncreated glory of Christ "seen" by the believer who has been purified, illumined, and is now in a state of deification.[3] Given this empirical knowledge, the Ortho-

---

[2] Ultimately, this understanding of inspiration and Holy Scripture is based on the fact that they do not believe that revelation takes place via the uncreated energies of the Holy Spirit, but through divinely created words. Ibid., page 478.

[3] We shall discuss these three stages in the Christian life at length in the following two chapters. In brief, purification refers to the purification of the passions, the thoughts, and deceitful desires of the heart; illumination refers to the Holy Spirit illumining the heart and the gift of unceasing inner prayer in the heart activated by the Holy Spirit; deification refers to the vision of Christ that likewise transfigures the one who sees Him. This final stage of deification is also referred to by the biblical terms "perfection" ("this also we wish, even your perfection." *2 Corinthians* 13:9) and glorification ("And the glory which Thou gavest Me I have given them; that they may be one, even as We are one" (*John* 17: 22).

dox Church teaches that Revelation and the Bible are not identical and that a real distinction exists between the written word and the experience that is the source of that written word. When the Prophets, Apostles, and Saints speak to men in their writings, the words that they speak are created words, words belonging to this world, but they are also a "translation" of the ineffable and unutterable uncreated words that the deified Prophet, Apostle, or Saint heard in a state of deification[4] and in precisely this sense his words are inspired. While the ineffable uncreated "words" that the Prophets, Apostles or Saints hear utterly transcend the expressions and concepts of man, the created spoken words that employ human expression and metaphor, nevertheless, are divinely inspired and "unerringly guide those in the Church

Although the concept of "deification" is most unfamiliar to Western Christians, it is for the Orthodox Church the ultimate goal of the believer and the deepest purpose of the incarnation. "For ye know the grace of our Lord Jesus Christ, that, though He was rich, yet for your sakes he became poor, that ye through his poverty might be rich" (*2 Corinthians* 8:9). The precise term deification was first employed by the champion of Orthodoxy Saint Athanasios who wrote, "God became man, so that man might become god (by grace)."

Saint Paul personally refers to this state of deification when he writes, "I knew a man in Christ above fourteen years ago, (whether in the body, I cannot tell; or whether out of the body, I cannot tell: God knoweth;) such an one caught up to the third heaven. And I knew such a man, (whether in the body, or out of the body, I cannot tell: God knoweth; How that he was caught up into paradise, and heard unspeakable words, which it is not lawful for a man to utter" (*2 Corinthians* 12: 2-4).

[4] Ibid., page 492.

who are walking on the path of the deified towards deification. Outside of this path, the same words lead to deception."[5]

The above theological framework has a direct bearing on our understanding of what is related in *Acts* and in Saint Paul's *First Epistle to the Corinthians*. A literal interpretation that ignores the experience of the deified as the source and reference of the text in question will not yield the intended meaning, but gross and wooden caricatures that no longer serve as apophatic metaphors for the uncreated energy of divine grace that transcends the mind of created man. If these caricatures then become the signposts for the spiritual life, those who follow them will necessarily "leave the paths of uprightness, to walk in the ways of darkness."[6]

It follows from what has been said, that in order to understand (and thus rightly employ) any divinely-inspired text (Patristic or Scriptural), one must be in turn inspired by the same Holy Spirit, and not merely equipped with the proper linguistic/cultural interpretive apparatus. In other words, to understand the texts of the deified one must be in the process of deification.[7] This means that in order to

[5] Father John Romanides, *The Dogmatic and Symbolic Theology of the Orthodox Catholic Church,* page 168 (in Greek).

[6] *Proverbs* 2:13.

[7] Fr. J. Romanides puts it so very well: "Not only he who writes, but also he who reads must know letters. Not only he who writes about mathematics, but also he who interprets what is written by the mathematician must know mathematics. The same holds true precisely for the delivered texts of every science

understand such texts properly one must have become a "vessel 'capable of containing' the divine energies and an icon representing Christ in some way," so that the "life of Christ that is human and divine interpenetrates the life of the believer" so that "all (of God) entirely interpenetrates all of the worthy, and all the saints entirely interpenetrate God, receiving in turn all of God."[8] For this reason, the use of patristic texts makes a study no more patristic than the use of Scripture makes it scriptural, for the crucial issue is leading the life that produces such texts. To acquire what Father Florovsky called "the patristic mind," it is necessary to acquire a "patristic heart," that is acquired only by walking along the same path of the Fathers: through participating in the Holy Mysteries under the direction of a spiritual father, leading a life of repentance, keeping the commandments, uprooting the passions, cultivating the virtues, and devoting oneself to prayer.

Hence, the best way to understand what is being described in *the Acts of the Apostles* and in

whatsoever. And for what reason should Holy Scripture be exempt? In it is recorded the experience of the deified prophets concerning God, His Kingdom, and His glory. How does the general scientific rule not apply in this case? That in other words, those who correctly read and interpret this experience of the deified be those who belong to the community of those deified in Christ?" Ibid., pages 174-175.

[8] Anestis Keselopoulos, *The Passions and the Virtues According to the Teaching of Saint Gregory Palamas,* (Domos Publishers: Athens, 1990) pages 208 and 200 respectively (citing Saint Gregory Palamas, *On Behalf of the Hesychasts,* 3, 1, 27) (in Greek).

Saint Paul's *First Epistle to the Corinthians* is to lead
a life in accord with the life that produced such texts.
Moreover by extension, to understand the very commentaries of the Holy Fathers on these passages, it is
likewise necessary to lead a life in accord with the
life that produced these commentaries. In fact, there
is but one life that all the deified friends of Christ
(Prophets, Apostles, and Saints) share which begins
with the purification of the passions through repentance and is made perfect in the self same vision of
the glory of Christ in the Holy Spirit. For those in the
middle stage of illumination, God does open "their
understanding, that they might understand the
scriptures."[9] For those of us who are still at the beginning stages of the life in Christ, however, the saf-
est and humblest path is to listen with faith and
simplicity of heart to the voices of those who "have
seen and heard"[10] and let their voices guide us in the
way we should go.

---

[9] *Luke* 24:45.
[10] *Acts* 4:20; 22:15, and *I John* 1:3.

2. Patristic Interpretations: Boldness, Truth, and Pastoral Needs

'The wicked flee when no man pursueth: but the righteous are bold as a lion."

— *Proverbs* 28:1

It has been rightly observed that "Orthodoxy is bolder than heresy," for the vision of Orthodoxy is based not on the puny reason of fallen man, but on the divine revelation of the glory of Christ to those purified souls who have been healed of the disease of sin. It is bolder, because its vantagepoint is not acquired through earthly investigations with speculations about eternity, but through the experience of eternity in this earthly life.[11] Thus, while the fallen logic of the unillumined Arius could not imagine how Christ could be anything greater than the highest of all creation, the illumined and god-bearing Fathers *beheld* and confessed Christ, Light of Light, True God of True God. And thus it is with so many passages of Scripture in the hands of the illumined and the unillumined. In the hands of the unillumined, the Scriptures resemble a chest full of all manner of jewels and precious stones that they carry about by quoting and commenting on, but that they cannot open (that is, understand or utilize), for the key is Christ Who opens the treasure chest of Scripture to those who become like Him.[12] The "boldness of Or-

[11] "and we beheld his glory" *John* 1:4
[12] Saint Simeon the New Theologian, "Discourse 24 on Spiritual Knowledge," *Catechetical Discourses*, Philokalia of

thodoxy" based on the vision of Christ in glory can especially be seen in the hesychastic[13] interpretation of both Pentecost and Saint Paul's often quoted, but seldom understood, discourse on tongues in his *First Epistle to the Corinthians.* From the onset, it must be stressed that the hesychastic interpretation is neither a spiritualization nor an allegorization of the Scriptural text, but an approach based on the experience of those perfected in Christ. Far from being subjective, it is an objective approach *par excellence,* for it employs the very tools appropriate to the subject being investigated.

In examining the patristic commentaries on Pentecost in *Acts* and on spiritual gifts in *Corinthians,* we find a general consensus concerning virtue and purification, but a divergence of opinion on the precise nature of tongues. The presence of two very different interpretations raises two fundamental questions that must be answered before one can proceed to examine the interpretations themselves: first why is there a divergence of opinion and second, how can one determine which opinion is the most correct.

In response to the first question, we know that the Truth to which the Fathers bore witness was one, but the needs which they faced were many indeed.

Neptic and Ascetic Fathers, 19D, text, trans. (into modern Greek), and comments by Demetrius Rizo and Katherine Goltsou, (Gregory Palamas Patristic Publications: Thessalonika, 1989) pages 290-294 (in Greek).

[13] Hesychasm is the spiritual and ascetic discipline accompanying the practice of stillness and inner prayer.

The Fathers were expert physicians who were compelled not only to respond to the various spiritual diseases that troubled man (sins and the passions) and to offer advice for leading a healthy life (of virtue and grace), but also to respond to unsound medical practice (the teaching of heretics[14]) that can wreak more far-reaching destruction than any epidemic. Hence, some Fathers wrote dogmatic works in order to safe-guard the saving Truth that enables man to be purified, illumined, and perfected. Other Fathers wrote specifically about the art of the spiritual life again to help their brethren at various stages of purification, illumination or perfection. In every case, unselfish love for their fellow man and a desire to see his glorification (or perfection) guided the Fathers in the words they would write or utter.

The various commentaries and comments by the Fathers on the passages of Holy Scriptures must be understood in this context. All the Fathers had a deep understanding of Holy Scripture, but in many cases their words were measured according to what those who listened to them were capable of "hearing." When Saint John Chrysostom, the King of the Exegetes, first began to speak as Patriarch in Constantinople, the faithful recognized his wisdom, but could not understand the concepts he was trying to ex-

---

[14] Those in positions of teaching authority (priests and bishops) who have not yet reached the stage of illumination or perfection. Cf., Fr. J. Romanides, "Justice and Peace in Ecclesiological Context," in *Come, Holy Spirit Renew the Whole Creation* ed. by Gennadios Limouris (Holy Cross Orthodox Press: Brookline, 1990) page 246.

press. Taking this to heart, the Saint henceforth began to speak to the people at a level that they could understand. He found himself speaking to people who were still given over to the passions of love for money, pleasure, and glory.[15] In other words, he had to speak to those who at best were progressing towards a state of purification. Thus, many of his interpretations remain on the surface simply because those who heard him were not sufficiently advanced in the spiritual life to dive deeper into the meaning of what is portrayed in Scripture. In spite of this fact (or perhaps because of it[16]), his interpretations became standard guides for Scriptural interpretation. Saint John Damascus, Blessed Theophylact of Bulgaria, and Saint Nicodemus of the Holy Mountain[17] basically provide the pious believer with Chrysostom's interpretations in a condensed version.

In order to find a deeper interpretation of Scripture, it is often necessary to turn to those Fathers whose words were directed to those close to or in a state of illumination. In other words, one needs to turn to many of the Fathers who shown forth in asceticism and whose writings are contained in *The Philokalia* and other such compilations of ascetic

---

[15] As the exhortations that close his many homilies bear witness.

[16] Since at the stages of illumination and especially glorification, the Holy Spirit leads the believer into all Truth.

[17] Saint Nicodemus does, however, annotate Saint Theophylact's commentaries with a variety of citations from other fathers as well.

writings. Their words are fewer, for they did not set out to provide those being purified with a comprehensive exegesis of Holy Scripture, but rather essayed to offer a few signposts for those being illumined. These signposts are quite precious, for they point to the heart of the reality that is portrayed in Scripture going beneath the letter to the life-giving Spirit.

3. Patristic Interpretations: The Spirit and the Letter

"The letter killeth, but the spirit giveth life."   — *2 Corinthians* 3:6.

Saint Maximus the Confessor often compares the distinction between the spirit and the letter in Scripture with the distinction between the inner *logos* and the appearance of created beings in creation and the *nous* and the senses in man.[18] Many falsely assume that the literal interpretation of Scripture which is based on both the senses and the appearances is the best reflection of "what really happened." In fact, such an interpretation which excludes the faculty of the soul that enters directly into communion with God (the *nous*) likewise excludes the possibility of even outwardly properly reflecting an event

---

[18] In this context, *logos* refers to the hidden message of the existence. In general, *nous* as an essence refers to the heart while as an energy, it refers to a kind of refined attention.

41

portrayed in Scripture,[19] for when the highest part of the soul (the *nous*) does not function properly, the senses themselves cannot properly function. And, since Scripture records in human created words man's experience of Christ's uncreated glory, an approach to Scripture uninformed by the prayer of the heart is in fact an approach to Scripture with inappropriate tools. It is as pointless as trying to understand poetry with a calculator (i.e., approaching it with the reason alone).

The outward or external interpretation, however, has its place. It is milk, and not firm food. It is what Saint Paul calls "thinking as a child." For those who are not purified, it can help lead them towards

---

[19] In one marvelous passage, the Saint writes, "He then who examines the symbols of the Law in a spiritual manner, and who contemplates the visible nature of created things with his *nous*, will discriminate in Scripture between the letter and spirit, in creation between inner essence and outward appearance, and in himself between *nous* and the senses; and in Scripture he will choose the spirit, in creation the inner essence or logos, and in himself the *nous*... In this way he will be delivered from all the things which deceive man and seduce him into innumerable errors—delivered that is to say from the letter, the outward appearance of things, and the senses, all of which posses quantitative distinctions and are the negation of unity. But if a man compounds the letter of the Law, the outward appearance of visible things, and his own senses with each other, he is 'so short-sighted as to be blind' (*2 Peter* 1:9), sick through his ignorance of the Cause of created beings." *The Philokalia: The Complete Text* comp. by St. Nikodimos of the Holy Mountain and St. Makarios of Corinth, trans. By G.E.H. Palmer, Philip Sherrard, and Kallistos Ware, vol. 2, (Faber and Faber: London, 1984), page 189.

an understanding, but to rely on it, or to make it exclusive, or predominant in the hands of those not yet illumined by the Holy Spirit can lead to shortsightedness. Saint Peter of Damascus in his discourse on the third stage of contemplation quite aptly treats this issue. He advises us not to be shocked or scandalized when we see apparent disagreements in the advice or interpretations of the Holy Fathers, but to realize that one kind of advice or interpretation is given to those whose *nous* functions properly (that is, to those who are united with God through unceasing prayer of the heart) and another kind is given to those whose *nous* does not yet function as it should. Following Saint John of Damascus, Saint Peter of Damascus likens the advice given to those whose souls are not yet healed to a ladder. It leads one up to the destination, but it is not the destination.[20]

4. The Sure and the Uncertain: A Choice of Interpretations

"The dream is certain, and the interpretation thereof sure."

— *Daniel* 2:45

When Saint Maximus the Confessor offered advice on the proper way to interpret Holy Scriptures, he commented, "If always understood in the same way, none of the persons, places, times, or any

---

[20] *The Philokalia: The Complete Text* comp. by St. Nikodimos of the Holy Mountain and St. Makarios of Corinth, trans. by G.E.H. Palmer, Philip Sherrard, and Kallistos Ware, vol. 3, (Faber and Faber: London, 1984), pages 119-120.

of the other things mentioned in Scripture, whether animate or inanimate, sensible or intelligible, will yield either the literal or spiritual sense intended. Thus he who wishes to study the divine knowledge of Scripture without floundering must respect the differences of the recorded events or sayings and interpret each in a different way, assigning to it the appropriate spiritual sense according to the context of place and time."[21] This counsel seems most appropriate as we begin to consider the second major explicit reference to speaking in tongues mentioned in Holy Scripture. We shall see that the first form we shall consider as recounted in *Acts* on the day of Pentecost is so inseparably linked to prophecy (utterances) and comprehensibility to those speaking other languages that some readers could overlook the presence of inner prayer and thus confuse the gift of tongues (inner prayer) with the other two more outward gifts, and thus conclude that gift of tongues was granted in order for the gospel of Christ to be proclaimed and understood.[22] Such readers would then suppose that the second form described in *First Corinthians* was a form of prayer that was employed in Christian worship and that excluded those without it. In fact, the great value of Saint Paul's discourse on tongues for the present study is that we encounter

[21] Saint Maximus, "Fourth Century of Various Texts," *The Philokalia*, v. II, page 253.

[22] Alevizopoulos, *Handbook of Heresies and Para-Christian Groups* (Preveza: Sacred Metropoliate of Nikopolis an Prevsezis, 1991), page 176 (in Greek).

the gift of tongues as distinct from the gifts of prophecy and comprehensibility that were united with it on Pentecost.

Our later examination of Saint *Paul's First Epistle to the Corinthians* and other epistles will make it clear that "speaking in tongues" is neither a matter of foreign languages nor strange sounds, but the ceaseless prayer of the heart by the Holy Spirit. This is moreover an interpretation of the early Christian writer Origen (185-255) which the Great Cappadocian Fathers did not reject. Unfortunately by the time of Saint John Chrysostom (344-407), most Antiochian circles began to teach that the "gift of the tongues" was the ability (gift) of the Apostles to speak in the languages of the people to whom they proclaimed the Gospel, instead of the gift of ceaseless prayer.[23] Noting the outward manifest gift of being able to communicate with those of other languages which the Apostles certainly possessed, the Antiochians failed to notice the more important inward gift of the prayer of the heart, referred to in Biblical terms as "speaking in tongues." Although Saint John Chrysostom clearly taught the absolute necessity of the gift of unceasing prayer, he, perhaps for pastoral reasons, perhaps under the influence of the prevailing interpretation, repeated the Antiochian interpretation of tongues as foreign languages.[24] The spirit of

[23] J. Romanides, "Jesus Christ- The Life of the World," in Despoinis Kontostergios' *The Ecumenical Councils* (Pournara: Thessalonica, 1997 page 346 (in Greek).

[24] We note that no Saint, even the greatest, is an infallible pope pontificating *ex cathedra* or uninfluenced by the particular

the entire patristic tradition and the New Testament, however, indicate that this interpretation is not adequate.

In Saint John Chrysostom's commentary on Saint Paul's *First Epistle to the Corinthians*, he identifies the kinds of tongues mentioned therein with the apostolic gift of comprehensibility on Pentecost and then confesses that "the whole passage is extremely unclear."[25] Assuming that what took place in the Church of Corinth had ceased to take place by his time (since people were not speaking in foreign languages in Church), Saint Chrysostom was compelled to provide an interpretation with which he himself

---

personal and historical context in which he has been placed. As a case in point, Saint Silouan the Athonite writes concerning the Most Pure Virgin, "The Mother of God never sinned even in thought. Thus did the Holy Spirit bear witness in my heart to her purity. But during her earthly life even she was not quite perfect and complete—she did make some mistakes that did not involve sin. We can see this from the Gospel when on the return from Jerusalem she did not know where her Son was, and together with Joseph sought Him for three days." Archimandrite Sophrony (Sakharov), *Saint Silouan the Athonite,* page 392.

[25] "The whole passage is extremely unclear. This lack of clairity is due to an ignorance of the situation and the absence of those things that happened then taking place now." Saint John Chrysostom, *Commentary on the First Epistle to the Corinthians* taken from *The Complete Works of Saint John Chrysostom,* 18A Discourse 29 Greek Fathers of the Church text, trans. (into modern Greek), and comments by Ioannis Pelitis, (Gregory Palamas Patristic Publications: Thessalonika, 1980) page 238 (in Greek).

was not satisfied.[26] The Saint's own doubts on this particular interpretation in turn prods the reader to question whether this assumption and identification are in fact true.

In contrast with Saint Chrysostom's misgivings on the subject, Saint Nikitas Stithatos with no uncertainty identifies the kinds of tongues mentioned in *First Corinthians* with the silent unceasing prayer by the Holy Spirit in the heart. It seems that by respecting "the differences of the recorded events" and interpreting "each in a different way, assigning to it the appropriate spiritual sense according to the context of time and place," Saint Nikitas was able both to make sense out of the situation in Corinth (and by extension of Pentecost), to draw out the deepest meaning of Saint Paul's passage on the gifts, and to provide practical instruction for the spiritual physicians of his day.[27]

---

[26] He asked in amazement, "what took place then? If someone was baptized he immediately began to speak in a foreign language, and not only languages, but also prophesied?" (Ibid.)

[27] Saint Chrysostom, on the contrary, by identifying the gift of Pentecost with the gift at Corinth, reached the conclusion that "the Church is now like a woman who has fallen from her former glory and possesses only the symbols in many areas of that ancient happiness, that points to the treasury where the gold was kept, but has lost her gold." Ibid., Discourse 36, page 512 (in Greek).

5. Spiritual Gifts, Prophecy, and Foreign Languages

"We... do not cease to pray for you, and to desire that ye might be filled with the knowledge of his will in all wisdom and spiritual understanding."

—Colossians 1:9

Since the proper interpretation of the relevant passages in *Acts* and *First Corinthians* are directly dependent upon one's understanding of spiritual gifts, prophecy and tongues, it seems prudent and only fair first to consider some of Saint Chrysostom's useful observations on prophecy and the spiritual gifts in accord with the universal opinion of the Fathers as well as his interpretation of the gift of tongues and the consequences of the same.[28] With this framework in place, we will be in a better position to patristically examine the texts.

According to the Fathers, spiritual gifts are given so that the struggling believer can more fully lead the Christian life by observing "all things what-

---

[28] In passing, we note that Saint John of Damascus and other commentators also followed Saint Chrysostom's treatment because of his well-earned reputation as an exegete of the epistles of the Apostle Paul. Cf., Saint John of Damascus *Commentary on the First Epistle to the Corinthians,* The Complete Works of John Damascus text, trans. (into modern Greek), and comments by Eleutherios Meretakis (Gregory Palamas Publications: Thessalonika, 1993) page 71 (in Greek).

soever Christ commanded the Apostles to do."[29] Saint
Maximus goes so far as to define a gift of the Spirit
as "every capacity for fulfilling a commandment," a
capability given according to man's faith and spiritual state.[30] This additional capacity, however, is
given only when the believer has shown himself to be
"faithful in very little"[31] by leading a life of virtue in
general and devoting himself to the life of inner
prayer in particular. God is quite ready to shed His
gifts upon His children, but his children first must
cleanse and ready the vessel (i.e., their entire existence: body and soul) in which the gifts can be received. Saint Basil the Great notes that God grants
His gifts not only with the benefit of others in mind,
but also according to the faith, peace, and purity from
the passions of the one receiving the gift.[32] In other
words, purification through repentance is required
before the believer reaches the stage of illumination
in which the gifts are given. Saint Maximus in one
passage notes the relation between the gift given and
man's receptivity: "Not even the grace of the Holy
Spirit can actualize wisdom in the saints unless
there is an intellect capable of receiving it; or spiritual knowledge unless there is a faculty of intelli-

[29] Cf., *Matthew* 28:20.

[30] Saint Maximus the Confessor, "First Century of Various
Texts," in *The Philokalia*, v. II, pages 186 and 187.

[31] *Luke* 19:17.

[32] Saint Nicodemus, *The Fourteen Epistles of the Divine and
Glorious Apostle Paul interpreted in Greek by Theophylact Archbishop of Bulgarius and translated in the more common dialect
and commented on by Nicodemus of the Holy Mountain.* Book 1
(Saint Nicodemus Press: Athens, 1971), page 326 (in Greek).

gence that can receive it, or faith unless there is the intellect and intelligence full of assurance about the realities to be disclosed hereafter or hidden from everyone; or gifts of healing unless there is natural compassion; or any other gift of grace without the disposition and faculty capable of receiving it."[33] Thus in order for a believer to receive spiritual gifts, he not only requires a general purity from the passions, but the good soil of a ready mind or heart well-fertilized with the virtue that most corresponds to that spiritual gift. The reception of spiritual gifts, like every aspect in the work of man's salvation, is the joint activity of (synergy between) the grace of God and the free will of man.

In addressing the issue of the use of tongues in the Church of Corinth, Saint Paul underlines the free will of the believer with spiritual gifts and the fact that they are not compelled to continue this practice even though they may be personally edified by it. He thus begins, "now concerning spiritual gifts, brethren, I would not have you ignorant. Ye know that ye were Gentiles, carried away unto these dumb idols, even as ye were led."[34] Here the Apostle points to one of the chief marks distinguishing between the gifts of the Holy Spirit and the false gifts of the fallen spirits: prudence and freedom. As Saint Maximus the Confessor puts it, "All the Saints show that God's grace

---

[33] Saint Maximus, "Fourth Century," in *The Philokalia*, v. II, page 239.

[34] *1 Corinthians* 12:1-2.

does not suspend man's natural powers."[35] This is in sharp contrast with the soothsayer or oracle who was possessed by an impure spirit and would be dragged about by the spirit not knowing what he was saying as if he were out of his mind. In fact, there are cases in antiquity in which the one making oracles would be slain by the evil spirit and fall to the ground wreathing on the floor because he could not endure the vehemence of the demon.[36] In passing, we note that the idolaters who were thus slain in the spirit considered their experience to be a divine one caused by the "gods" who cared for man, for they did not know that "all the gods of the nations are demons."[37] Only the heretical Montanists would be foolish enough to suggest that the Prophets similarly did not know or understand the meaning of what they said.[38]

Saint Basil the Great, Saint John Chrysostom and Saint Theophylact, on the other hand, insist that the Prophets were not in some sort of ecstasy[39] which

[35] Saint Maximus the Confessor, Fourth Century, *The Philokalia*, v. II, page 238.

[36] Saint John Chrysostom, *Commentary on the Epistle to the Corinthians*, Discourse 29 pages 244 and 246. Cf., Saint Nicodemus, *Commentary on the 14 Epistles*, page 322 (both in Greek).

[37] *Psalm* 95:5 (LXX).

[38] Saint Nicodemus, *Commentary on the 14 Epistles*, page 352 (in Greek).

[39] When we employ the term "ecstasy"/"ecstatic" here and elsewhere throughout this text, we are not referring to "intense joy or delight," but to "a state of emotion so intense that one is carried beyond thought and self-control." *Webster's II New College Dictionary*, (Houghton Mifflin Company: Boston, 1999) page 358.

would be the sign of a demonic influence.[40] Instead, the Prophets were "free to speak or not to speak," for this reason Jonah was able to flee, Ezekiel was able to postpone, and Jeremiah was able to give up.[41] When the Prophets spoke, they would do so with a watchful mind and sober heart in a calm state and with full awareness of what they were saying.[42] They were not subjected to "a spiritual gift," but the gift was subjected to them.[43] While the devil with violence causes an uproar, lunacy and a darkened mind, the Spirit of God enlightens and teaches by a means that befits the understanding.[44]

Given Saint Chrysostom's general understanding of spiritual gifts and the freedom, calmness and prudence of the prophet in particular, his identification of tongues with the supposed foreign languages of Pentecost[45] and liturgical prayer[46] is indeed

---

[40] Ibid., page 323 (in Greek).

[41] Saint John Chrysostom, *Commentary on the Epistle to the Corinthians,* Discourse 29 page 248 (in Greek).

[42] Ibid., page 244. Cf., Saint Nicodemus, *Commentary on the 14 Epistles,* pages 322-323(in Greek).

[43] Saint Nicodemus, *Commentary on the 14 Epistles,* page 359(in Greek).

[44] Saint John Chrysostom, *Commentary on the Epistle to the Corinthians,* Discourse 29, page 248 (in Greek).

[45] Ibid., Discourse 35, page 452 (in Greek).

[46] Ibid., Discourse 35, page 466 (in Greek). He writes, "the layman cannot answer and respond with the 'Amen,' because he did not hear the 'unto ages of ages,' that is the end of the exclamation." Cf., also, Saint Nicodemus, *Commentary on the 14 Epistles* page 353 and Saint Cyril of Alexandria, "On the First Epistle to the Corinthians," The Extent Works, volume 7 PA-

problematic. If kinds of tongues means speaking in foreign languages, where is the prudence for one to speak a language whose meaning he does not know?[47] If the gifts require a certain preparation and certain corresponding attributes in the soul, what preparation and what attributes in the soul would be required for speaking a foreign language? Finally, if each of the gifts is a means of fulfilling the commandments, what commandment is fulfilled by praying in a foreign language that one does not know, especially if there is no one else present who knows that particular language?[48]

Saint Chrysostom readily admits that when interpreted in this way the whole situation does not make a great deal of sense. While, the Antiochian interpretation that the Holy Apostles spoke in many languages at Jerusalem before a multilingual crowd at Pentecost as a sign to them is at least reasonable even though it is erroneous; while it is likewise rea-

---

TROLOGIÆ CURSUS COMPLETUS, 74, ed. by J. P. Migne: Paris, 1859) page 893 (both in Greek).

[47] The Saint notes the existence of those in ancient times who could make the sounds of the words in a foreign language without knowing what those words signify. Ibid., pages 454 and 464 (in Greek).

[48] In passing, we note that these difficulties do not arise if kinds of tongues are interpreted as silent prayer of the heart. The proper preparation being the cleansing of the passions and the stilling of the uproar of the various thoughts (*logismoi*) and the faculty being the heart itself. The prayer of the heart enables the believer to fulfill the Lord's commandment to persist in prayer and the Apostle's commandment to "pray without ceasing."

sonable, albeit superficial, to suggest that the Apostles had the ability to speak foreign languages in order to go to the ends of the earth with the Gospel of Christ, it would be absolutely pointless for those in Corinth where all spoke Greek for some to speak in Indian, Persian, or Latin with no Indians, Persians, or Latins present.[49] Furthermore, whenever Saint Chrysostom is required to comment on a verse dealing directly with the issue of tongues, his own identification of the gift with foreign languages pushes him to always put Saint Paul's words on the gift in the darkest possible light as mere figures of speech or even worse as means of appeasing the wounded pride of the supposed multilingual Corinthians, to such a point that one wonders how it can be called a gift at all. Thus, he asserted that Saint Paul did not hold the gift in high esteem and did not use it because he was free of vainglory. This, in turn, compels the Saint to interpret Saint Paul's assertion "I speak with tongues more than ye all" as merely a ploy to win the Corinthians' sympathy.[50] In fact with this interpretation, the very gift that brought unity on Pentecost was cause for schism in Corinth.[51]

One can rightly ask what is the spiritual nature of this gift when interpreted in this matter.

---

[49] Saint Nicodemus of the Holy Mountain, *Commentary on the 14 Epistles*, page 348 (in Greek).

[50] Saint John Chrysostom, *Commentary on the Epistle to the Corinthians*, Discourse 35, page 468 (in Greek).

[51] Ibid., Discourse 29, page 240 and Saint John of Damascus, page 372 (both in Greek).

Even further, when Saint Chrysostom maintains that the Corinthians justified their concern with this gift because it was the first given to the Apostles and therefore impressive,[52] we are no longer dealing with a gift of the spirit, but a spiritual exhibitionism that is much more of a vice than a virtue. Saint Chrysostom goes so far as to say that they "are possessed by an intense passion for the gift of tongues out of love of glory."[53] This interpretation in fact raises more questions than it answers. Why would Saint Paul who prays in tongues more than all the rest be more edified praying in Persian for example than in Hebrew? Even more so, how would the Greek speaking Christian be edified who prays in Persian or any other foreign language and has no idea what he is saying?

6. A Preliminary Answer: Kinds of Tongues as the Prayer of the Heart

> "Therefore did my heart rejoice and my tongue was glad."
>
> — *Psalm* 15:9 (LXX)

Saint Nikitas' interpretation does not merely answer such questions, it makes them utterly irrelevant. In the steps of his own spiritual father, Saint Simeon the New Theologian,[54] Saint Nikitas quickly

---

[52] Ibid., Discourse 35, page 452 (in Greek).

[53] Ibid., Discourse 36, page 500 (in Greek).

[54] For example, when Saint Simeon considered the scriptural passage in which Christ said "for I was an hungered, and

passes through an external or superficial examination of the passage under discussion to the serious deeper meaning and significance contained therein. To those who are ignorant of the purpose of the Christian life, to those unacquainted with the gift of the prayer of the heart, to those whose thoughts are guided more by the darkened logic than the enlightened heart, his interpretation may seem revolutionary and even far-fetched (especially if one is not acquainted with Saint Paul's original text), for God has "hid these things from the wise and prudent, and revealed them unto babes."[55] A careful and pious examination of his words, however, indicate an inner unity between his interpretation of this passage and the experience of the Church throughout the centuries.

According to Saint Nikitas, the kinds of tongues referred to by Saint Paul are neither foreign languages nor inarticulate utterances (an interpreta-

---

ye gave me meat: I was thirsty, and ye gave me drink: I was a stranger, and ye took me in," he rejected the most outward social interpretation of good deeds to the needy that seems obvious to many, but in fact excludes some of the desert-dwelling Saints from the Kingdom of Heaven and includes those who have not in the least purified themselves and have simply taken from what was not theirs in the first place and given it back to the poor. Instead, he understood Christ's words as a call to feeding Christ by hungering for Him with tears, repentance and faith, a revolutionary interpretation, but completely in accord with the heart of the Tradition and the Gospel. (Cf., Saint Simeon the New Theologian, "Discourse 9 on Almsgiving," *Catechetical Discourses*, pages 38-41 (in Greek).

[55] *Luke* 10:21.

tion that cannot be found anywhere in two thousand years of Christian tradition), but "praying or psalmodizing inwardly with the tongue,"[56] otherwise

[56] This passage is of such importance that we will quote it in full at this point:

"If in your aspiration for spiritual gifts you have pursued and laid hold of love, you cannot content yourself with praying and reading solely for your own edification. **If when you pray and psalmodize you speak to God** *in private* **you edify yourself, as Saint Paul says.** But once you have laid hold of love you feel impelled to prophesy for the edification of God's Church (cf., *I Corinthians* 14: 2-4), that is to teach your fellow men how to practice the commandments of God and how they must endeavor to conform to God's will. **For of what benefit can it be to others, if, while charged with their guidance,** *you always converse with yourself and God alone through prayer and psalmody, and* <u>*do not speak*</u> **to those in your charge,** whether through the revelation of the Holy Spirit, or out of knowledge of the mysteries, of God, or by exercising the prophetic gift of foresight, or by teaching the wisdom of God (cf. *I Corinthians* 14:6)? **For which of your disciples will prepare for the battle against the passions and the demons** (cf. *I Corinthians* 14:8) **if he does not receive clear instructions from you either in writing or by word of mouth?** Truly, if it is not in order to edify his flock that the shepherd seeks to be richly endowed with the grace of teaching and the knowledge of the Spirit, he lacks fervor in his quest for God's gifts. **By merely** <u>**praying and psalmodizing inwardly with your tongue, that is, by praying in the soul**</u>—**you edify yourself, but your intellect is unproductive** (cf., *I Corinthians* 14:14), **for you do not prophecy with the language of sacred teaching or edify God's Church.** If Paul, who of all men was the most closely united with God through prayer, would have rather spoken from his fertile intellect five words in the church for the instruction of others than ten thousand words of psalmody in private (cf., *I Corinthians* 14:19). Surely those who have responsibility for others have strayed from the path of

known as the prayer of the heart. This interpretation in turn radically alters one's understanding of the entire issue that Saint Paul was addressing in his *First Epistle to the Corinthians.* The problem was not that some Christians were saying their prayers in a foreign language under the inspiration of the Holy Spirit in order to show that they had the same gift as the Apostles, but "the innovation of silent *corporate* prayer in the heart."[57]

Although in Saint Nikitas' writings we find the first extensive and explicit commentary on this passage with the gift of tongues understood as the prayer of the heart, his interpretation is in no way idiosyncratic. As early as the first half of the third century, Origen commenting on *Psalm* 15:9 writes that the Prophet David "calls a tongue *the gift of the Holy Spirit...*, for the tongue *that is within the soul* rejoices, is joyful as it speaks and makes others rejoice."[58] Even more explicitly commenting on Saint Paul's words, "the Spirit itself maketh intercession for us with groanings which are not spoken."[59] and "I will pray with the spirit, and I will pray with the

---

love if they limit the shepherd's ministry solely to psalmody and reading." St. Nikitas Stithatos, "On Spiritual Knowledge," in *The Philokalia,* v. IV, pages 169-170 (emphatic formating mine).

[57] Fr. John S. Romanides, "Justice and Peace in Ecclesiological Context," page 239.

[58] Origen, "On the Psalms," *Library of Greek Fathers and Ecclesiastical Writers,* v. 15, part 6 (Apostolic Diaconia of the Church of Greece: Athens, 1958), page 326 (in Greek).

[59] *Romans* 8:26.

mind also,"[60] Origen understands this to mean that the Spirit prays in the heart and the mind follows the words of the prayer. "The Spirit prays truly spiritual prayers in the heart of the Saints, prayers that when recorded are full of ineffable and wonderful teachings."[61] It is significant that his works that were not destroyed were saved because the Holy Fathers recognized that in these works he was speaking truly and not philosophizing vainly.

For those accustomed to understanding "speaking in tongues" as "speaking in foreign languages," Saint Nikitas' interpretation may seem far-fetched. For those acquainted with the practice of inner prayer, however, his interpretation is not only natural, but makes sense not only of the scriptural passages in question, but also of the continuing practice of the Church throughout the centuries. If the kind reader will give this interpretation "the benefit of the doubt," if he will be willing to make "a paradigm shift" if necessary, he will encounter an unimagined depth of meaning both in Saint Luke's account of Pentecost in *Acts* and in Saint Paul's discourse on tongues in *First Corinthians,* a depth of meaning that can lead to the transfiguration of his life. This being said, we will close these preliminary remarks and open the Scriptures and Patristic commentaries on the same. May our hearts and minds be opened as well.

[60] *1 Corinthians* 14:15.

[61] Origen, "On Prayer," *Library of Greek Fathers and Ecclesiastical Writers,* v. 10, part 2 (Apostolic Diaconia of the Church of Greece: Athens, 1957), pages 236-237 (in Greek).

A Patristic Reading
of Pentecost

"Once, when He descended and confounded the tongues, the Most High divided the nations; and when He divided the tongues of fire, He called all men into unity; and with one accord we glorify the All-Holy Spirit."[1]

Kontakion for the Feast of Holy Pentecost.

"And **when the day of Pentecost was fully come,** they were all with one accord in one place. And suddenly there came a sound from heaven **as** of a rushing mighty wind, and it filled all the house where they were sitting. And there appeared unto them cloven tongues **like as** of fire, and it sat upon each of them. And they were all filled with the Holy Ghost, and **(i) began to speak with other tongues, (ii) as the Spirit gave them utterance.** And there were dwelling at Jerusalem Jews, devout men, out of every nation under heaven. Now when this was noised abroad, the multitude came together, and were confounded, because that **(iii) every man**

---

[1] *A Prayer Book for Orthodox Christians,* translated by Holy Transfiguration Monastery (Holy Transfiguration Monastery: Boston, 1995) page 196.

heard them speak in his own language. And they were all amazed and marveled, saying one to another, **Behold, are not all these which speak Galilaeans? And how hear we every man in our own tongue, wherein we were born?** Parathions, and Medes, and Elamites, and the dwellers in Mesopotamia, and in Judaea, and Cappadocia, in Pontus, and Asia, Phrygia, and Pamphylia, in Egypt, and in the parts of Libya about Cyrene, and strangers of Rome, Jews and proselytes, Cretes and Arabians, **we do hear them speak in our tongues the wonderful works of God.** And they were all amazed, and were in doubt, saying one to another, What meaneth this? **Others <u>mocking</u> said, These men are full of new wine.** But Peter, standing up with the eleven, lifted up his voice, and said unto them, Ye men of Judaea, and all ye that dwell at Jerusalem, be this known unto you, and hearken to my words: For **these are not drunken,** as ye suppose, seeing it is but the third hour of the day. **But this is that which was spoken by the prophet Joel; And it shall come to pass <u>in the last days</u>,** saith God, I will pour out of my Spirit upon all flesh: and your sons and your daughters shall prophesy, and your young men shall see visions, and your old men shall dream dreams: And on my servants and on my handmaidens **I will pour out in those days of my Spirit; and they shall prophesy.**" (Acts 2: 1- 17—emphasis mine).

1. Preparation: the Proper Time, the Proper Place, and the Appropriate Persons

"Ready is my heart, O God, ready is my heart."
— *Psalm* 56:10 (LXX).

As a wise farmer awaits the proper time and season to send forth his laborers to gather in the fruits from his fields, so the Husbandman of our souls and bodies awaited the fullness of time to send forth His Holy Spirit upon His Divine Apostles to harvest the crop of the nations. On the one hand, there were practical considerations. "It was necessary," Saint John Chrysostom exclaims, "for it (the descent of the Holy Spirit) also to take place during a feast so that those who were present at Christ's Crucifixion might see these things as well."[2] The salvation of mankind required the general setting, time and place to be Jerusalem during a feast and shortly

---

[2] Saint John Chrysostom, *Commentary on the Acts of the Apostles*, "Homily 4," taken from volume 15 of *The Complete Works of John Chrysostom, Commentary on the Acts of the Apostles* in the series *Greek Fathers of the Church* text, trans. and comments by Christos Krikonis (Gregory Palamas Patristic Publications: Thessalonika, 1983), page 120 (in Greek).

after Christ's Passion, Death, and Resurrection. On the other hand, the precise details were also divinely chosen for theological and spiritual reasons. The Holy Spirit descended at the third hour in order to reveal that God is three Persons,"[3] but He did so on the first day, Sunday, "to reveal the one nature of the divinity."[4]

Every detail that the Holy Apostle Luke relates about Pentecost is a precious vessel containing a treasure of meaning. That the sound from heaven came suddenly alludes to the fact that the Apostles were not in need of further purification or preparation in order to receive the Holy Spirit as they were already pure and prepared for receiving Him. There was no need for them to push themselves into an ecstatic or emotional state through evocative hymns or fiery words, for they had already prepared themselves by their very way of life. Saint Nicodemos of the Holy Mountain notes that God the Word healed the hearts of the Apostles, purified them from sin, and prepared their souls to become pure and unde-

---

[3] Nicephoros Theotokis, *Way of the Sundays*, volume iv, ed. by Mathaios Laggis, (Monastery of the Transfiguration of the Savior: Athens, 1976), page 66 (in Greek). Compare with Saint Peter of Damascus in Nicodemos of the Holy Mountain and St. Makarios of Corinth, *The Philokalia: The Complete Text* trans. by G.E.H. Palmer, Philip Sherrard, and Kallistos Ware, vol. 4, (Faber and Faber: London, 1995), page 192 and Saint Nicodemos of the Holy Mountain, "Interpretation of the Canons for Pentecost," *Way of the Feasts*, volume iii (Orthodox Kipseli: Thessalonica, 1987), page 206 (also in Greek).

[4] Saint Nicodemos of the Holy Mountain, *Way of the Feasts*, page 207 (in Greek).

filed dwellings of the Holy Spirit. And this Christ did by sharing His life with them, a life that is both human and divine. He transformed them through "His life-giving words, His heavenly teachings, His revelation of His mysteries, His godly works, His supernatural miracles, His divine example, and His deifying commandments."[5] To put it simply, proper belief (Orthodox doctrine) and the proper way of life (obedience to all of Christ's commandments) are what gradually healed the Apostles' souls and transfigured them by grace.

If one desires to be convinced that the Apostles were in fact both prepared and purified by their way of life and belief, one need only observe the veritable transfiguration that gradually took place in the Apostles' very way of understanding the world and those around them, a transformation that can vividly be seen by comparing the behavior of the Apostles when they were following Christ before His Crucifixion (in the process of purification) and their behavior on the very day of Pentecost (in a state of deification). While Christ was still purifying the Sons of thunder, they coveted positions of prominence, but at Pentecost they readily yielded before Peter allowing him to speak publicly and considering it to be the same honor. The disciples who earlier desired to call down fire from heaven to devour those who would not receive them now at Pentecost address those who handed their beloved Lord over to torture and death as brethren and by every means struggle to save

[5] Ibid., page 195 (in Greek).

64

those who persecute them. While at the time of the Savior's Passion they were so filled with the desire for self-preservation that, "one left his Teacher and fled naked, another denied Him with an oath, and the rest trembled like rabbits and fled and hid themselves for fear of the Jews," but "on this day, they came forth iron-clad with super-human courage and a unique boldness to proclaim the Crucified as God."[6]

Thus having passed through the stages of purification and illumination, the Apostles were prepared for the descent of the Holy Spirit through their years spent with Christ from the moment He called them until His Ascension in glory. This significant process points to a basic law of the spiritual life: in order for the believer to become a vessel of the Holy Spirit, he must first cleanse the vessel of his soul "from all pollution of the flesh and spirit" through a life of self-denial.[7] Saint Peter of Damascus expresses this teaching as follows: "in this life, all things go in pairs: practice and spiritual knowledge, free will and grace, fear and hope, struggle and reward. The second does not come until the first has been actualized; and if it seems as if it does, this is an illusion."[8] Thus, the Apostles (and every Christian after them) first had to offer up their free will to Christ, to be obedient

[6] Theodore Zographos, *Delights and Echoes of Glorious Greece: Way of the Sundays,* book 2, (Literary Press of Athanasius Plataniptos: Volo, 1914), page 115 (in Greek).

[7] Saint Nikitas Stithatos, "On Spiritual Knowledge," *Philokalia,* vol. 4, page 139.

[8] Saint Peter of Damaskos, "Twenty-four Discourses," *Philokalia,* vol. 3, page 237.

to what He commanded them, and to struggle to follow Him, so that He could then enable them to understand the depths of His teachings and grant them His spiritual gifts. And as the Apostles themselves required years to fully purify themselves for the full reception of the Holy Spirit, even though they forsook all to follow Christ and dwelt daily with God Incarnate, so every Christian must labor long and hard at purification from the passions and the acquisition of the virtues in order to become a vessel of the All-Holy Spirit. The more the believer purifies himself of the passions, the more he labors to fulfill all of Christ's commandments, the more he makes them the law of his very existence, the more receptive he then becomes to the grace of the Comforter.[9]

If the suddenness and the third hour denote the fact that the Apostles were already purified and illumined through serving the Divine Word through obedience to His commandments, the "upper room" indicates that they dwelt in "the upper room of this life." In other words, their minds were already on things above and their way of life was guided not by the laws of earth, but of heaven.[10] And not only were all of the Apostles gathered together in prayer in that upper room where the Lord made them communi-

---

[9] Saint Nicodemos, *Way of the Feasts*, page 129 (in Greek).

[10] Saint Gregory of Nyssa, "Discourse on the Holy Spirit or On Pentecost" taken from vol. 11 of *The Complete Works of Gregory of Nyssa, Commentary on the Acts of the Apostles* in the series *Greek Fathers of the Church* text, trans. (into modern Greek), and comments by Ignatios Sakalis, (Gregory Palamas Patristic Publications: Thessalonika, 1991), page 54 (in Greek).

cants of the Divine Mysteries,[11] each one of them personally was also gathered in that upper room of his soul (the *nous)* praying undistractedly to God with supplication and hymns of thanksgiving.[12] Through these prayers, they further readied the soil of their hearts for the Holy Spirit to descend, to bring them ineffable peace and to continue that same supplication ("speaking in tongues") now in their hearts. Saint Gregory the Theologian notes that for there to be union with God, it is always necessary for man to ascend towards God and for God to descend towards man. If God were to remain in His uncreated, unapproachable Light on high and man in his spiritual lowliness on earth, that chasm which separated Lazarus from the rich man would also prevent God's grace from reaching man on the one hand and man from receiving that grace on the other.[13] A meeting of wills must take place, for "neither the grace of the Spirit is given unless the man about to receive it is fit to receive it, nor can man receive any gift of the Spirit by his natural faculties alone, without the supernatural power of God."[14]

[11] Saint Gregory the Theologian, "Discourse 41 on Pentecost," page 138 (in Greek).

[12] Saint Gregory Palamas, "Homily 24 on Pentecost" taken from *The Complete Works of Gregory Palamas, 76 Homilies 21-42 Greek Fathers of the Church* text, trans. (into modern Greek), and comments by Panagiotos Christos, (Gregory Palamas Patristic Publications: Thessalonika, 1985), page 102 (in Greek).

[13] Saint Gregory the Theologian, "Discourse 41 on Pentecost," page 141 (in Greek).

[14] Saint Nicodemos, *Way of the Feasts,* page 128 (in Greek).

Thus, the purified and partially illumined disciples whose hearts were more in heaven than on earth were united in prayer awaiting the promised Comforter. Saint John of golden discourse comments, "please note, when they were concentrated in supplication, when they had love, then the Spirit comes."[15] The Disciples were thus not only generally prepared, but more specifically they were prepared by their unity in prayer and by the love that reigned in their hearts. In other words, the Apostles were at peace with themselves and with one another, as the words they "were of one accord," indicate. With the Descent of the Holy Spirit, this peace, "not as the world giveth,"[16] would be perfectly received as a gift of the Holy Spirit. Saint Nicodemos beautifully describes their peaceful condition as follows:

> Until the divine Apostles received the grace of the Holy Spirit, they did not have perfect peace and calmness in their hearts, but were divided by different thoughts. When, however, they received the grace and energy of the peace-giving and pacifying Spirit, then they became perfectly peaceful, their thoughts were settled and their hearts became more meek, peaceful, and calm than the sea appears at a time of great calm. As when the sea is calm it receives the rays of the sun on its surface and reflects them on its own, so that one cannot

[15] Saint John Chrysostom, *Commentary on the Acts of the Apostles,* Homily 4, page 124 (in Greek).
[16] *John* 14:27.

look upon it, in the same way, the hearts of the Apostles received the rays of the super-substantial Sun of the Holy Spirit. On their own, they reflected those rays by the deep peace they had, so that they appeared as another sun to transmit the radiance of the Spirit to others.[17]

2. The Meaning of "As"

"Is not my word like as a fire? saith the Lord"

— Jeremiah 23:29

Then, "there came a sound from heaven." In our Lord's words, "this voice came not because of Me, but for your sake."[18] The sound was the first outward sign for those present: on the one hand, it directed the attention of those outside the house to the upper room where Christ's Disciples were gathered,[19] and on the other hand, it placed a bridle in the mouths of those inclined to scoff and who later accused the Apostles of drunkenness.[20] In order to describe the indescribable, the mystery of the descent of the Holy Spirit, the Apostle Luke at this point turns to various metaphors and symbols and this he does with a very significant little word: "as." "There came a sound

[17] Saint Nicodemos, *Way of the Feasts,* page 174 (in Greek).
[18] *John* 12:30.
[19] Theotokis, *Way of the Sundays*, page 70 (in Greek).
[20] Saint John Chrysostom, *Commentary on the Acts of the Apostles,* 15, Homily 4, page 120 (in Greek).

from heaven *as* of a rushing mighty wind, and it filled all the house where they were sitting. And there appeared unto them cloven tongues like *as* of fire, and it sat upon each of them."

It is certainly worth stressing that for the Fathers, Holy Pentecost was a vision of the glorified Christ in the Holy Spirit (i.e., glorification or deification). We know this both beforehand from Christ's own prophetic words in Saint John's Gospel and from the effects of this vision expressed through Saint Peter's discourse, even though this new presence of Christ among the Disciples as a state of deification defies description. Since the grace that the Apostles received at Pentecost was *uncreated* and since the glory of Christ that the Apostles beheld in the Holy Spirit was uncreated, this means that there are **no** *created* words or conceptions (tongues, fire, mighty wind....) that can express it.[21] Ultimately, this experience in the Holy Spirit can be properly understood only by those who have beheld the same uncreated glory of Christ. Using the term "as," the Apostle Luke simply underlines this fact.

The Apostle does not tell us that the sound was brought by a rushing wind, but that it was *like* one brought by a rushing wind. Likewise, he does not say that the tongues were fire, but that they were *like* fire.[22] According to Saint John Chrysostom, Saint Luke writes in this way so that we "do not form any

---

[21] Fr. J. Romanides, "Jesus Christ-The Life of the World," pages 309-310 (in Greek).

[22] Theotokis, *The Way of the Sundays*, page 67 (in Greek).

sensual idea about the Spirit,"[23] for the Holy Spirit is neither wind, nor fire, nor anything else material. These are but created "metaphors" that ultimately can be understood properly only by those who attain to the same state of deification to which they bear witness.[24] Thus, when the Evangelist relates that the Holy Spirit appeared as a dove at Jordan or as fire in the upper-room, these are in fact the best symbols for expressing the meaning of the Spirit's action or movement.[25] Even as the vision of the light of the Transfigured Christ on Mount Tabor was dependent upon the Apostles' spiritual preparation and not on the prevailing meteorological conditions, "for the light that shown from Christ's flesh illuminating from without also illumined them from within" their hearts,[26] so also the mighty wind and tongues of fire were "seen" and "heard" by the Apostles first of all in their purified hearts and secondarily by their out-

---

[23] Saint John Chrysostom, *Commentary on the Acts of the Apostles,* 15, Homily 4, page 122 (in Greek). Cf., Saint Gregory Palamas, *Homily 24 on Pentecost,* page 108 (in Greek).

[24] Theotokis, *The Way of the Sundays,* page 67 (in Greek).

[25] Bishop Nikolai Velmirovicv, *Homilies,* vol I, trans. by Mother Maria (Lazarica Press: Birmingham, 1996), page 311. If one were to describe a landscape to a blind man, one could describe the color of the sun as warm and the color of the sea as cool, although yellow objects can certainly be cold and blue objects warm. Ultimately without sight, the landscape cannot really be seen as it is. Nevertheless, there are certain metaphors that are more appropriate than others, with an appropriateness that only those who "see" can fully appreciate.

[26] Father John Romanides, "Notes on the Palamite Controversy and Related Topics II," *Greek Orthodox Theological Review* 9:2, 1963-64, page 240 and 241.

ward senses. As the Apostles' vision was itself transfigured in order to behold the uncreated glory of Christ transfigured,[27] so here the Apostles themselves were filled with the divine fire of the grace of the Holy Spirit in order for the Spirit to rest upon them as tongues of fire.

On the one hand, the "tongues" show that the Holy Spirit Whom they received was of the same nature as God the Word (for what is more related to the Word than the tongue?); on the other hand, they symbolize the grace of teaching, since Christ's teachings require a grace-filled tongue.[28] The tongues were "as of fire" again to show that the Holy Spirit is God, for when God descended on Mount Sinai, He descended in fire.[29] Moreover, fire has the property of either devouring or purifying, and God is like a fire that devours the dross of wickedness, but purifies the gold of virtue.[30] In receiving this fire, the Apostles' preaching would itself be a fire that brings light to the obedient but delivers the rebellious to eternal fire and torment.[31] Finally, the fire indicates the abundance of grace that the Apostles received transfigur-

[27] "In thy light shall we see light." *Psalm* 36:9

[28] Saint Gregory Palamas, *Homily on Pentecost,* page 106. See also Saint Gregory the Theologian, "Discourse on Pentecost," page 138 and Saint Nicodemos, *Way of the Feasts*, page 139 (all in Greek).

[29] Saint Nicodemos, *Way of the Feasts*, page 169 (in Greek).

[30] Saint Gregory the Theologian, "Discourse on Pentecost," page 138 (in Greek).

[31] Saint Gregory Palamas, *Homily on Pentecost,* page 106 (in Greek).

ing them into "angels of light and ministers of the things on high."[32]

3. Prayer, Prophecy, and Comprehensibility: Purposeful and Timely Gifts

> "There is a time there for every purpose and for every work."
> — *Ecclesiastes* 3:17

When Saint Luke relates that the Apostles "began to speak with other tongues," "as the Spirit gave them utterance," and that "every man heard them speak in his own language," he is referring to *three* manifestations of the grace of the Holy Spirit in the Apostles that must neither be confused nor merged. "To speak with other tongues" refers to the words of their common supplications becoming words no longer simply uttered in one's mind or with the reason, but words spoken in the heart by the Holy Spirit. "As the Spirit gave them utterance" refers to the gift of prophecy, the ability to open Scriptures, even as Christ opened the Scriptures to the Apostles on the way to Emmaus.[33] Finally, that "every man heard them speak in his own language" refers to the fact that the Apostles' words were comprehensible to

---

[32] Saint John Chrysostom, *Commentary on the Acts of the Apostles,* 15, Homily 4, page 128-130 (in Greek).
[33] *Luke* 24:13-42.

those whose native tongue was not Hebrew.[34] In other words, first the Apostles' purified hearts received the gift of unceasing prayer in the Holy Spirit, then with hearts illumined by the prayer they began to prophesy, and finally through the grace of the Holy Spirit the words of their prophecy were understood by those who spoke other languages. "When someone receives the gift of tongues (prayer of the heart), then the Holy Spirit may or may not cause such situations as those described by Luke in *Acts* (2:6-13)."[35] The fact that certain Corinthians spoke in tongues (received the gift of inner prayer) and yet neither prophesied nor interpreted indicates quite clearly that "speaking in tongues" and the "utterances given by the Holy Spirit" are by no means one and the same.[36]

It is significant that the Fathers maintain that the Apostles were on the one hand "instruments of the Divine Spirit acting and being moved according to His will,"[37] and on the other hand, responsible persons acting according to their own sanctified volition. The Spirit inspires them, but does not force them. Neither the text of *Acts* nor the interpretation of the Spirit-bearing Fathers give any reason to construe

[34] J. Romanides, "Jesus Christ: The Life of the World," page 326 (in Greek).

[35] Ibid., page 326 (in Greek).

[36] Ibid., page 332 (in Greek). The case of Cornelius and others who spoke in tongues, but did not prophesy also support this interpretation.

[37] Saint Gregory Palamas, *Homily on Pentecost*, page 108 (in Greek).

the gift of speaking in tongues (inner prayer) as a means of entering into or a result of an enthusiastic spiritual state. Scripture and Tradition both indicate that this is not how God, Who speaks to man with a "still small voice,"[38] operates. As Saint Nicodemos of Mount Athos writes, "the light-bearing grace of the Comforting Spirit did not cause an uproar in a tumultuous way, but moves us the faithful reverently, calmly and in a way befitting God."[39] If there was tumult, it was certainly not among the Apostles who received the Spirit, but among the crowds outside who as of yet had not.

Saint Cyril of Alexandria notes that the ability to be understood by those of other languages was given at a specific time in response to a concrete need,[40] for what benefit would their proclamation in a given language (prophecy) have had for those who spoke another language.[41] And truly, how could Christ's Apostles have gone to teach all nations without the ability to communicate with them in their languages? Since this ability was the most necessary

---

[38] *I Kings* 19:12.

[39] Saint Nicodemos, *Way of the Feasts*, page 203 (in Greek).

[40] Saint Cyril of Alexandria, "Commentary on First Corinthians," PG 74, page 888 (in Greek).

[41] Saint Gregory of Nyssa, *Discourse on the Holy Spirit*, page 54 (in Greek). He also adds, "Now, however, that there is agreement in language, we must pursue the fiery tongue of the Spirit so that those who are darkened by deceit might be enlightened." Compare with Saint John Chrysostom's "Second Homily on the Holy Spirit" The Complete Extent Works, volume 4 *PATROLOGIÆ CURSUS COMPLETUS, 50,* ed. by J. P. Migne (Paris, 1859) (in Greek).

at the time, this gift of comprehensibility was among the first to be bestowed upon them.

While it is truly amazing for men who know no foreign language to speak to those of another language and be understood, this is the lesser part of the miracle, for as the Saint Chrysostom, the peer of the Apostles, notes, "they were not simply speaking, but they said things worthy of admiration."[42] Thus, they spoke about the greatness of God with the luminous thoughts of the Holy Spirit.[43] Saint Nicodemos again comments, "revivified by that living breath of the Holy Spirit and made firm by the fiery tongues like iron made firm by fire, the Apostles spoke eloquently about the greatness of God even though they were illiterate fisherman. They spoke fearlessly and boldly with a free tongue and with such great wisdom that the wise and literate stood amazed and remained stunned and ecstatic."[44] Once more we note that those who heard the Apostles prophetic words were ecstatic, not the Apostles themselves. Fr. J. Romanides significantly writes,

> In accord with the Fathers of the Church, Christ's words and prayer referred to in *John* 13:31-17:26 containing the promise that the Spirit of Truth will come and 'He will guide you into all Truth,' was fulfilled on Pentecost which became a continuous experience of those who from that point

[42] Saint John Chrysostom, *Commentary on the Acts of the Apostles*, 15, Homily 4, page 132 (in Greek).

[43] Zographos, page 111 (in Greek).

[44] Saint Nicodemos, *Way of the Feasts*, page 157 (in Greek).

were united with the community of the glorified. This does not mean that the Prophets were not led into the Truth or that the Apostles were not led into the Truth, some by enlightenment others by glorification as well, but that the Apostles were about to be lead into all Truth in the revelation of Pentecost... Christ's words and prayer for unity is for the unity of the Apostles and the faithful in the experience of glorification, in other words the vision of the uncreated glory of the Holy Trinity in the human nature of Christ, granted in its fullness by the participation in the experience of Pentecost."[45]

4. What was heard?

"And thine ears shall hear a word behind thee, saying, this is the way, walk ye in it."
— *Isaiah* 30:21

In the patristic literature, two opinions can be discerned concerning the nature of what was heard. The literal interpretation favored by Saint Gregory the Theologian is that the Apostles were not speak-

---

[45] Fr. J. Romanides, "Jesus Christ the Life of the World," pages 309-310.

ing in Hebrew, but in foreign languages.[46] Saint
Gregory of Nyssa on the other hand seems to indicate
that they were speaking in Hebrew, but that "every
man heard them speak in his own language."[47] Although both interpretations can be supported by the
actual text if one is free with the punctuation, both a
practical consideration of the event and an understanding of the primary faculty of the soul involved
in the working of grace point to the preferability of
Saint Gregory of Nyssa's intuitions.

Saint Gregory the Theologian asserts that the
phrase "each one heard them speak in his own language" requires punctuation for the best interpretation. He suggests that a comma should be inserted
after the word "heard" so that the text would have
the sense "they spoke the languages of those who
heard them." What prompts the Theologian to add
this punctuation and provide the text with this interpretation is his pious desire to honor the Holy Apostles. He notes that otherwise this aspect of the
miracle would refer to the crowds who were listening
rather than to the Apostles who were speaking and
that the magnitude of the miracle would be de-

---

[46] Saint Gregory the Theologian, "Discourse on Pentecost,"
page 144 (in Greek).

[47] Saint Gregory of Nyssa, "Polemic Against Eunomios,"
*The Complete Works of Gregory of Nyssa, 2 Dogmatics 2,
Antirhetiorical Discourses Against Eunomios, Greek Fathers of
the Church* text, trans. (into modern Greek), and comments by
Ignatios Sakalis, Gregory Palamas Patristic Publications, Thes-
salonika, 1987, pages 446-448 (in Greek).

creased.[48] Following Saint Gregory the Theologian's interpretation, Saint Nicodemos likewise adds that the miracle belonged not to the Jewish opponents of Christ, but to the Apostles, for some of the Jews accused the Apostles of drunkenness.[49] Strictly speaking, however, the miracle was neither of the Apostles, nor those listening, but of the Holy Spirit acting through the Apostles for the benefit of the foreign Jews present.

An alternative interpretation that Saint Gregory the Theologian himself mentions is that "one voice came forth, but they heard many."[50] Saint Gregory of Nyssa apparently follows this interpretation when he speaks of the "divine power being portioned out into many languages" for the benefit of all.[51] For Saint Gregory of Nyssa, each person received the one "proclamation in his own dialect... comprehending the meaning of what was said by words familiar to him." Thus, for Saint Gregory of Nyssa, the words uttered by the Apostle and the words heard by each foreigner were not the same. The Holy Spirit "translated" Saint Peter's words in the hearts of each listener into his own respective language. This is what leads Saint Gregory of Nyssa to exclaim, "we must realize that the Holy Spirit

[48] Saint Gregory the Theologian, "Discourse on Pentecost," pages 144 and 146 (in Greek).

[49] Saint Nicodemos, *Way of the Feasts*, page 164 (in Greek).

[50] Saint Gregory the Theologian, "Discourse on Pentecost," pages 144 (in Greek).

[51] Saint Gregory of Nyssa, "Polemic Against Eunomios," pages 446-448 (in Greek).

speaks to us in our own words as we have learned from the narration of *Acts*."[52]

When the late, blessed Elder Porphyrios (†1991) was asked which of the two interpretations was correct, he chose the interpretation of Saint Gregory of Nyssa on the basis of his own experience of being understood by one who spoke another language, an occurrence related in full in the appendix to this study. According to the Elder, when the grace of the Holy Spirit suddenly descended from above and the crowd gathered hearing the sound "as by a violent wind," grace was poured forth upon all. And while the Apostle would speak in his own language, those listening would hear in their own languages. For example, if the Apostle would say, "go to your homes," the Frenchman would not hear "homes," but *"maisons,"* for the words would be transformed within his heart. One sound would be heard and strike the ears, but within the heart the mind enlightened by God would grasp what was said by another kind of "hearing." And so everyone would understand the sound and what was said would become comprehensible to each individual.[53] Thus as the visitor conversing with the Elder commented, while the Apostles spoke Hebrew, the foreigners present heard the apostolic proclamation in their own languages. Their hearing became spiritual through a type of clairvoyance that was temporarily granted to

---

[52] Ibid., page 438.

[53] Constantine Yiannitsiotis, *Near the Elder Porphyrius,* (The Sacred Women's Monastery of the Transfiguration of the Savior: Athens, 1995), pages 148-150 (in Greek).

the hearers of the Apostles. Thus, when the Apostle Peter spoke to the crowds, thousands simultaneously heard him in their own languages. And he asks, "How else would it be possible to say each individual word in 15-20 languages?"[54]

Practical considerations seem to favor Saint Gregory of Nyssa's interpretation. The most visible aspect of the miracle of Pentecost was the comprehensibility of the word of God spoken by the Apostles. There is no reason to suggest that the Apostles were all speaking simultaneously in different languages (for even if they were speaking the same language, it would be difficult for one to understand what was being said), since such is not characteristic of modest and sensible men. It also seems unlikely that one would speak of the wonders of God in Hebrew, followed by another speaking in Persian, followed by another in Latin..., for then the majority of the discourse would be incomprehensible to most listeners (since it would be in foreign languages that they did not know). Such is not reported in *Acts*, but rather that "every man heard them speak in his own language." This seems to indicate that the Apostle Peter spoke in one language, but those present heard him in their own languages.

Finally, the miracle for the multitude was the revelation of the Person of Christ to the human

---

[54] Ibid., 149-150. Father Porphyrius contends that the Fathers in general were well aware that the miracle of comprehensibility took place in this way, but that the mystery is so very awesome that they were afraid even to comment on it (Ibid., page 151).

hearts of those present. Having the Holy Spirit praying silently within them through the gift of tongues and having beheld the uncreated glory of Christ, the Apostles were now more than ever before fully prepared to proclaim Him to those present. They were men speaking from concrete experience. The Apostle Luke does not write that "when the multitudes heard this, *they were convinced in their minds*," but "when they heard this, *they were pricked in their heart*."[55] The heart has another immediate and direct way of knowing and apprehending the Truth, quite distinct from the reason. With the grace of the Holy Spirit, the Apostles did not become mathematicians or linguists, but all-wise teachers of the wisdom of God and profound speakers to the *hearts* of men. Consistent with this given, it is not at all unreasonable to suppose that their grace-filled words could penetrate the language barrier and speak directly to the heart, where the real miracle took place among those who heeded to the Apostles' words.

5. The Sobriety of the Spirit

"For God hath not given us the spirit of fear; but of power, and of love, and of a sound mind."

— *2 Timothy* 1:7

---

[55] *Acts* 2:37.

While many of the well-dispositioned were amazed on "hearing" the Apostles speak in their native languages, others who find fault in all things dared to mock the Apostles and accuse them of drunkenness. This accusation, however, had no foundation whatsoever in the Apostles' behavior, demeanor, or words. The Pharisees who once said that Christ cast out demons by the prince of the demons now say that the Apostles spoke freely because they were full of new wine.[56] In both cases, their words were nonsense and blasphemy; the reality was precisely the opposite. The Holy Spirit ever rested upon the Son; the Apostles were the most sober of men. The words and actions of the Apostles inspired by the All-Wise Spirit were sober, measured, and wise. To speak "eloquently about the great and supernatural mysteries of God and the supernatural and all-powerful activity and Grace of the Holy Spirit"[57] is not the mark of drunkenness. The Apostles were neither drunk, nor in some spiritual ecstasy like the pagan oracles who were possessed by the necessity to speak.[58] Saint Peter's response to such accusations was in fact clear, peaceful, fearless, and calm, reflecting the very characteristics of the sober activity of the Holy Spirit. It is in fact, the opposing Spirit, the devil who produces drunken behavior and drunken words, full of agitation, fear, turmoil and

[56] Saint John Chrysostom, *Commentary on the Acts of the Apostles,* 15, Homily 4, page 132 (in Greek).

[57] Saint Nicodemos, *Way of the Feasts*, page 150 (in Greek).

[58] Saint John Chrysostom, *Commentary on the Acts of the Apostles,* 15, Homily 4, page 134 (in Greek).

confusion.[59] Saint Nicodemos of Mount Athos himself full of the Spirit eloquently answers the foolish words of those who maligned the Apostles,

> What are you saying, ye senseless men? Were the Apostles drunk who spoke eloquently about the great things of God? Were they drunk whose words were a philosophy about things spiritual and heavenly? Were they drunk who heard the glad tidings about those good things that 'eye hath not seen, nor ear heard, neither have entered into the heart of man,' as Paul says? And to say what is greatest, were the disciples of the Savior drunk who preached the Life-creating Trinity Who is the One God of our Fathers? O your chatter and blasphemy! Truly unbelief has made you drunk, or rather the father of unbelief the devil has done so.[60]

6. Holy Pentecost: A Unique Fulfillment of Prophecy and Figure

> "I have also spoken by the prophets, and I have multiplied visions, and used similitudes, by the ministry of the prophets."
> — *Hosea* 12:10

[59] Saint Nicodemos, *Way of the Feasts*, page 175 (in Greek).
[60] Ibid., page 151.

A Patristic Reading of Pentecost

When the Apostle Peter stood up to address
the multitude, he turned to an Old Testament prophecy in order to help them to understand the fulfillment that was taking place among them even as
Christ Himself did when He began His outward
teaching ministry among His chosen people.[61] Thus
Saint Peter refers to a prophecy that the Jewish
scribes had overlooked, the prophecy of Joel, "And it
shall come to pass in the last days, saith God, I will
pour out of my Spirit upon all flesh: and your sons
and your daughters shall prophesy, and your young
men shall see visions, and your old men shall dream
dreams: And on my servants and on my handmaidens I will pour out in those days of my Spirit; and
they shall prophesy."[62] With these words, the Prophet
Joel "filled with godly and divine grace sees into the
future to the day of Pentecost."[63] And Peter then
filled with the same grace sees its fulfillment, for to

[61] "And there was delivered unto Him the book of the
prophet Esaias. And when He had opened the book, He found
the place where it was written, The Spirit of the Lord is upon
Me, because He hath anointed Me to preach the gospel to the
poor; He hath sent Me to heal the brokenhearted, to preach de-
liverance to the captives, and recovering of sight to the blind, to
set at liberty them that are bruised, to preach the acceptable
year of the Lord. And He closed the book, and He gave it again
to the minister, and sat down. And the eyes of all them that
were in the synagogue were fastened on Him. And He began to
say unto them, This day is this scripture fulfilled in your ears."
Luke 4:17-21.

[62] *Joel* 2:28-30.

[63] Saint Nicodemos, *Way of the Feasts*, pages 204-205 (in
Greek).

85

interpret prophecy correctly is itself a gift of prophecy that can initiate the listener into the Truth about Christ.[64]

It is important to realize that Holy Pentecost belongs to that series of saving and unrepeatable divine actions that includes the Incarnation of God the Word, His Passion, Death, Resurrection and Ascension.[65] When the various Prophets prophesied about different aspects of this economy, they would use the term "in the last days." In this case, "the last days" do not refer specifically to our own times, but to the days beginning with Christ's Incarnation and continuing through Holy Pentecost. "The last days" are those days beyond which we await nothing else.[66]

Even as it would be unthinkable for a Christian to read the Prophet Isaiah's prophecy concerning the virgin birth and to interpret it in terms of someone born recently or about to be born, in precisely the same way, it is unthinkable for a Christian to read the Prophet Joel's prophecy concerning Holy Pentecost and to interpret it differently from the Apostle Peter as though it referred to some contemporary experience or event. The Old Testament prophesies in detail what would be described in the New Testa-

---

[64] Saint Cyril of Alexandria, "On the First Epistle to the Corinthians," PG 74, page 892 (in Greek).

[65] Anthony Alevizopoulos, *Handbook of Heresies and Para-Christian Groups*, page 168 and Saint Cyril of Alexandria, "On the First Epistle to the Corinthians," PG 74, page 889 (both in Greek).

[66] Ibid., page 167. The "former days" are those of the patriarchs and the prophets.

ment both openly and veiled through types, anti-types, and figures. To understand these prophecies, our hearts must be purified and illumined by the grace of the Holy Spirit through the prayer of the heart, so that we can "see Christ." As Saint Maximus the Confessor teaches, "the mystery of the incarnation of the Logos is the key to all the arcane symbolism and typology in Scripture."[67] In other words, the key to understanding what the Old Testament prophesies are referring to is an understanding of the entire economy from the Annunciation of the Archangel to the Holy Virgin to Christ's sending down His Consubstantial Spirit from the Throne of the Father. Any other interpretation is not simply wrong, it can lead to delusion. Those who would apply Joel's prophecy to a new or "second Pentecost" do not differ in the least from those who will use other messianic prophecies in the Old Testament in order to welcome the Anti-Christ. As for the teaching from the New Testament, "before Christ's Second Coming, we do not await another 'outpouring' of the Holy Spirit or a 'second Pentecost,' but the 'outpouring' of the spirit of the antichrist (*2 Thessalonians* 2:3)."[68]

Like the other great mysteries accomplished by God the Word, Holy Pentecost was foreshadowed by many types and figures to the people of Israel, even though it far transcended them all. The Apostles themselves were prefigured by the hosts of

[67] Saint Maximus the Confessor, "First Century on Theology," *The Philokalia,* v. II, page 127.
[68] Alevizopoulos, *Handbook of Heresies and ParaChristian Groups,* pages 167-168 (in Greek).

Prophets (or to be more precise the Apostles were the Prophets of the New Testament or in the same tradition as the Prophets of the Old). As Elisha received grace through Elijah's mantle, as David did so when anointed with oil, as Moses did so when he beheld the burning bush, so did the Apostles with the fiery tongues that rested upon them.[69] And as Pharaoh said of Joseph, "Can we find such a one as this is, a man in whom the Spirit of God is?" so would the nations say of the Apostles. Like the fashioners of the tabernacle of old, they were "filled with the spirit of God, in wisdom, and in understanding, and in knowledge, and in all manner of workmanship," now to adorn new temples of the living God, the soul's of men.[70] Like the formerly slow-tongued and stuttering Moses who after initiation into the ways of God became the most fluent transmitter of His law, so the formerly ignorant and uneducated Apostles strengthened by the Spirit became "the wisest of the wise and the most eloquent of the eloquent."[71] And it is important to note that the same spiritual law is at work both in the Prophets (Moses, Samuel, David, Elisha, Elijah, Ezekiel...) and in Christ's Apostles: first, they proved their own virtue, first they showed themselves to be worthy, and then they were vouchsafed

---

[69] Saint John Chrysostom, *Commentary on the Acts of the Apostles,* 15, Homily 4, page 126 (in Greek).

[70] Saint Nicodemos, *Way of the Feasts,* page 130 with citations from *Genesis* 41:38 and *Exodus* 31:3 respectively (in Greek).

[71] Ibid., page 172.

to receive the Spirit.[72] In other words, the stages of purification, illumination and deification that are clearly seen in the Apostles can be seen with equal clarity in the lives of the Prophets.[73] "According to the Fathers of the Church, the Prophets also had unceasing prayer which was the natural path towards glorification... These experiences however were not yet the gift of tongues of Pentecost. Thus, the latter gift contains the former, but not vice versa."[74] In many and varied ways the Prophets who served the pre-incarnate Word prefigured the Apostles who served God the Word Incarnate. Nevertheless, the grace that the Apostles received was much greater than that of the Prophets,[75] for the Prophets were directed only towards one nation, their own nation, while the Apostles were directed towards the entire inhabited world and to those who did not know them.[76]

Of course, Pentecost was more than the moment when the Apostles abundantly received the grace of the Holy Spirit. The Apostles had already received from the Lord the grace to "to heal sicknesses and to cast out devils."[77] Pentecost, furthermore, belongs to that class of divine interventions

[72] Saint John Chrysostom, *Commentary on the Acts of the Apostles,* 15, Homily 4, page 128 (in Greek).

[73] Cf., Saint Gregory of Nyssa, *The Life of Moses.*

[74] Fr. J. Romanides, "Jesus Christ, the Life of the World," page 340 (in Greek).

[75] Theotokis, *The Way of the Sundays,* page 67 (in Greek).

[76] Saint John Chrysostom, *Commentary on the Acts of the Apostles,* 15, Homily 4, page 126 (in Greek).

[77] *Mark* 3:15.

that altered the very course of human history. Thus, it is not surprising that the two most clear prefigurements of Holy Pentecost as type and anti-type are likewise events that left an indelible mark on the spiritual history of man: the giving of the Law at Mount Sinai and the Confusion of the Tongues at the Tower of Babel.

The parallels and the differences between what transpired when God the Word spoke with Moses on Mount Sinai and when He sent the Holy Spirit upon the Apostles in the upper room are striking. Both the giving of the Law and the descent of the Holy Spirit took place according to the sovereign will of the Holy Trinity. This is symbolically manifest by the third hour when the Holy Spirit descended upon the Apostles and the third day when the Lord descended upon Mount Sinai. Nevertheless, comparing Sinai and Pentecost is in many ways like comparing a glowing candle and the brilliant sun. To use the very imagery both events provide, on Sinai the unpurified children of Israel experienced the Uncreated Light as a dark cloud and smoke, "a shadow of the good things to come, while in the upper rooms the Apostles experienced it as tongues shining like fire removing the veil of the law." In fact, it is said that the Law was given near the beginning of the morning, because it gave the first rays of the written legislation, but the Holy Spirit descended near noon, because the Gospel of Christ would shine forth as radiantly as the sun. On Sinai, there was smoke and lightening, because the experience of "glorification before Pentecost was temporary and did not continue after death," but in the upper room the tongues of fire were seated upon the Apostles signifying that the temporary experience of deification becomes "the permanent experience of the Saints in Christ in their very bodies after death. In fact glorification in the Body of Christ is not restricted to the heart or expressed only by the face as with the Prophets, but extends to the entire bodies of those who have been glorified."[78] On Sinai, the twelve tribes of Israel required an advanced warning in order to prepare themselves, but the pure Apostles were already prepared so that the Spirit could arrive suddenly. On Sinai, the hard-hearted Jews required shouts and the loud sounding of trumpets, while at Pentecost, it was not simply the sound of a violent wind, but one "as the sound of a violent wind."[79]

If Sinai positively prefigured Pentecost, Babel negatively did so. Although at Babel and at Pentecost there was oneness of mind and concord, at Babel the unity was for an evil and harmful end, while at Pentecost, unity was good and beneficial. At Babel, men pridefuly strove to reach heaven by fashioning a tower, but at Pentecost, the Apostles were humbly gathered together with the desire to raise men up to heaven.[80] To prevent the evil concord from reaching its end, the Most High divided the languages at Babel and the prideful enterprise was stopped, whereas

[78] Fr. J. Romanides, "Jesus Christ the Life of the World," pages 320-321 (in Greek).

[79] Theotokis, *Way of the Sundays*, page 67-68 (in Greek).

[80] Saint Nicodemos, *Way of the Feasts*, pages 132-133 (in Greek).

to enable the blessed concord of the Apostles to bear fruit, the grace of the Spirit united the many languages into one harmony[81] and the many nationalities into one nation, the Christian nation.[82]

These and other foreshadowings of Holy Pentecost found in the Old Testament underscore the fact that Pentecost was a unique fulfillment of prophecy, of God's wondrous and loving design for man's salvation. While the believer can partake of the grace of Pentecost by passing through the stages of illumination and deification, Pentecost remains a unique event in the life of the Church along side of Christ's Nativity, Passion, and Resurrection. Those who have received the humble and meek Spirit of God would naturally be most hesitant to refer to any current spiritual phenomena among those who have not been purified as a second Pentecost of the same stature as the first.

In referring to Old Testament prophecies with respect to Pentecost, we must not overlook Christ's own prophecies about Pentecost recorded in *John* 13:31-17:26. When Christ told His Apostles at the mystical supper, *"At that day ye shall know that I am in my Father, and ye in Me, and I in you,"* (*John* 14:20), He was referring to *the day of Pentecost "when He, the Spirit of truth, is come, He will guide you into all truth."* Christ is the Truth that was revealed fully to the Apostles in the Holy Spirit on Pentecost. Thus,

[81] Saint Gregory the Theologian, "Discourse on Pentecost," page 146 (in Greek).

[82] Theotokis, *Way of the Sundays*, page 67 (in Greek).

when Christ prayed "Father, I will that they also, whom Thou hast given Me, be with Me where I am." He was referring to His glory, the unapproachable light in which Christ dwells. In other words, He was referring to the glorification or deification of the Apostles by the grace of the Holy Spirit. Thus with hearts illumined by prayer (speaking in tongues), on Pentecost, "they truly beheld His glory, which the Father had given Him (*John* 17:24). Thus "it was expedient for the Apostles that Christ go away" (*John* 16:7), so that He could "return for a new presence of His human nature that is shared among the many faithful without being divided." There is, in fact, reason to suppose that when Christ ascended in glory and the two men in white apparel said, "this same Jesus, which is taken up from you into heaven, shall so come in like manner as ye have seen him go into heaven," that they were referring to His descent in glory in the Holy Spirit on Pentecost,[83] for those who saw Him ascend in glory at Ascenscion would live to see Him come with glory in the descent of the Holy Spirit on Pentecost.

7. The Characteristics of Holy Pentecost

Following Saint Peter's grace-filled words, the hearts of some "three thousand souls" were touched. The Apostle showed them the way of repentance and

---

[83] J. Romanides, "Jesus Christ: The Life of the World," pages 325-326 (in Greek).

brought them into the Church through the Mystery of Holy Baptism so that they might receive the grace of the Holy Spirit and thus pass through the same stages of purification (of the passions), illumination (through inner prayer or in Biblical terms "speaking in tongues), and deification through which the Apostles had already passed. The new Christians then devoted themselves to learning the Apostles' teaching (dogma), sharing in the life of the Apostles (observing the Commandments of the Lord) and being strengthened through Holy Communion and prayer.[84] It is worth noting that speaking in foreign languages and highly-charged spiritual experiences are *not* what characterize the life of these first Christians, but repentance founded on the rock of the right belief in Christ reflected by the corresponding way of life and guided by inner prayer and nourished by "the breaking of the bread."

In looking back upon the unique mystery of Pentecost as described in *Acts* and interpreted by the Fathers, it is helpful to note both those characteristics which are present and those which are absent. The Fathers indicate that the time and place were specifically chosen for the salvation of man. The Apostles were already purified vessels who led an exalted way of life and were well acquainted with the way of repentance and humility. At the time, they were united in prayer and in a most peaceful state. Reading the account of *Acts*, there is no indication that an emotionally charged atmosphere was induced

[84] *Acts* 2:38-42.

94

by suggestive hymnody or fiery words, but quite simply "the wind bloweth where it listeth."[85] There is nothing ecstatic about the Apostles' behavior or words, nor is there anything to suggest that they were speaking with their eyes shut or with swaying hands upraised. On the contrary, their actions and words were sober and watchful.

The distinction between "speaking in tongues," the words spoken, and their comprehensibility is crucial for a proper understanding of Pentecost. Without this clear distinction, inward prayer, prophecy, and foreign languages can be so thoroughly confused, that one can reach the peculiar conclusion that speaking in a foreign language (or even worse, making strange incomprehensible sounds) is a more spiritual form of prayer than the many prayers and examples of prayer that the Lord gave His disciples before His Passion and Resurrection. If, however, the reader of *Acts* realizes that "speaking in tongues" refers to the inner prayer of the heart by the Holy Spirit, then he will note the complete harmony with Christ's teaching about the "kingdom of heaven being within," about the need to pray day and night (without ceasing), and about Christ taking up His abode in the believer's heart. The reader will also no longer confuse Saint Peter's prophetic words (utterance) with his inner prayer ("speaking in tongues"). The Holy Apostle Peter's prophetic words on the Day of Pentecost were the fruit of his inward prayer (the gift of tongues) and his vision of the glorified Christ, but not

[85] *John* 3:8.

a more perfect way to pray. Even more categorically, his prophetic words were neither the fruit of nor a means of entering into a higher or ecstatic spiritual state, for how can one in an ecstasy persuade those who are in their right mind. No, the Apostle Peter's prophetic words were uttered in order to proclaim the Gospel so that those present might hear and come to the knowledge of all Truth and repent. Saint Peter's words recorded in the *Book of Acts* are not described as a way of praying to God, but of proclaiming the Gospel to one's brother who otherwise would not be able to understand it. Thus from a heart illumined by inward prayer (speaking in tongues) and glorification (the vision of Christ in glory), Saint Peter proclaimed the Word of Truth (being led into all Truth by the experience of deification), and through the Grace of the Holy Spirit, all present understood precisely what Saint Peter was saying in their own language. Furthermore, the words were not simply understandable to all, they were also wise and able to change the hearts of men.

From what has been said, it is clear that the grace-filled experience of Pentecost was an experience of deification through which the Apostles were led into the most complete knowledge of the Truth (Who Christ is), an experience that graced the Apostles with clarity of understanding, comprehensibility, sobriety and peace. The gift of comprehensibility that was a particular characteristic of Pentecost[86] was

---

[86] There are other clear cases of "speaking in tongues" (silent prayer of the heart by the Holy Spirit) in which no utter-

given for the building up of the Church and the salvation of mankind. Through it, those divided were brought into unity. Through it, the Gospel was proclaimed and the lost sheep from every nation and language were given the opportunity to repent. From a careful study of Saint Luke's description of Pentecost, we learn both the preconditions that must be present for the three gifts observed on Pentecost to be given and the qualities that are manifested in those gifts. With respect to the gift of comprehensibility to those who speak another language, there must be a pressing need for such and those found worthy of the gift must be virtuous and humble. On the other hand, what is uttered (the prophecy) must be comprehensible to all, wise, and touch the human heart. The genuine gifts of Pentecost both well forth from peace, sobriety, and unity (that are present in the soul with inner prayer, "the gift of tongues") and bear the fruits of peace, sobriety and unity. As "every tree is known by his own fruit,"[87] so the many experiences of the spirit that are manifested today can be judged by comparing them with the genuine fruits that were manifested on Holy Pentecost.

ance is given and hence in which there is no comprehensibility because nothing is heard.

[87] *Luke* 6:44.

A Patristic Reading of Saint Paul's Discourse on Spiritual Gifts in His First Epistle to the Corinthians

1. The Aim of the Incarnation and Gifts of the Spirit

> "For I will restore health unto thee, and I will heal thee of thy wounds, saith the Lord."
>
> — *Jeremiah* 30:17

The question of spiritual gifts, their function and their purpose in the life of the faithful, is ultimately a question about the purpose and activity of the Church in general and the Incarnation of God the Word in particular. Taken outside of this context, Saint Paul's words in his *First Epistle to the Corinthians* (12-15) can be misconstrued into an ideology on the workings of the Spirit that is at odds with the most basic teachings of the Christian faith. When viewed in its proper context, however, Saint Paul's discourse unveils the most profound mystery and sublime heights of the life in Christ: the purification, illumination, and perfection of man. Since Saint Paul's words remain in a foreign and incomprehensible tongue as long as the basic alphabet of man's spiritual healing is not known, it seems prudent to spell out briefly the background of man's sickness and restoration to health before proceeding to Saint Paul's words as interpreted by Saint Nikitas Stithatos and in agreement with the entire ascetic and hesychastic tradition of the Church.

In an overabundance of love, God created man, adorned him with the virtues, placed him in Paradise, and entrusted him with a single commandment so that through obedience man could also express his love for God[1] and thus proceed from the image of God traced in his soul to the beauty of the divine likeness. In other words, man was meant voluntarily and actively to make his own the virtues nascently present in his soul (the image) by cooperation (synergy) with divine grace.[2] Already pure by nature and illumined by his intimate converse with God, man was to grow in virtue and unselfish love eventually becoming like God by divine grace. By accepting, however, the prideful suggestion of the serpent, by breaking God's commandment, and by refusing to repent for his transgression, the image of God in man's soul was cloaked with the thick garment of the passions and every aspect of man's soul was distorted and enfeebled. The blameless passions of death, corruption, sleep, hunger, thirst, and fatigue entered man's life and were transformed by his now darkened heart into blameworthy ones. His desires became selfish. His will and aggressive faculty were directed towards the acquisition of his selfish desires. His intelligence

---

[1] Dorotheos of Gaza, *Discourses and Sayings*, trans. by Eric Wheeler (Cistercian Publications: Kalamazoo, 1977), page 77.

[2] Jean-Claude Larchet, *The Healing of Spiritual Diseases* (Les Editions de l'Ancre: Suresnes, 1993), page 21 (in French).

was employed to devise ways in which his selfish desires could be fulfilled using his selfish will. And his prayerful union and communion with God, which was meant to direct and enlighten every activity and faculty of his soul, was broken and that aspect of the soul (the *nous* or spiritual heart) through which man was to commune with God became functionally dead. Furthermore, man's memory, which was to be utilized to remember God through ceaseless prayer, became forgetful and engrossed in sensible realities.[3] Dominated by the senseless passions of the love of money, glory, and pleasure, man was no longer able to think or to feel properly. Thus, only a few rare examples were able to rise above the disease that darkened man's heart and that can be summarized with a single word: self-love.

Christ the Word, however, in His great mercy and love, labored to gradually heal man first by curtailing the outward expressions of the passions through the Mosaic Law, secondly by prodding man towards an honest and sincere fulfillment of the Law through the Prophets, and finally by taking on human flesh and becoming man in order to be the Way and provide the means for man to be completely healed: i.e., to purify his body and soul from the passions, to continue the work that was set before Adam in Paradise, and by grace to enter communion with Christ again. The Incarnate Christ now is able to heal man through His teachings, His example, His

---

[3] Ibid., pages 117-118.

Person, and His Church. In His teachings, the Lord Christ revealed to man the nature of his sickness in his selfish relationship with God, his fellowman, and the world. He gave him self-emptying commandments that could heal his heart through repentance, humility, and love. By His example, Christ practically revealed how to be humble, how to pray, how to fast, how to love God and how to love one's enemies. In His Person, He healed human nature itself conquering both corruption and death by resurrecting His own human body. Finally Christ ascended with His resurrected human body to the very throne of the Father, raising it to the state of *permanent* glorification and thereby making it the *natural* source of divine glory. In so doing, He raised human nature through His glorified body to a state higher than that of Adam in Paradise thus reconciling him with His Father, offering Him His glorified human body that He allowed to be crucified, and sending the Holy Spirit, the Comforter to sanctify creation. And finally the Good Physician of our souls and bodies established His Church on the day of Pentecost as the most perfect hospital in which spiritually sick man could be healed.

The Church continues to heal man through diverse means. In Holy Baptism, man is healed of the consequences of the ancestral sin, cleansed of his own personal sins, and clothed with Christ. The new-believer thus dies with Christ "in order to be raised with Him and to lead the new life that His Resurrection has granted to mankind."[4] In Chrismation, he receives the seal of the Holy Spirit and the grace to help him turn fully to God.[5] Through Confession, the believer has the opportunity to cleanse himself of his sins committed after Holy Baptism. And in Holy Communion, the most powerful medicine for healing the soul, man receives not simply the grace of Christ, but Christ Himself. In addition to the Holy Mysteries, the Church directs the believer towards the goal of health (through the commemoration of the Saints) and teaches him how to repent, how to believe, and how to pray.[6] The believer learns to follow Christ's commandments, to make them the law of his existence, acting according to them rather than according to sinful habit (the passions). Through the ceaseless prayer of the heart, he reacquires the permanent memory of God that Adam had in Paradise, while through watching over his thoughts, he gains control over the deluding effects of the imagination. And thus gradually, the Church leads the believer through the stages of purification and illumination to that of glorification.

This, the broader context of the healing of man's personality (heart) of selfish love within the Church, is the framework within which Saint Paul's discourse on spiritual gifts must be understood in his *First Epistle to the Corinthians*. The gifts are the sign

[4] Ibid., page 349.

[5] Ibid., page 353.

[6] Cf., especially the texts of Vespers and Matins during Great Lent.

that one is in fact a member of the Body of Christ and indicate the particular stage of the spiritual life (purification, illumination, or glorification) which the believer has reached. The specific context of Saint Paul's words, however, is the use of "kinds of tongues" in the liturgical worship of the Church of Corinth. In order to comprehend this passage, one must first determine what the original Greek text reveals to us about the nature of "kinds of tongues" and on that basis to interpret the text in the light of the hesychastic tradition of the Church.

2. The "Traditional" English Text: Its Translation and Interpretation

"They know not the ways thereof, nor abide
in the paths thereof."
— *Job* 24:13

Unfortunately, the translators of the King James Version of the Bible, the most influential of the English translations,[7] were unfamiliar with the practice and experience of inner prayer since the West had been cut off from the hesychastic tradition many centuries before. Hence, various crucial expressions in this passage were unwisely translated or mistranslated into English, thus opening the entire passage up to interpretations not fully based on Saint Paul's actual words. The translators of the

[7] And more to the point, this translation was the one used by the first American Pentecostals.

King James Bible apparently had already decided that the passage in question referred to speaking in unknown foreign languages, so they translated the text accordingly even if this meant infidelity to the plain sense of the original text.

Although the King James version of *I Corinthians* 14:2 reads "For he that speaketh in an *unknown* tongue speaketh not unto men, but unto God: for no man *understandeth* him," indicating that the one speaking in a tongue is speaking in a foreign language, the word "unknown" is not present in the original in this case or in the other five cases in which the authors of the KJV insert it.[8] Moreover, the verb in the last half of the verse is not "to understand," but "to hear." A more accurate translation would have been, "for he who speaks with a tongue does not speak to men, but to God, for no one *hears*."[9] In other words, Paul states quite clearly that when one speaks in a tongue "no one hears," that is, no one hears, because speaking in a tongue is offered up silently within the heart. In like manner, the authors of the King James version translate *I Corinthians* 14:10 as "there are, it may be, so many kinds of voices in the world, and none of them is without *signification*" again pointing to the incomprehensibility

[8] The word "unknown" is added to the word "tongue" in the KJV version of *First Corinthians* 14:2, 3, 4, 16, 20, and 29 presumably for clarity's sake. Fortunately, the RSV has removed these additions.

[9] ὁ γὰρ λαλῶν γλώσσῃ οὐκ ἀνθρώποις λαλεῖ, ἀλλὰ τῷ Θεῷ· οὐδ-ε ὶς γὰρ ἀκούει." This verse is also not mistranslated in the RSV.

of a foreign language to one who does not speak it, although a more precise rendering of the Greek text would have been "there are, it may be, so many kinds of voices in the world, and none of them are *mute* (or silent),"[10] again indicating that the inaudible speaking in tongues is an exception, since it takes place without the use of the voice (*a phonon* literally means "no voice"). In a similar vein, the same translators render *I Corinthians* 14:8 as "for if the trumpet give an *uncertain sound*, who shall prepare himself to the battle,"[11] although Saint Paul here speaks not of an "uncertain sound," which would be an allusion to speaking in an unknown language or making inarticulate sounds, but of an "unmanifested sound," which alludes to silent prayer. Thus a better translation would have been "For if the trumpet *does not manifest* its sound, who shall prepare himself for battle," with the implication that if one does not use one's voice and pray out loud (and thus "sound the trumpet"), how will the others who do not yet have the prayer of the heart be edified. Finally, those who do not have the gift of speaking in tongues (inner prayer) need to hear "the loudness of the voice,"[12]

---

[10]"τοσαῦτα, εἰ τύχοι, γένη φωνῶν ἐστὶν ἐν κόσμῳ, καὶ οὐδὲν α ὐτῶν ἄφωνον." (The RSV here follows the questionable translation of the KJV).

[11]"καὶ γὰρ ἐαν ἄδηλον φωνὴν σάλπιγξ δῷ, τίς παρασκευάσεται εἰς πόλεμον." (The RSV here follows the questionable translation of the KJV).

[12] "δύναμιν τῆς φωνῆς," other possible translations include, the volume, power, or strength of the voice (The RSV here follows the questionable translation of the KJV).

(which the KJV renders "meaning of the voice") in order to respond by saying their "Amen" and thus be benefited,[13] for if everyone is praying the psalms silently in their heart by the Holy Spirit, how would one without this gift "know"[14] what is being said.

Thus at every cross-roads, the translators based on their own experience (or, to be more precise, inexperience) selected expressions that would prevent the English-speaking reader from understanding the very nature of the gift of speaking in tongues to which Saint Paul was referring in any way other than the most external and superficial. If, however, one translates the text more simply, and if one realizes that in *Corinthians* 14:24-37 Saint Paul is already considering the separate issue of women speaking in Church,[15] the interpretation of kinds of tongues as prayers offered up silently in the heart through the Holy Spirit is not only not far-fetched, it fits squarely within the parameters of the Biblical text, not to mention the tradition, teaching, and experience of the Church.

---

[13] Father John Romanides, *The Ancestral Sin* (Domos: Athens, 1992), pages xxiix-xxix (in Greek).

[14] "τί λέγεις οὐκ οἶδε" which the KJV again mistranslates as "he understandeth not what thou sayest," although the RSV correctly translates this verse.

[15] Father John Romanides, *The Ancestral Sin*, page xxxi (in Greek).

3. Kinds of Tongues in *Corinthians* and other Pauline Epistles

"And because ye are sons, God hath sent
forth the Spirit of his Son into your hearts,
crying, Abba, Father."
— *Galatians* 4:6

In Corinth, the gift of kinds of tongues referred to the kinds of prayers and psalms from the Old Testament offered up silently by the tongue in the heart through the Holy Spirit as Saint Paul clearly describes it in *I Corinthians* 14: 17: "I will *pray with the spirit*, but I will also pray with the mind. I will *sing psalms with the spirit*, but I will also sing psalms with the mind." When the prayers and psalms are transferred by the fear of God (which is the first gift leading to repentance) from the reason to the spirit or inner man or heart, man's personality begins to be healed, he enters the stage of repentance, his heart is gradually emptied of both good thoughts and bad, his blameworthy passions begin to be transformed into blameless ones, and he begins his journey towards illumination.[16] By speaking in tongues, this silent prayer "with the spirit," the Corinthians were simply following the Lord's advice, "when thou prayest, enter into thy closet, and when thou hast shut thy door, pray to thy Father which is in secret."[17] Thus, they would descend deep into the heart "where their

[16] Ibid., page 28.
[17] *Matthew* 6:6.

treasure is" and pray to the Lord. If there was any question why they would be particularly edified praying in Persian instead of in Greek, there is no question why they would be especially edified praying silently within their hearts in the Holy Spirit following the Lord's command. In this light, it becomes quite understandable why Saint Paul, who encouraged the Thessalonians to "pray without ceasing"[18] and the Ephesians to speak "to yourselves in psalms and hymns and spiritual songs, singing and making melody in your heart to the Lord,"[19] would likewise thank God that he speaks in tongues, that is, prays silently in his heart through the Holy Spirit, more than all the rest. Quite understandably, he wishes that they all would speak in tongues, for there is no treasure more precious and no joy more sweet than man's intimate converse with Christ deep in the Paradise of the heart.

Father J. Romanides notes that speaking in tongues is not peculiar to Corinth and that Saint Paul refers to this gift in his other epistles, even if he does not employ the same term (tongues) to denote it. These passages are worth quoting at length. To the Galatians, Saint Paul writes, "And because ye are sons, God hath sent forth *the Spirit of his Son into your* <u>*hearts*</u>*, crying, Abba, Father.* Wherefore thou art no more a servant, but a son; and if a son, then an

---

[18] *1 Thessalonians* 5:17.
[19] *Ephesians* 5:19.

heir of God through Christ. (4:6-7)[20] In other words, prayer activated by the Holy Spirit in the heart (N.B., not with the mouth) is the indication that the Christian has become a son of God by grace and entered the stage of illumination. Saint Paul reiterates this objective fact in his *Epistle to the Romans*:

> For as many as are led by the Spirit of God, they are the sons of God. For ye have not received the spirit of bondage again to fear; but *ye have received the Spirit of adoption, whereby we cry, Abba, Father. The Spirit itself beareth witness with our spirit,* that we are the children of God... Likewise the Spirit also helpeth our infirmities: for we know not what we should pray for as we ought: but *the Spirit itself maketh intercession for us with groanings which <u>cannot be uttered.</u>* And He that searcheth the hearts knoweth what is the mind of the Spirit, because He maketh intercession for the saints according to the will of God"[21] (8:14-16; 26-27).

---

[20] Father John Romanides, "Jesus Christ: the Life of the World," page 332 (in Greek).

[21] According to the Fathers, Saint Paul here is clearly speaking about the grace-filled and Spirit-activated prayer of the heart that is received when the believer has purified himself of the passions. (cf., Saint Hesychios the Priest, "On Watchfulness and Holiness," and Saint Diadochos of Photiki, "On Spiritual Knowledge," *The Philokalia*, v. 1, page 164 and page 271 respectively, "A Discourse on Abba Philemon," *The Philokalia*,

That "the Spirit itself beareth witness to our spirit" indicates that one who has the gift of tongues "hears" or "follows" with his *nous* the prayer said by the Spirit in his heart. This gift of tongues or the prayer of the heart is "the law of God after the inward man" in which Saint Paul delights and "the reasonable worship" (λογικὴ λατρεία) by which the believer "is transfigured by the renewing of the nous" (*Romans* 7:22,12:1-2).[22]

Saint Paul likewise describes the gift of tongues in detail when he writes to the Ephesians, "Be filled with the Spirit; *Speaking to yourselves* in *psalms and hymns* and spiritual songs, singing and making melody *in your heart* to the Lord. Giving thanks *always* for all things unto God and the Father in the name of our Lord Jesus Christ" (*Ephesians* 5:18-20). In other words, Saint Paul is saying that in order to have the gift of tongues the believer must have the Spirit in his heart (making intercessions as we saw in *Romans* and *Galatians*). Simultaneously, Saint Paul describes speaking in tongues as *speaking to yourself,* as opposed to out loud, with the comprehensible words of prayer (psalms and hymns and spiritual songs) in the heart. This is precisely the same advice Saint Paul gives to the Corinthians, "But if there be no interpreter, let him keep silence in the church, *and let him speak to himself and to God*"

v. 2, page 354, Saint Gregory of Sinai, "On the Signs of Grace and Delusion," *The Philokalia,* v. 4, page 260).

[22] Father John Romanides, "Jesus Christ: the Life of the World," page 333.

(14:28). Finally, this prayer of the heart called speaking in tongues is continuous or unceasing prayer by which man "gives thanks *always* for all things unto God and the Father in the name of our Lord Jesus Christ." Because this prayer continues to repeat itself in the heart through the Holy Spirit, Saint Paul could say to the Corinthians, "I thank my God, I speak with tongues more than ye all."[23]

In Saint Paul's *First Epistle to the Thessalonians,* he also refers to the gift of tongues summarizing the above teachings, "Rejoice *evermore. Pray without ceasing.* In every thing give thanks: for this is the will of God in Christ Jesus concerning you. *Quench not the Spirit.* Despise not prophesyings. Prove *all things; hold fast that which is good. Abstain from all appearance of evil"* (5:16-22).[24] In this passage, Saint Paul also stresses that this unceasing prayer of the Holy Spirit (that should not be quenched) also enables the believer to acquire watchfulness over the thoughts "proving all things"

This unmanifested prayer of the heart as a gift of the Spirit, however, must be distinguished from emotional prayer, silent prayer in one's mind, or even one's attempt to pray in the heart. Man's struggle, labor, insistence, persistence and attention in prayer express human virtue that must be first exercised in order to acquire the prayer of the heart, but for the prayer to well up from the heart ceaselessly, effortlessly and naturally filling the soul with joy and

---

[23] *1 Corinthians* 14:18.
[24] Ibid., page 334.

light, one must receive the gift of prayer enlivened by the grace of the Holy Spirit. The kinds of tongues in *First Corinthians* refer not to the *virtue* of silent prayer, but to the *spiritual gift* of silent prayer[25] that is far deeper than simply the words of prayer, for through it one's entire soul is cleansed and illumined. Through it, man regains the memory of God that Adam had in Paradise. Through it, the heart is healed and takes a place of prominence in the soul watching over the thoughts, controlling the desires, and governing the will. This in fact is the primary work of repentance. It is no wonder that a gift such as this would be greatly desired and avidly cultivated in Corinth and elsewhere.

Thus in addressing the Corinthians, Saint Paul begins by stressing the freedom of the one who has spiritual gifts[26] and then by characterizing both the gift of tongues and the distinguishing trait of the one who possesses that gift. He writes, "no one who *speaks by the Spirit of God* can say 'anathema Jesus,' and no one is able to say 'Lord Jesus' except by the

[25] Cf., Saint Simeon the New Theologian's more general discussion on the difference between virtues and the gifts of the spirit in his 18th Catechetical Discourse, pages 190-192 (in Greek). Saint Theophan the Recluse refers to this distinction as follows, "Inner prayer consists of two states, one *strenuous,* when the man strives for it, and the other *self-impelled,* when the prayer exists and acts on its own." *The Art of Prayer*, page 71.

[26] Cf., our earlier discussion on the Prophets in both chapters 1 and 3.

Holy Spirit."[27] The gift of tongues is the gift of praying in the heart by the Spirit and through Christ to the Father. Here, "Saint Paul speaks about real and ceaseless prayer *of the Holy Spirit* in the heart, and not heart-felt feelings."[28] The believer who has received this gift, who does not merely call upon Christ with his mind, but does so deep in his heart by the Holy Spirit, cannot renounce Christ even under torture. If he were to renounce Christ, it would mean that he did not in fact have the gift of tongues, that he had not reached the state of illumination by the Holy Spirit, and was not truly member of the Body of Christ. This is the most basic gift of the Spirit shared by all those who have passed through the stage of purification of the passions to that of illumination by the grace of the Holy Spirit,[29] and seen so clearly in the lives of the Martyrs from Saint Stephen the Protomartyr onwards.

---

[27]οὐδεὶς ἐν Πνεύματι Θεοῦ λαλῶν λέγει ἀνάθεμα Ἰησοῦς, καὶ ὑδεὶς δύναται εἰπεῖν Κύριον Ἰησοῦν εἰ μὴ ἐν Πνεύματι, which the KJV renders "no man speaking by the Spirit of God calleth Jesus accursed: and that no man can say that Jesus is the Lord, but by the Holy Ghost." This version implies that one cannot make the statement Jesus is Lord without the Holy Spirit. In this particular case, however, there is no need to insert the verb "to be" as with adjectives in the predicative position, for Saint Paul may well have been referring here to the first words of a known prayer (e.g., Lord Jesus have mercy on me).

[28] Father John Romanides, *The Ancestral Sin*, pages xxx-xxxi (in Greek).

[29] Fr. John S. Romanides, "Justice and Peace in Ecclesiological Context," page 240.

4. The Illumined and the Perfected: Spiritual Gifts and Ministries

"And this also we wish, even your perfection."

— *2 Corinthians* 13: 9

With this foundation in place, Saint Paul then notes that although there are differences among the various gifts, ministries, and activities in the Church, they all have the same source. "The grace of the Spirit is one and unchanging; but energizes each one of as He wills (*1 Corinthians* 12:11). When rain falls on the earth, it gives life to the quality inherent in each plant: sweetness to the sweet; astringency to the astringent. Similarly when grace falls upon the hearts of the faithful, it gives to each the energy appropriate to the different virtues without itself changing."[30] Here, we encounter more openly the idea of synergy that Saint Paul already pointed to in speaking about "not being carried away by the dumb idols." Simultaneously, Saint Paul emphasizes the sovereignty of the Spirit "that bloweth where it listeth."[31] At each stage in man's spiritual healing, man offers up his good will and honest effort, but the

[30] Saint Mark the Ascetic, "No Righteousness by Works," *The Philokalia: The Complete Text* comp. By St. Nikodimos of the Holy Mountain and St. Makarios of Corinth, trans. By G.E.H. Palmer, Philip Sherrard, and Kallistos Ware, vol. 1, (Faber and Faber: London, 1979), page 134.

[31] *John* 3:8.

114

Spirit effects the change through purifying, illumining, or deifying grace as He sees fit.

Having identified the Source of all true gifts, the Apostle Paul then speaks at length about the spiritual gifts describing their use, purpose, and relative importance in the life of the Church. The gifts themselves point to where the believer is found in the process of the healing of his personality. Among these gifts, Saint Paul numbers the word of wisdom, the word of knowledge, faith, healing, the working of miracles, prophecy, discerning of spirits, kinds of tongues, and the interpretation of tongues. The "word of wisdom" means to be wise and be able to make other wise.[32] This is a gift that the Apostles possessed and is observed in the very epistles of Saint John the Theologian and Saint Paul. The word of knowledge, on the other hand, is the knowledge of and ability to recognize the Truth, but not necessarily the ability to express it.[33] Following these teaching gifts, Saint Paul mentions faith that is able to move mountains, healing, and the working of miracles. Whereas healing refers only to the restoration of health, the working of miracles includes the grace to bind or punish as well. The latter gift Saint Paul employed when he blinded the sorcerer and Saint Peter did so when at his word Ananias collapsed and died. The gift of comprehensibility observed on Pentecost

[32] Saint John of Damascus, *Commentary on the First Epistle to the Corinthians,* chapter 12, page 326 (in Greek).

[33] Saint John Chrysostom, *Commentary on the Epistle to the Corinthians,* page 256. Cf., Saint Nicodemos,*Commentary on the 14 Epistles,* page 326-327 (both in Greek).

as a type of clairvoyance would seem to be a positive manifestation of the more general category of working miracles. Prophecy, whose source is a direct experience of revelation, the glory of Christ, refers mainly to the ability to express the will of God at every moment and place ("thus saith the Lord"), but also to the ability to interpret the Prophets (having seen the same vision of Christ as they did) and to see the past and future as present. Discerning the spirits refers to the ability to discern who is genuine and who is not, who is a prophet and who is not.[34] Kinds of tongues refers to the ceaseless prayer of the heart in the Holy Spirit, whereas the interpretation of tongues to the translation of that prayer or hymn into audible prayer as expressed by the hymnology of the Church. Fr. Romanides further notes that "the difference between those who prophesied and those who interpreted was that the first had direct eye-witness experience of the Truth of Scripture and knew exactly how he reached glorification and so could guide others unerringly in the same experience. Those who interpreted Scripture did so with the guidance of the Holy Spirit praying in the heart and under the guidance of the Prophets and Apostles."[35]

---

[34] Ibid., page 258. Cf., St. Nicodemos, *Commentary on the 14 Epistles,* page 327; St. John of Damascus, *Commentary on the First Epistle to the Corinthians,* chapter 12, page 334 (all in Greek).

[35] Father John Romanides, "Justice and Peace in Ecclesiological Context," pages 240-241.

This list of gifts, however, is not unique in Holy Scripture. Both Saint Gregory Palamas and Peter of Damascus note that the Prophet Isaiah has another such list that includes the spirit of wisdom and understanding, the spirit of counsel and strength, the spirit of knowledge and reverence, the spirit of the fear of God. And these "spirits" known as the "seven gifts of the Holy Spirit" are the energies of the Holy Spirit that act in purified man.[36] These gifts are not seen as "supernatural powers" that the believer can wield when he enters some semi-conscious "mystical state," but quite simply ministries or capabilities (*diaconia*) with which the believer is entrusted in order to serve and minister unto his neighbor.[37] As Christ came "not to be ministered unto, but to minister,"[38] so the Christian who is purified of the passions and illumined by the grace of the Holy Spirit is able to employ the gifts he receives from Christ in like fashion, in a self-offering of love. If the gift received is not used to edify, it in fact will be to the condemnation of the one who received it.[39] For this reason, Saint

[36] Saint Peter of Damascus In *The Philokalia,* v. III, page 93 and Saint Gregory Palamas' "Topics of Natural and Theological Science" in *The Philokalia,* v. IV, page 378.

[37] Saint Nicodemos of the Holy Mountain, *Commentary on the 14 Epistles,* page 325 quoting from an unidentified manuscript by Saint Photius the Great. Later Saint Nicodemos adds, "for absolutely everything is for the gift that you have to be beneficial for others." Ibid., page 350 (in Greek).

[38] *Matthew* 20:28 and *Mark* 10:45.

[39] Saint John Chrysostom, *Commentary on the Epistle to the Corinthians,* page 506 and Saint Nicodemos, *Commentary on the 14 Epistles,* page 357 (both in Greek).

Theognostos advises "do not even ask for spiritual gifts unless they contribute to your salvation and help you to remain humble."[40] If the gifts are not "equal," this is due to the fact that "the vessels of the Spirit are not equal."[41] Saint Macarius of Egypt expresses this insight in this way, "Just as many lamps may be lit from the same oil and from a single light, and yet often do not give out an equal radiance, so the gifts that come from different virtues reflect the Light of the Holy Spirit in different ways."[42]

Having listed the gifts and likened the interdependence of the members of the Body of Christ with the same physiological interdependence of the human body, Saint Paul lists the members of the Church that correspond to the previous list of gifts. "And God hath set some in the church, first apostles, secondarily prophets, thirdly teachers, after that miracles, then gifts of healings, helps, governments, diversities of tongues" (12:28). Commenting on this passage, Saint Nikitas writes,

> No one baptized into Christ and believing in Him is left without a share in the grace of the Spirit, so long as he has not succumbed to any diabolic influence and defiled his faith with evil actions or does not

[40] Saint Theognostos, "On the Practice of the Virtues" in *The Philokalia*, v. II, page 369.

[41] Saint Nicodemos, *Commentary on the 14 Epistles*, page 326 quoting Saint Gregory the Theologian (in Greek).

[42] Saint Macarius of Egypt, "Patient Endurance & Discrimination," *The Philokalia*, v. III, page 302.

live slothfully and disolutely... He may after worthily engaging in the spiritual combat be blessed through the plenitude of the Spirit with the consciousness of God's wisdom and so become a teacher in the Church or he may through the same Spirit be given knowledge of God's mysteries or come to understand the mysteries of the Kingdom of heaven; or from the same Spirit he may acquire deep-rooted faith in God's promises, as Abraham did. He may receive the gift of healing, so that he can cure diseases, or of spiritual power, so that he can expel demons and perform miracles; or of prophecy, so that he can foresee and predict things of the future; or of the ability to distinguish between spirits, so that he can discern who is speaking in the Spirit of God and who is not, or of interpretation of various tongues, or of helping the weary, or of governing God's flocks and His people, or of love for all men and the gifts of grace that go with it, long-suffering kindness and the rest. If you are bereft of all these qualities there is no way in which I could call you a believer or number you among those who have 'clothed themselves in Christ' through divine baptism.[43]

Briefly put, the gifts of the Spirit indicate that the receiver is indeed a temple of the Holy Spirit and

---

[43] Saint Nikitas Stithatos, *The Philokalia,* v. IV, page 168.

a member of the Body of Christ. Thus, Saint Paul writes, as "one star differeth from another star in glory,"[44] so the members of the Church differ according to the stage of spiritual healing through which they are passing. Saint Nikitas puts it in this way, "Of those granted the grace of the Holy Spirit in the form of various gifts, some are still immature and imperfect with regard to these gifts, while others are mature and perfect enjoying them in their fullness."[45] According to Fr. Romanides, "Paul lists 'kinds of tongues' as the bottom of the line of membership. This is why all the members have this gift of grace. But there were those who had gifts of the Spirit in addition, a fact which puts them at a higher level."[46] The gift of ceaseless prayer (tongues) is, in fact, so taken for granted by Saint Paul that when he lists the various ministries corresponding to the gifts in *Ephesians* and *Romans*, he does not even mention that gift in particular,[47] although he clearly instructs

[44] *1 Corinthians* 15:41.

[45] Saint Nikitas Stithatos, *The Philokalia*, v. IV, pages 168-169.

[46] Fr. John S. Romanides, "Justice and Peace in Ecclesiological Context," page 239.

[47] "And he gave some, apostles; and some, prophets; and some, evangelists; and some, pastors and teachers; For *the perfecting of the saints*, for the work of the ministry, for the edifying of the body of Christ;" (*Ephesians* 4:11-12) and "Having then gifts differing according to the grace that is given to us, whether prophecy, let us prophesy according to the proportion of faith; Or ministry, let us wait on our ministering: or he that teacheth, on teaching; Or he that exhorteth, on exhortation: he that giveth, let him do it with simplicity; he that ruleth, with dili-

both the Thessalonians (5:17) and the Ephesians (5:19) to cultivate it.

5. Illumination and Glorification: Unceasing Prayer and the Vision of Christ

"When Christ, who is our life, shall appear, then shall ye also appear with Him in glory."

— *Colossians* 3:4

According to Saint Paul, the foundation stones of the Church are those who have reached a state of glorification (perfection or deification) and in whom the entire Church rejoices.[48] Here, it is important to realize that Saint Paul is not using the term "glorified" metaphorically for praise or honor by men

gence; he that showeth mercy, with cheerfulness" (*Romans* 12:6-8).

[48] Once again, the KJV obscures the meaning of this passage translating *1 Corinthians* 12:26, "And whether one member suffer, all the members suffer with it; or one member *be honored*, all the members rejoice with it." There is, however, no reference to "being honored," but to "being glorified" (Εἴτε δοξάζεται ἕν μέλος, συγχαίρει ὅλα τὰ μέλη) which means perfected, united with Christ and deified. "And the *glory* which thou gavest me I have given them; that they may be one, even as we are one: I in them, and thou in me, *that they may be made perfect* in one; and that the world may know that thou hast sent me, and hast loved them, as thou hast loved me." (*John* 17:22-23)

(which is no reason for a Christian to rejoice),[49] but ontologically for the new reality of those who have become "partakers of the divine glory"[50] and consequently have both beheld the glorified Christ and "received from His fullness."[51] They are the Apostles or Prophets among whom Saint Paul numbers himself without separating himself from those who pray in the heart (kinds of tongues). The essential trait that distinguishes an Apostle or a Prophet is neither "missionary activity" nor "forecasting capabilities," but an experience of revelation granted to a properly illumined vessel, a vision of Christ that transfigures the one who beholds Him. This Paul summarizes in *Ephesians* (3:5) as the mystery of Christ "which in other ages was not made known unto the sons of men, as it is *now revealed* unto his holy Apostles and Prophets by the Spirit."[52] As the glorified Christ was fully revealed by the Holy Spirit to the Apostles on Pentecost thus leading them to *all* Truth, in like manner is Christ now revealed to the Prophets of the New Covenant.

As important as the prayer of the heart (kinds of tongues) is in the process of man's healing and il-

---

[49] "For they loved the *glory* (δόξαν) of men more than the *glory* (δόξαν) of God." *John* 12:43 (Not "honor" as the KJV typically mistranslates it).

[50] *2 Peter* 1:4. In theological terms, Saint Peter means glory when he writes nature.

[51] *John* 1:16: "And of his fullness have all we received, and grace for grace."

[52] Fr. John Romanides, "Justice and Peace in Ecclesiological Context," page 240.

lumination, it is neither the goal of the Christian life nor the complete healing of man's soul, for although those who pray in the heart (not by their own effort, but with a prayer activated by the grace of the Holy Spirit) are in a state of illumination and may have even acquired some of the other lower gifts, they can still fall into pride and thus become "a sounding brass" or "nothing." The complete healing takes place with the vision of Christ in glory that grants perfect love which never fails and which Saint Paul describes in *1 Corinthians* 13:4-7: "Love suffereth long, and is kind; love envieth not; love vaunteth not itself, is not puffed up, Doth not behave itself unseemly, seeketh not her own, is not easily provoked, thinketh no evil; Rejoiceth not in iniquity, but rejoiceth in the truth; Beareth all things, believeth all things, hopeth all things, endureth all things." This love, however, must not be confused with sentimentality nor with mere ethical perfectionism. It is rather the highest gift of the Holy Spirit. It entails man's complete self-emptying[53] through keeping Christ's command-

---

[53] Purification is self-emptying by nature. What vessel can be cleansed unless it is not first emptied?

ments[54] to the point of the Cross being perfected in "his face to face encounter with Christ" in glory through the Holy Spirit. Only in this way, can man become one with God and "like" God "Who is love." Obedience to Christ's commandments directs man to this perfect love. Strengthened by grace, man implements the commandments and again by grace gradually grows in love, until Christ loves him and reveals Himself to him granting him perfect love that never fails. This is what He Himself said to His holy Apostles, "he that hath My commandments, and keepeth them, he it is that *loveth* Me: and he that *loveth* Me shall be loved of My Father, and I will love him, and *will manifest Myself to him*."[55]

At this point, Saint Paul speaks even more concretely about the stages of illumination and glorification and the operation of the gifts at each stage. Saint Nikitas comments, "the mature and the perfect, having attained the summit of God's love and knowledge, cease from exercising partial gifts, whether of prophecy, or of distinguishing between

[54] Saint Paul summarizes this in his discourse on love. The following commandments of Christ exemplify this point: "But I say unto you, That whosoever looketh on a woman to lust after her hath committed adultery with her already in his heart" *Matthew* 5:28. "But I say unto you, Love your enemies, bless them that curse you, do good to them that hate you, and pray for them which despitefully use you, and persecute you" *Matthew* 5:44. "But I say unto you, That every idle word that men shall speak, they shall give account thereof in the day of judgment" *Matthew* 12:36.

[55] *John* 14:21.

spirits, or of helping, or of governing, and so on. Once you enter the palace of love, you no longer know in part the God, Who is Love, but, conversing with Him face to face, you understand Him fully even as you yourself are fully understood by Him."[56] The state of glorification or deification that is reached in the vision of Christ in the Holy Spirit is not relegated to the safely remote region of life after death, but is a reality experienced in this life. This is clearly revealed in the lives of Saint Paul,[57] Saint Stephen the first Martyr,[58] Saint John the Theologian,[59] and the countless hosts of Saints throughout the centuries who have progressed through the same stages of purification, illumination until they reached that of deification.[60] The words, "but *we see* Jesus, who was

---

[56] Saint Nikitas Stithatos, *The Philokalia,* v. IV, page 169.

[57] "I knew a man in Christ above fourteen years ago, (whether in the body, I cannot tell; or whether out of the body, I cannot tell: God knoweth;) such an one caught up to the third heaven" *2 Corinthians* 12:2.

[58] "And said, Behold, I see the heavens opened, and the Son of man standing on the right hand of God" *Acts* 7:56.

[59] "I was in the Spirit on the Lord's day, and heard behind me a great voice, as of a trumpet, Saying, I am Alpha and Omega, the first and the last" *Revelation* 1:10-11.

[60] "Thus, it is clear that the resurrection of Christ and his appearances in glory took place and take place only for the deification of those appropriately prepared. This appearance did not take place only for a certain "lucky few" who were in Jerusalem at the time of His Passion, the Resurrection, the Ascension, and Pentecost, but takes place for all who wish to follow the same way of the healing of the disease of selfishness in order to acquire the health of unselfishness. Deification, then, does not refer only to those who were in Christ's surroundings,

made a little lower than the angels for the suffering of death, crowned with glory and honor,"[61] in *The Epistle to the Hebrews are not* metaphorical, nor rhetorical, nor an expression for the Church's witness to the resurrection, but the common experience of the believer whose heart has been fully healed and is thus reckoned with the saints, the perfected members of the Church (those in a state of glorification or deification).

Fr. Romanides commenting on Saint Paul's words to the Corinthians writes, "'For when the perfect is come,' the face to face encounter with Christ in glory, 'then that which is in part is abolished' (13:10), but 'love never fails. For whether there be prophecies, they will pass away, whether tongues, they will cease, whether knowledge, it will pass away' (13:8-9). During glorification, the prophetic witness to Christ is replaced by Christ Himself, the prayer of the Holy Spirit in the heart temporarily ceases and returns when the vision is terminated, and concepts and words about Christ in the glory of His Father are

---

but to everyone in all the world. This is precisely what is meant by the presence of prophets in the parishes founded by the Apostles far from Jerusalem. After His Resurrection, Christ appears only for the deification and perfection of His disciples, and not to the world. 'Yet a little while, and the world seeth me no more; but ye see me' (*John* 14:19). For the world, there is only the empty tomb." Fr. Romanides, *The Ancestral Sin,* page xxx (in Greek).

[61] *Hebrews* 2:9.

abolished by the reality itself."[62] Tongues (the ceaseless prayer of the heart), knowledge, and prophecy that are gifts proper to the stage of illumination disappear not merely in the future age, but for a time in this age as well when the illumined beholds Christ Who in this way glorifies and perfects him. Elsewhere Father Romanides writes:

> Deification, before the glorious appearance of Christ as arisen from the dead is the perfection of the illumined, certainly a temporary state, since after the vision of Christ, the deified returns to a state of illumination... He who is in a state of illumination is a child and speaks as a child, thinks as a child (*I Corinthians* 13:11). He who is in a state of deification becomes a man and childish things are put away. All those in a state of illumination 'see through a glass, darkly; but (those in a state of deification) face to face.' Paul continues referring to himself, now (in a state of illumination) 'I know in part; but then (in a state of deification) I shall I know even as also I have been known.' In other words, Paul will be known by God as he had been known by him in the past. He who prays in the spirit sees Christ 'as in a glass dimly.' While he

---

[62] Fr. John Romanides, "Justice and Peace in Ecclesiological Context," page 241.

who is in a state of deification sees Him 'face to face.'[63]

This process that Saint Paul describes in *First Corinthians* can be clearly observed in the lives of the Saints. Saint Anthony the Great first underwent a long period of struggles and tribulations devoting himself to prayer and fasting (purification) before he obtained the gift of prayer (illumination), and then saw Christ in glory (glorification) and became himself the professor of the desert (healing the spiritual sicknesses of those who turned to him for help). In the life of Saint Simeon the New Theologian, we likewise note first strict obedience to his conscience (purification), his acquisition of prayer in the heart (illumination), and then his vision of Christ in the divine light (glorification). In the life of Saint Gregory Palamas, we note first his absolute obedience to his spiritual father (purification), then his acquisition of inner prayer as he would cry out day and night "enlighten my darkness" (illumination), and then his vision of the divine light (deification). Precisely, the same stages in the process of the healing of the heart can be easily outlined in the lives of more recent saints and saintly men such as Saint Seraphim of Sarov, Saint Silouan the Athonite, the Elder Joseph the Hesychast the Athonite and the Elder Paissios the Athonite.

Having described the gifts, their relation to the stages in man's progressive spiritual healing, and the

---

[63] Fr. John Romanides, *The Ancestral Sin,* page xxix.

ultimate goal that lies before him, Saint Paul is now in a position to address the disturbance caused by the Corinthians' use of tongues, silent prayer of the heart, in their services. If everyone were at a state of illumination, if every believer had the gift of unceasing prayer in his heart, there would presumably be no problem. The fact of the matter is, however, that in addition to those in a state of illumination (with the gift of tongues) and glorification (with prophetic/apostolic witness stemming from the vision of Christ), there were also those private individuals (*idiotai*) who were "baptized by water unto remission of sins and in a state of purification who had not yet received the transfer by the Holy Spirit of the prayers and psalms from the reason to the spirit recurring in the heart," and unbelievers "who have not yet come into the arena of purification."[64] It is Saint Paul's pastoral concern for the proper instruction and healing of those in or prior to the process of purification that leads him to comment on the use of tongues in Corinth.

Thus, Saint Paul notes that while those illumined who pray silently in the heart (pray in tongues) are edified in their converse with God, he rightfully asks how will those without that gift be edified since they will enter Church and will not hear anything (*I Corinthians* 14:2). Thus, Saint Nikitas comments, "If when you pray and psalmodize you speak to God in private you edify yourself, as Saint Paul says. But once you have laid hold of love you

[64] Ibid., page xxix.

feel impelled to prophesy for the edification of God's Church (cf., *I Corinthians* 14: 2-4), that is to teach your fellow men how to practice the commandments of God and how they must endeavor to conform to God's will. If when you pray and psalmodize you speak to God in private you edify yourself, as Saint Paul says. But once you have laid hold of love you feel impelled to prophesy for the edification of God's Church (cf., *I Corinthians* 14: 2-4), that is to teach your fellow men how to practice the commandments of God and how they must endeavor to conform to God's will." In other words, love requires those who have reached a state of spiritual health or perfection to teach those who are still lacking in health how to be healed as well. It is not enough that those with the gift of the prayer in the heart edify themselves silently. They are called to interpret their inward prayer into words of encouragement and instruction for those without the gift. Fr. J. Romanides notes,

> Paul no where says that someone inter-
> prets what another 'says in tongues.' One
> interprets what he himself 'says in tongues'
> in his heart. Consequently, *1 Corinthians*
> 14:27-28 means 'If any man speak in a
> tongue, let it be by two, or at the most by
> three, and that by course; and let one in-
> terpret. But if there be no interpreter, let
> him keep silence in the church; and let him
> speak to himself, and to God.' The inter-
> preter is clearly he who has the grace to
> transfer the prayer of the Spirit in the

130

heart to his intellect to be heard for the edification of others.[65]

Obviously, those who have reached a state of glorification are the most able to speak and teach thus "edifying the Church" on the basis of their own face to face encounter with Christ. Next in capability, those who speak in tongues are to speak on the basis of the psalms and prayers that they ceaselessly sing in their heart under the inspiration of the Holy Spirit if in fact they have the ability to outwardly express their inward prayer to God or the fruit of their inward prayer to God (in other words to interpret their inward prayer). Saint Paul asks the Corinthians how they would be benefited if he were to come to them and only pray silently to God in his heart. It is only by translating those ineffable uncreated words that he "heard" in a state of deification (*2 Corinthians* 12:4) that he could benefit those in need of instruction in a manifold number of ways: by revelation (revealing the thoughts of their hearts), or by knowledge (of the mysteries of God), by prophecy (the revelation of the will of God in their lives as well as revealing things past or to come), or by teaching (about virtue or dogma).[66] Saint Paul goes so far as to say that if the Church services are conducted silently, they are like a trumpet that is not sounded or like a barbarian whose words are not understood.

[65] Fr. J. Romanides, "Jesus Christ: the Life of the World," page 331.

[66] Saint Nicodemos, *Commentary on the 14 Epistles*, page 349 (in Greek).

Thus, Paul exhorts them to pray with the spirit and with the mind by prophesying "with the language of sacred teaching."[67] Otherwise how will those without the gift of the prayer of the heart (tongues) be able to say, "Amen" and participate since they do not hear anything (if all are simply praying silently in their hearts). This is why "Paul, who of all men was the most closely united with God through prayer, would have rather spoken from his fertile intellect five words in the Church for the instruction of others than ten thousand words of psalmody (the prayer of the heart) in private."[68] At best, the services conducted in silence are a sign to the unbelievers that there is something taking place here beyond what meets the eye. At worse, they will simply think those praying silently in their hearts are mentally ill. Instructive words from the prayer of the heart as well as from the vision of Christ in glory, however, will ignite the zeal in those not yet at a state of illumination to worship God and will convince them that God dwells in the hearts of the saints (the illumined and deified). Not only was this observed in the effect of Saint Peter's words on Pentecost, but even in our times we have contemporary verifications of Saint Paul's words in the effects of conversations with spirit-bearing elders (such as the late blessed Elders Paissios and Porphyrios) on the souls of those who would come to them for help.

[67] St. Nikitas Stithatos, "On Spiritual Knowledge," in *The Philokalia*, v. IV, page 169.
[68] Ibid.

Bearing in mind Saint Paul's advice, the innovation of Corinth (services being conducted silently) was for the most part brought to an end in the practice of the Orthodox Church. It is worth noting, however, that on the Holy Mountain of Athos to this day, there are certain small communities which observe the practice of completing the divine services by praying silently with the prayer-rope (saying the Jesus Prayer) if there are no pilgrims present, but in obedience to the Apostle Paul if there is but one guest present, they read from the divine service books as in all the other Churches and Monasteries, so that the guest may also say his "Amen," be instructed, and edified.

6. Pentecost and Corinth

"Jesus Christ the same yesterday, and to day, and for ever."
— *Hebrews* 13:8

When considered together Saint Luke's description of Pentecost in *Acts* and Saint Paul's description of spiritual gifts in *First Corinthians* form a single complementary vision on the stages, nature, and purpose of the spiritual life. The more inward analytical character of *1 Corinthians* in contrast with the more outward descriptive character of *Acts* is no doubt due to the simple fact that Saint Paul's letters "were directed to those *already* initiated into the mysteries of the Church" whereas Saint Luke's ac-

133

count was directed to those who were not.[69] Thus while at Pentecost, we see in part the aim of the process of purification, illumination, and glorification in the revelation of all Truth in the glorified Christ, at Corinth, we observe the continuation of Pentecost in the lives of the faithful at every stage of the healing process: those at a stage of purification (without the gift of tongues), those at a stage of illumination (with the gift of tongues), and those who have tasted a state of glorification (the Prophets and Apostles who have beheld Christ in glory). If we juxtapose *Acts* with *1 Corinthians,* we note that normally purification precedes illumination, which precedes glorification. At each stage, the believer remains free and sober. And under no condition can drunkenness or ecstasy be construed as an experience of grace or effects of the calm and gentle Holy Spirit.

We note that a correct understanding of the gift of tongues based on a careful and precise reading of the relevant passages is crucial for a proper understanding of both Pentecost and Saint Paul's discourse on spiritual gifts. Unless one distinguishes tongues from what is uttered (prophecy or interpretation) and from comprehensibility (in *Acts)* and unless one notes that tongues are "not heard," while interpretation and prophecy are heard (in *1 Corinthians),* one will find oneself in a hermeneutically awkward and apologetically precarious position. When tongues are mistakenly identified with foreign languages (or even

---

[69] Father John Romanides, "Jesus Christ: the Life of the World," page 323.

worse strange sounds), one is posed with a series of fabricated and in reality non-existent problems such as: Why did Christ not teach His disciples to pray in foreign languages when they asked Him how they should pray? Why did this gift, given at the threshold of Pentecost, seemingly vanish in the Church? Why did Saint Paul pray in tongues more than all the rest? Why would praying in a foreign language be edifying to the early Christians who prayed in this way? How can praying in foreign languages be reconciled with the entire tradition of prayer in the Old Testament, in the New Testament, and in the writings of the Holy Fathers?... *ad absurdum ad infinitum.*

If, however, one does observe the distinctions mentioned above, it becomes clear that "speaking in tongues," "praying in the Spirit," "praying without ceasing," "speaking to oneself in psalms and hymns and spiritual songs, singing and making melody in one's heart to the Lord," "the Spirit of his Son in one's heart, crying, Abba, Father," that "treasure hid in a field," all refer to one and the same prayer that later tradition would call the prayer of the heart. Then, one realizes that "tongues" is neither the "big miracle" of Pentecost, nor a "peculiarity" of Corinth to be explained away, but an inward activity intrinsic to the genuine life in Christ and an objective indication that the believer is in fact a temple of the Holy Spirit and living member of the Body of Christ.

Notwithstanding the pivotal role of the gift of tongues in the life of the Church and each believer, the new commandment of love prods those who have been purified and illumined to speak and help those who have not yet begun the process of purification. This can be clearly seen both at Pentecost and in Saint Paul's advice to the Corinthians. Thus, having beheld the glorified Christ and being in continuous communion with Him by the unceasing prayer of the Holy Spirit in the heart, the Apostles would speak about the Truth "as ones that had authority, and not as the scribes."[70] Even as "the Jews marveled," over Christ's words "saying, how knoweth this man letters, having never learned,"[71] so also "when they saw the boldness of Peter and John, and perceived that they were unlearned and ignorant men, they marveled."[72] For in both cases, the words are the fruit of the experience of deification (in Christ's case by nature, in the Apostles' case by grace). Precisely the same prerequisites of glorification (or at least illumination) should be demanded for one to speak (prophecy) in Church. Thus, the vision of the glorified Christ, which is the secret heart of Pentecost becomes the manifest goal to be pursued by the Corinthians. In like manner, that love which seeks not its own that Saint Peter outwardly expressed in his care for the crucifiers of his Lord is most beautifully hymned by Saint Paul for the benefit of those Corinthians still at the earliest stages of the Christian life.

Orthodoxy is truly bolder than heresy, for its foundation is not feeble human reasoning, but the

[70] *Mark* 1:11 and *Matthew* 7:29.
[71] *John* 7:15.
[72] *Acts* 4:13.

136

revelation of the uncreated glory of Christ. It nevertheless remains calm and sober, wise and true. To those who have not yet entered the process of purification and illumination, Orthodoxy's words may be a "hard saying; who can hear it."[73] And yet anyone who reads the lives of the Saints, who considers their struggles and who studies their words will recognize the same tradition described in the Old Testament and the New and will meet a spiritual profundity not encountered elsewhere in the "Christian world." The process of purification, illumination, and glorification observed in *Corinthians* 12-14 and culminated in *Acts* 2 is the process observed in the life of every Saint unto the present day. It is the key to the purpose of the Church (Who is a mystery) and the backbone of the Orthodox Christian Tradition. It is the theory and practice of hesychasm which is the heart of the Orthodox Christian life that today unfortunately is experienced chiefly in Orthodox monastic communities, although in the early Church it was experienced by every Christian community existing in the world. It seems only sensible that it be used as the lens through which the believer reads Scripture with the help of those already in a state of illumination or glorification. Only then, can spiritual gifts in general and kinds of tongues in particular be seen in their true light, the light of Christ Who comes and reveals Himself to those who properly purify themselves for Him.

[73] *John* 6:60.

A Matter of Experience

1. Discerning the Spirits:
The Safe Experiences of the Church

"The name of the Lord is a strong tower:
the righteous runneth into it, and is safe."
— *Proverbs* 18:10

In our examination of Pentecost and the gifts
of the Spirit in the Church of Corinth, certain principles emerged concerning Christian spiritual experiences. On Pentecost, we noted that the Apostles were
well prepared and purified vessels for the coming of
the Comforter through their lives of humble repentance and obedience to Christ. They were already in
a state of illumination and had tasted the state of
glorification. In Corinth, we likewise observed that
the gifts of the Spirit (beginning with the gift of the
prayer of the Holy Spirit in the heart) were found in
those members of the Church who were in a state of
illumination or glorification. In both cases, we noted
that the gifts of the Spirit were not characterized as
ecstatic experiences, but as experiences of peace,
freedom, prudence, and wisdom in which spiritual
gifts were employed for the edification or salvation of
one's brother.

The gifts of the Spirit that range from prayer
of the heart (kinds of tongues) to the apostolic vision
of Christ have never ceased in the Church. It would
not be difficult to compose a study of the lives of the

Saints from any period of Church history (including present day) in which one can observe the gifts of Pentecost and the gifts that Saint Paul records in his *First Epistle to the Corinthians* fully active in the lives of those members of the Church who have come "unto a perfect man, unto the measure of the stature of the fullness of Christ."[1] There are, however, other experiences that the believer may encounter as he more closely approaches Christ, experiences from the right hand as well as from the left. In order to help the believer to navigate his course through the possible experiences that may cross his path, it would seem prudent to both define spiritual experience in general and then to characterize those experiences of grace and delusion.

Although everyone is intuitively aware of what a spiritual experience is, the outlines delimiting such are often not clearly drawn. An experience of God is by its very nature an experience of the soul that is personal, intimate, inward, and precious. The Abbott George of Gregoriou Monastery on Mount Athos aptly defines this the subjective aspect of spiritual experience as follows: "An experience of God is first of all, an inner assurance that through faith in God, the Christian finds the true meaning of life. He feels that his faith in Christ is a faith that satisfies him internally, that gives meaning to his life and guides him, that is a strong light which enlightens him."[2] This

[1] *Ephesians* 4:13.
[2] Archimandrite George Capsanis, *Experiences of the Grace of God* (Holy Monastery of Saint Gregorios: Mount Athos, 1995), page 17.

inward assurance, satisfaction, and enlightenment form the subjective pole of an experience of God and is an inward knowledge that increases one's faith. This faith that has been received and believed forms the concrete, stable, and unshaken foundation of the Christian life. As Christ known through the Holy Spirit is the center of the Christian faith, so any genuine Christian experience in the Church is naturally both Christ-centered and marked by the presence of the Holy Spirit.[3] The term "faith," moreover, implies not simply acknowledging a set of beliefs, but more concretely confessing and embracing a whole way of life in accord with them. Fr. Alevizopoulos quite eloquently writes,

> The personal link of love with Christ in freedom that is founded on the dogmatic faith of the Church and expressed by keeping the Lord's commandments leads us on the unique road of spiritual experiences, which is prayer, participation in the sacred mysteries of the Church, the study of God's Word and communion with the Saints, that bring us closer to the Lord. This road was not found by us with our own thought or by means of logic.[4]

The proper living faith expressed through the proper way of life (asceticism and the mysteries) is

[3] Fr. Anthony Alevizopoulos *The Occult, Ghurus, and the New Age,* (Anthony Alevizopoulos: Athens, 1990) page 292 (in Greek).

[4] Ibid., page 290.

then the most sure context for genuine spiritual experiences that range from the most modest sigh of repentance of those just turning to Christ to the vision of Christ in glory that characterizes those in a state of deification. Of course, the proper way of life and proper faith imply being an obedient member of the Church which preserves the faith and way of life with which Christ entrusted the Apostles—the Holy Orthodox Church. Archimandrite George, thus, numbers being in the Church, together with humility and repentance, as primary presuppositions that ensure the authenticity of spiritual experiences.[5]

Within this context, there are a number of genuine experiences of grace of which every sincerely active believer partakes even at the stage of purification. The most basic experience, the heart of the Gospel, is repentance, for the remembrance of one's sins, the desire to confess, and to make a fresh start in life takes place in the soul through a visitation of purifying grace. The peace, the relief, and the joy that follow sincere repentance is another fundamental experience in the Christian life. The peace and joy that accompany Holy Communion, the joyful sorrow of tears of repentance, the joy of tears of love for God, the consolation and joy that one feels venerating the Holy Icons, venerating the Holy Relics, reading Scripture and Patristic writings, or being present for the Divine Services are all genuine experiences of the grace of God.[6] Even for those being purified, there is

---

[5] Archimandrite George Capsanis, pages 21-23.
[6] Ibid., pages 18-20.

no great danger of being deluded by such experiences.

The danger arises when some, out of pride, are influenced by the evil one and suppose that they have experiences which characterize states of illumination and glorification. For those in a state of spiritual health whose humble hearts are healed from the passion of selfish love, it is not difficult "to discern the spirits," which are of God and which are of Satan. For those, however, who are still sick with pride and struggling to purify themselves of the passions, the waters are a bit murkier. If such people cannot recognize their spiritual illness and refuse to turn to a qualified physician (one in a state of glorification or at least one in a state of illumination who follows the teachings of the deified), the situation is nearly hopeless as Saint Nilos explains.

> It is difficult to treat those who suffer from chronic disease. For how can you explain the value of health to people who have never enjoyed it, but have been sickly from birth. Because this is their customary state, they regard it as a misfortune of nature and even as perfectly normal. It is useless to offer advice to those who have no intention of taking it, but continue regardless on their downward path.[7]

---

[7] Saint Nilos the Ascetic, "Ascetic Discourse," *The Philokalia,* v. I, page 205. Saint Gregory of Sinai expresses the same idea as follows: "people who are a law unto themselves cannot

If, however, they are willing to accept the wise advice of the healthy, they are already proceeding towards the path towards their cure.

2. Discerning the Spirits: Experiences of Deception

"Beloved, believe not every spirit, but try the spirits whether they are of God."
— *1 John* 4:1

Notwithstanding a proper faith and a seemingly ascetic way of life, the believer can still fall prey to false spiritual experiences, especially at the time of prayer. This being said, we must affirm that "there are many differing methods of prayer. No method is harmful. If it were, it would be not prayer but the activity of Satan."[8] Prayer can be defined in diverse ways. In terms of form, prayer is either public and liturgical or private and solitary.[9] In terms of content, "every prayer is a supplication, or a request, or a thanksgiving, or an offering of praise."[10] In terms of essence,

> prayer is the *reason's* dialogue with God in which the words of petition are uttered

---

avoid being conceited, and the natural result of conceit is delusion." *The Philokalia,* v. IV, page 268.

[8] Saint Mark the Ascetic, "On the Spiritual Law," Ibid., page 111.

[9] John Warren Morris, *The Charismatic Movement: An Orthodox Evaluation,* (Holy Cross Press: Boston, 1994), page 30.

[10] Saint Isaac the Syrian, page 117.

with the *nous* (i.e., *the heart*) riveted wholly on God. For when the *reason* unceasingly repeats the name of the Lord and the *nous* gives its full attention to the invocation of the divine name, the light of knowledge overshadows the entire soul like a luminous cloud. *The exact memory* of God (i.e., *the prayer of the heart*) is followed by love and joy.... Pure prayer is followed by divine knowledge and compunction. When *nous* and *reason* stand attentive before God, compunction of the soul will ensue. When the *nous*, the *logos (the faculty of the soul by which the nous and reason express themselves)* and spirit prostrate themselves before God, the first through attentiveness, the second through invocation, and the third through compunction and love, the whole of your inner self serves God.[11]

This description of the essence of prayer as a state of illumination in which the primary faculties of the soul function properly is of course a description of the prayer of the heart or "kinds of tongues" that we discussed in the past chapter. This prayer entails both a calm, yet attentive synergy between the facul-

---

[11] Saint Theoliptos of Philadelphia, "On Inner Work In Christ," *The Philokalia,* v. IV, page 181. Italicized words are more faithful translations based on the original text; explanatory words in parenthesis are added for clarity's sake, but are not in the original.

ties of the soul (the reason and the *nous)* working together towards the same aim and divine grace. It is consequently spiritual as well, for through it, the purified soul partakes of the energies of the Holy Spirit.[12] The sign that the believer has entered into such prayer is "warmth of the heart that scorches the passions, fills the soul with joy and delight, and establishes the heart in unmoving love and unhesitating surety."[13] It is precisely at this point, however, in the evaluation of the believer's spiritual experience that he must exercise caution lest he fall into delusion.

What is most necessary in the beginning is discrimination or discernment which according to Abba Moses, "comes to us only as a result of true humility and this in turn is shown by revealing to our spiritual father not only what we do, but also what we think."[14] The spiritual father in turn listens and discerns both the state of his spiritual child's soul and the nature of any spiritual experiences that his spiritual child may have. Saint Makarios of Egypt compares this spiritual discernment with the sense of taste: "Just as the throat through its sense of taste distinguishes the difference between vinegar and wine, although they look alike, so the soul through its *noetic (of the heart)* sense and *activity (in other words, the activity of the prayer of the heart)* can dis-

---

[12] Saint Isaac the Syrian, page 182.

[13] Saint Gregory of Sinai, "On Stillness," *The Philokalia,* v. IV, page 270.

[14] Saint John Cassian, *The Philokalia,* v. I., page 103.

tinguish the gifts of the Spirit from the fantasies of the devil."[15]

Two points are worth stressing in this passage: first, a fantasy of the devil can externally appear very much like a gift of the Spirit. As one Athonite elder put it, "when dealing with spiritual gifts, one must be so very careful. One must realize that the devil, who can create nothing on his own, counterfeits the gifts of the Holy Spirit in order to beguile the believer and lead him astray. And while outwardly (like vinegar!) the devil's gifts mimic those of the Holy Spirit, they are utterly different both inwardly and in the effect they have on the believer (as are vinegar and wine!)." Secondly, in order to taste the difference (to have the noetic sense), the believer's heart must function properly, which implies a state of illumination, the presence of ceaseless prayer of the heart that Saint Makarios refers to here as *noetic activity* and that Saint Luke and Saint Paul refer to as "tongues."

Those who are still struggling to fulfill the most basic commandments of Christ and set their bearings according to their own personal experi-

---

[15] Saint Makarios of Egypt, "On Patient Endurance and Discrimination," *The Philokalia*, v. III, page 304. Saint Gregory of Sinai says as much, "as the palate discriminates between different kinds of foods, so the spiritual sense of taste clearly and unerringly reveals everything as it truly is." "On Stillness,"*The Philokalia*, v. IV, page 271. Italics mine—see note 11 in the present chapter.

ences[16] or even simply "naively trust their own experiences"[17] open themselves up to being deceived. This is why it helps to admit and realize that "in many, although grace is active, evil is still present together with it lying hidden: the two spirits that of light and that of darkness are at work in the same heart."[18] Although there is no replacement for humbly opening one's heart up before an experienced spiritual father, it is nevertheless instructive to note the characteristics of spiritual gifts and experiences that the devil apes, for such can serve as a rough indicator of whether or not a spiritual experience or gift is in fact genuine.

Saint Paul, the most wise of spiritual guides, wrote in his *Second Epistle to the Corinthians:* "For such are false apostles, deceitful workers, transforming themselves into the apostles of Christ. And no marvel; for Satan himself is transformed into an angel of light. Therefore it is no great thing if his ministers also be transformed as the ministers of righteousness; whose end shall be according to their works" (*2 Corinthians* 11: 13-15). From this passage, we can conclude that experiences and gifts that

[16] Fr. Anthony Alevizopoulos, *Handbook of Heresies and Para-Christian Groups,* pages 153-154 (in Greek).

[17] Fr. Seraphim Rose, *Orthodoxy and the Religion of the Future* (Saint Herman of Alaska Brotherhood, Platina: 1996), page 149.

[18] Saint Makarios of Egypt, "On the Raising of the Intellect," *The Philokalia,* v. IV, page 318. "Bishop Ignatius writes, 'We are all in deception. The knowledge of this is the greatest prevention against deception.'" taken from Fr. Seraphim Rose, *Orthodoxy and the Religion of the Future,* page 150.

might seem genuine and true can in fact be deceitful and false. Even on the surface, the very fact that the devil's delusion is a lie brings a subtle atmosphere of agitation and confusion. The presence of chaos, disorder, disturbance and confusion in spiritual experiences point to a demonic origin. Saint Isaac the Syrian very descriptively writes, "Confusion should be called (if permissible) the chariot of the devil, because Satan is ever wont to mount upon it as a charioteer and bearing with him the throng of the passions, he invades the wretched soul and plunges her into the pit of confusion."[19] Saint Peter of Damascus writes, "all that the demons produce is disorderly;"[20] while "Saint Barsanuphius universally says that every disturbance is of the devil."[21] Thus, confusion, disorder, and disturbance are the means by which the devil enters a soul which would otherwise not admit him entry. This confusion and disorder then become a condition that enshrouds the soul with a cloak of spurious spiritual experiences.

When Saint Gregory of Sinai writes about the feelings that one encounters in deceitful spiritual experiences, he notes that the energy of delusion "is entirely amorphous and disordered, inducing mindless joy, presumption, and confusion, accompanied by a mood of ill-defined sterile levity and fomenting above

---

[19] Saint Isaac the Syrian, page 269.
[20] "A List of Passions," *The Philokalia*, v. III, page 206.
[21] Saint Nicodemos, *Way of the Feasts*, page 175 (in Greek).

all the soul's appetitive power with sensuality."[22] In sharp contrast to the clarity, humility, and sobriety of Pentecost, the counterfeit spiritual experience is foggy, conceited and confused. There is a type of joy present, but the mind cannot pinpoint the reason for such joy (for example, as in joy over the mercy or love of God). Meanwhile, the recipient of such an experience begins to form a high opinion of himself. He desires to act, but not to create or to serve. Sensual things (outward beauty, foods, smell, touch) all become more stimulating and attractive. In fact, the very desire for spiritual experiences makes us open prey for the devil who leads the naïve astray primarily through the desiring faculty. Using the imagination and man's desire, the devil "substitutes his own unruly heat for spiritual warmth, so that the soul is oppressed by deceit. For spiritual delight, he substitutes mindless joy and a muggy sense of pleasure, inducing self-satisfaction and vanity."[23] Continuing on a similar note, Saint Diadochus of Photiki writes,

> Through this joy, amorphous and disordered, the devil tries to lead the soul into an adulterous union with himself. For when he sees the *nous* unreservedly proud of its own experiences of spiritual perception, he entices the soul by means of certain plausible illusions of grace, so that it is seduced by that dark and debilitating

[22] "On the Signs of Grace and Delusion," *The Philokalia*, v. IV, page 262.

[23] Ibid., pages 270-271.

sweetness and fails to notice its intercourse with the deceiver.[24]

In speaking about delusion in prayer, Saint Simeon the New Theologian notes that "the good is not good when it is not done in the right way."[25] For as great a good as prayer is, as great a blessing as experiences of grace are, if the believer does not approach them "in the right way," that is "with humility," they are no longer good at all. When those still entangled in the passions seek exalted visions appropriate to those in a state of glorification or the heart-felt prayer of those in a state of illumination,[26] they reveal a lack of knowledge about their own state, an unconcern for working in the vineyard set before them (repentance and uprooting the passions), and most importantly a lack of humility. Thus, it is not surprising that they fall into delusion, since whether they are deluded by their own imaginings or by demonic influence, "the sole cause and origin is always arrogance."[27] And arrogance in turn "arises from superficiality,"[28] from preferring a counterfeit world of spiritual states along with all the necessary array of

---

[24] *The Philokalia*, v. I, page 262-263.

[25] "Three Methods of Prayer," *The Philokalia*, v. IV, page 69.

[26] Fr. Seraphim Rose, *Orthodoxy and the Religion of the Future*, pages 144-145.

[27] Gregory of Sinai, *The Philokalia*, v. IV, page 249.

[28] Ibid., page 250.

false ideas and feelings[29] needed to keep such a world together in lieu of the real world of one's spiritual poverty and need for the Lord's mercy. In other words, lurking behind an experience of delusion is often found a refusal to take a close, serious, and deep look at oneself and the thoughts and feelings that one might hold dear.

Although delusion may start off by seemingly small failings, the final outcome can be fearful indeed. Not a few ascetics have ended their lives with suicide by starting along that dangerous road of arrogant trust in self. Saint John Cassian records how Abba Hiron spent fifty years in the desert leading a life of great asceticism and self-denial, but because he arrogantly trusted in his own judgment rather than that of the fathers, he fell into delusion, worshipped Satan who appeared as an angel of light, and committed suicide casting himself down a well. Another Mesopotamian monk likewise deluded ended up renouncing the faith and converting to Judaism.[30] And alas, such instances continue down to the present day (and this is still within the confines of the Orthodox Church!). And while those who arrogantly seek exalted states often receive them, though not from the hand of God, genuine spiritual experiences "cannot be forced, and genuine spiritual states are

[29] Fr. Seraphim Rose, *Orthodoxy and the Religion of the Future*, page 162.

[30] Saint John Cassian, "The Holy Fathers of Sketis," *The Philokalia*, v. I, pages 100-101.

gifts of the love of God and stem from His free Divine Will."[31]

3. Discerning the Spirits: Experiences of Grace

"But the fruit of the Spirit is love, joy, peace, long-suffering, gentleness, goodness, faith, meekness, temperance."
— *Galatians* 5:22-23

As a knowledge of the characteristics of demonic experiences can provide a rough guide to discern the nature of a given experience, likewise a rudimentary knowledge of the characteristics of genuine experiences of grace can complete the positive end of this rough scale. As glorious and full of light as the deceptive experiences of the devil may seem to be, he cannot "produce within us the effects of grace... For the devil cannot bring about love either for God or for one's neighbor, or gentleness or humility, or joy or produce equilibrium in one's thoughts or hatred of the world, or spiritual repose, or desire for celestial things, nor can he quell the passions or sensual pleasure."[32] In other words, as

---

[31] Fr. Anthony Alevizopouos, *The Occult, Ghurus, and the New Age*, page 329 (in Greek).

[32] Saint Makarios of Egypt, "Patient Endurance and Discrimination," *The Philokalia*, v. III, page 304. Saint Gregory of Sinai puts it quite similarly, "you must be aware that the effects of grace are self-evident and that even if the devil does trans-

"every tree is known by his own fruit,"[33] so the spirit that abides in each man is known by the fruits of the Spirit: love, joy, peace, meekness, abstinence, and every other virtue, in place of hatred, sorrow, disturbance, audacity, intemperance and every other vice.[34]

As disorder, confusion, and disturbance are traits that characterize false spiritual experiences, so good order, clarity, and peace are the traits that characterize genuine ones. In fact, the activity of grace "stills the provocation of the thoughts and for a time suspends the body's impulses,"[35] thus bringing clarity of thought and freedom from the blameless passions. Saint Gregory Palamas writes, "And the Father first bestows upon the soul peace of thoughts, the gift which contains within it all the gifts."[36] Saint Isaac the Syrian similarly comments, "good order generates peace, peace gives birth to light in the soul, and peace makes the pure air in the mind radiant."[37]

form himself he cannot produce these effects. He cannot induce you to be gentle or forbearing or to be humble or joyful or serene, or stable in thoughts. He cannot make you hate what is worldly or cut off sensual indulgence and the working of the passions as grace does. He produces vanity, haughtiness, cowardice, and every kind of evil." *The Philokalia,* v. IV, page 286.

[33] *Luke* 6:44.

[34] Zographou, pages 113-114. Or as Saint Makarios of Egypt puts it, "the fruits of the Spirit are love, peace, and so on (cf., *Galatians* 5:22), while the devil is most apt and powerful in promoting vanity and haughtiness" in "Patient Endurance and Discrimination," *The Philokalia,* v. III, page 304.

[35] Saint Gregory of Sinai, "On the Signs of Grace and Delusion," *The Philokalia,* v. IV, page 262.

[36] "To the Most Reverend Nun Xenia," Ibid., page 315.

[37] *Ascetical Homilies,* page 253.

Above all, peace, humility and unselfish love for God mark the genuine experience of grace. Saint Diadochos of Photiki writes,

The feeling of warmth which the Holy Spirit engenders in the heart is completely peaceful and enduring. It awakes in all parts of the soul a longing for God; its heat does not need to be fanned by anything outside of the heart, but through the heart it makes the whole man rejoice with a boundless love.[38]

In other words, a genuine experience of grace has a lasting and calming effect upon the entire soul and body. The experience prods the mind to think about God, the desire to long for God, and the will to be employed to labor for God. At the same time, there is no need for external or mechanical means to be employed to maintain this state, but in natural way love for God precedes from this state and in turn preserves the effects thereof.

4. Which Comes First, Faith or Experience?

"They said therefore unto Him, What sign showest Thou then, that we may see, and believe Thee? what dost Thou work?"'For

---

[38] Saint Diadochus of Photiki, *The Philokalia,* v. I, "On Spiritual Knowledge," page 278.

had ye believed Moses, ye would have believed Me: for he wrote of Me. But if ye believe not his writings, how shall ye believe
My words?"

— *John* 6:30, 5:46-47.

Having outlined the characteristics of false
and genuine experiences of grace, having noted the
need for humility and repentance, one can not over-
emphasize (i) the priority of faith over experience at
the early stages of man's spiritual healing and (ii) the
spiritual law that God does not show His grace to
someone unless he believes *and* obeys His commandments. The great importance of a concrete
dogmatic conscience as a means of safeguarding and
properly interpreting one's experience is repeatedly
manifested in the Gospels with the phrases such as
"that it might be fulfilled which was spoken of the
Lord by the prophet,"[39] "for thus it is written by the
prophet"[40] "that the scriptures of the prophets might
be fulfilled,"[41] "as it is written in the prophets,"[42]
"that all things must be fulfilled, which were written
in the law of Moses, and in the prophets, and in the
psalms concerning me,"[43] and so forth. Likewise,
Philip confirms the genuineness of his experience of
Christ on the basis of the teaching (concrete faith or

---

[39] *Matthew* 1:22, 2:15, 13:35.
[40] *Matthew* 2:5.
[41] *Matthew* 26:56.
[42] *Mark* 1:2.
[43] *Luke* 24:44.

dogma) expressed by the law and the prophets, re-vealed Truth that had been handed down to him.

This initial faith[44] is in some way analogous to the trust that a sick patient places in his physician in particular and in medical science in general rather than in his own uninformed experimentation with his health. This initial trust is not in medicine as an abstraction, but in concrete principles and postulates (such as germ theory, blood analysis, x-rays...) that he may nevertheless neither thoroughly understand nor personally have tested. In like manner, by faith *at the initial stage,* we do *not* mean some nebulous abstract "faith in God," but a concrete and well-defined set of beliefs about the Holy Trinity, about the person, life and teachings of Christ, about the Church, and Her mysteries, about the Theotokos, the Saints, the Icons, man's union with God in prayer, and other subjects formulated by the Holy Ecumenical Councils and set forth in Scripture and Holy Tradition. These initial teachings are part of the initial catechism that is addressed mainly to the reason. Similarly by reading the Gospel and accepting it intellectually, an intellectual faith is founded. This faith, however, is not sufficient. It resembles the faith with which the hearer happily accepts the Word of God, but because he does not have much "soil'

[44] We note that when Saint Paul employs the term faith (e.g., justification by faith), this faith "is not the acceptance of dogmas, but the gift of tongues in the heart." Fr. J. Romanides, "Jesus Christ: the Life of the World," page 334. Here, we are employing the term in its more conventional sense.

(faith of the heart), he quickly denies it. This faith becomes sound (gains soil) only when it is accompanied by a new illumination.

Notwithstanding, dogmatic faith even as a faith of the mind (an intellectual faith) precedes experience. In asserting this, we are merely underlining the fact that dogmatic faith is necessary for Baptism. Once one is baptized and chrismated, the energy of the Holy Spirit can create in him an inward faith through experiences. For this to take place, however ascetic struggle and the implementation of Christ's commandments are required. Healing of the soul begins with the formation of the faith of the mind, since this faith heals the reason. The end of this healing process is the state of glorification we discussed earlier. The untrained (those who have not reached a stage of illumination or glorification) are neither in a position to evaluate their own state of health, nor the efficacy of the procedures (prayer, obedience to a spiritual father, the sacramental life) and principles (the dogmas and teachings) of the medical establishment (the Church).

Thus, the personal experience of the untrained can neither judge faith, nor the genuineness of the proclaimer of the Gospel "for false Christs and false prophets shall rise, and shall show signs and wonders, to seduce, if it were possible, even the elect."[45] For this reason, when Father Seraphim Rose was speaking to those outside of the Church who had not yet acquired even a faith of the mind, he asks, "how

[45] *Mark* 13:22.

can a religious seeker avoid the traps and deceptions which he encounters in his search. There is only one answer to this question: a person must be in the religious search not for the sake of religious experiences that can deceive, but for the sake of the Truth."[46] Ultimately, however, the believer must establish the house of his soul on the bedrock of the teachings of Christ, the faith of the heart based on the genuine experience of grace[47] rather than the sand of an intellectual faith (that philosophy can overturn).[48]

The centrality and priority of Orthodox dogmatic faith over individual logical explanations means that doctrinal relativism (or the ecumenical movement which minimizes or clouds over doctrinal differences) is perhaps the most dangerous of deceptions, for it erodes away the very Rock capable of protecting the faithful from delusion. Once faith in Christ and His Church have been eroded, once the tested findings of this medical establishment have been rejected, the devil (the chief agent of sickness) can make the naïve believe that they are "one in the Spirit, one in the Lord" with those of other confes-

---

[46] Fr. Seraphim Rose, *God's Revelation to the Human Heart* (Saint Herman of Alaska Brotherhood, Platina: 1997), page 17. Of course, for those in the Church, the safe procedure is to be obedient to a spiritual father and to reveal to him all thoughts and experiences.

[47] Cf., those safe experiences of grace enumerated at the beginning of this chapter.

[48] Fr. Anthony Alevizopoulos, *Handbook of Heresies and Para-Christian Groups,* page 152 (in Greek).

sions, when they in fact neither agree about Who is Christ or Who is the Holy Spirit. The fact of the matter is, if one changes the content of one's faith, one inevitably will change the form of one's spiritual experiences.[49]

"In order to protect ourselves from counterfeit experiences, we must link purity with the Truth, that is 'correct dogma,' so that as Saint John Chrysostom notes, 'both our life confirms the dogmas and the dogmas make our life appear credible.'"[50] "Whoever does not keep the commandments of the Lord does not receive the Holy Spirit, nor have genuine spiritual experiences that are fruits of the Holy Spirit. Obedience to the teaching of the Apostles, that is, keeping the commandments of God is the mark of true knowledge of God,"[51] for "the Holy Spirit is not acquired through ecstatic 'charismatic' experiences, but by the long and arduous path of asceticism."[52] This is why one Athonite Elder in a talk to his monks advises them,

> Don't be afraid of the alternations of spiritual states. When you will feel dryness, when grace withdraws, don't be afraid. It's nothing to be concerned with, but is in the

[49] Archimandrite Sophrony, *Saint Silouan the Athonite,* page 144.

[50] Fr. Anthony Alevizopoulos, *The Occult, Ghurus, and the New Age,* page 289 (in Greek).

[51] Fr. Anthony Alevizopoulos, *Handbook of Heresies and Para-Christian Groups,* pages 154-155 (in Greek).

[52] Fr. Seraphim Rose, *Orthodoxy and the Religion of the Future,* page 158.

very nature of things. When you feel
within you the consolation of divine grace,
don't bank on it, it won't remain; it will
withdraw again. We don't base ourselves
on our feelings or emotions. We don't make
our feelings our criteria, neither dryness,
nor the exultation of consolation. No, our
criterion is the faith, active faith, believing
in Christ, applying His All-holy Will, and
having it as the goal of our life. From this
we take our criteria: how much we have
submitted ourselves to His Holy Will, how
we have labored in order to follow our conscience with exactness. That is the criterion."

Thus, while genuine experiences of grace are a
great blessing for the soul and while experiences of
deception are the soul's great curse, the wise struggler in the Christian life keeps his focus not on the
experiences that come his way, but on the extent to
which he lives the faith he confesses. Of course, he is
grateful if the Lord is merciful to him and grants him
His purifying, illumining, or deifying grace, but he
also is well aware that the treasure of grace is *not* his
personal property, but a trust that can be withdrawn
at anytime. This in turn makes him more watchful
lest he become the cause for the loss of grace. He
knows his weakness and frailty as a human and a
sinner. He knows that if Adam could be beguiled in
Paradise when he began to listen to another voice
apart from the voice of God, that he too is not beyond

160

the reach of deception's charms. This, in turn, makes him look to the faith of the Fathers as his anchor of hope, for the faith that has sanctified and made fragrant the bones of men, women, and children of the same nature as himself, is more than able to sanctify him as well if he will but follow the same path and live the same faith.

PART TWO

THE PENTECOSTAL CHURCHES

Quotations on "Tongues" as Supernatural Unintelligible Prayer

And *they were all filled with the Holy Ghost,* and *began to speak with other tongues.*

> — Saint Luke,
> *The Acts of the Apostles* 2:4

Right then and there came a slight twist in my throat, a glory fell over me and I began to worship in the Swedish tongue, which later changed to other languages and continued.

> — Charles Parham,
> "The Father of Pentecost"[1]

I will pray with the spirit, and I will pray with the mind also: I will sing with the spirit, and I will sing with the mind also.

> — Saint Paul,
> *The First Epistle to the Corinthians* 14:15

Praying in tongues will birth the will of God in your spirit, you will no longer depend on your intellect or the direction of others."

> — Roberts Liardon[2]

---

[1] Roberts Liardon, *God's Generals Why They Succeeded and Why Some Failed,* (Aubury Publishing: Tulsa, Oklahoma, 1996), page 120.

[2] Ibid., page 121.

A Tale of Sound and Fury[1]

1. The Enthronement of Experience in American Protestantism

In order to properly evaluate the Pentecostal movement, it is helpful not only to examine what it professes and practices, but also to investigate its historical origin, context, and development. Our intention is not to judge the many sincere religious seekers who discovered something quite vibrant in Pentecostalism, for there is Another Who will judge us all. We can and must, however, pass judgement on actions and ideas whose repetition is harmful. A dead-end is a dead-end, a path no wayfarer need take twice. If we love the Truth revealed by Christ and if we love our brother, our study of the past must not be indifferent to the traps, dangers, and deceptions that have prevented the believer from walking on that strait and narrow path that leads to the Kingdom of Heaven. Our aim then is to unearth Pentecostalism's foundation and to determine whether it be sand or stone. Before we reach this foundation where we shall listen to the voices of the first Pentecostals, we first need to uncover two layers whose imprint can be clearly seen in Pentecostalism: its American and its Protestant heritage.

[1] "It is a tale told by an idiot, full of sound and fury, signifying nothing." William Shakespeare, *Macbeth*, Act 5; Scene 5.

Whatever may be one's evaluation of the Pentecostal movement in any of its forms or with any of its creeds, there is no denying the fact that as a phenomenon it is every bit as American as Plymouth Rock, the Wild West, Hollywood, or McDonald's. In fact, the remnant ideology of the Puritans, the rugged individualism of the Western frontier, the heightened sensationalism of the film industry, and the instant gratification of the fast-food business all find their expression now in the American popular religious sphere. The first Pentecostals were usually very simple and rather uneducated Americans. It is not surprising that in their quest for the Holy Spirit, they would be shaped by or express themselves in the language of these currents in American culture, currents whose captivating or enticing power any student of American cultural or religious history can recognize. What most cultural historians fail to notice, however, is that the moral aspect of these currents at their best express the noble virtues of courage and trust in Providence, but at their worst the age-old passions of the love of glory, the love of money, and the love of pleasure that have afflicted the human race since the fall of Adam.[2]

Thus, the "American garb" with which Pentecostalism is girt is the natural fallen accompaniment to the "clothes of skin" that cover Adam's nakedness. This is not to condemn all things American. The American proclivity for the simple and the practical

[2] The presence of the passions in turn introduces another factor into an already complex equation, that of the instigator of the passions, the deceiving spirit.

in speech and thought together with a desire to trust one's neighbor is also found in these sincere seekers. In any event, the fact that this distinctive "American garb" of the Pentecostal is weaved from decided Protestant thread compels us to briefly outline the historical relationship between Protestantism and Orthodoxy (whose interpretation of Pentecost and the gifts of the Spirit we previously examined.)

It is a well known fact that for the first thousand years of ecclesiastical history in spite of the appearance of various heresies, there was one Holy Catholic and Apostolic Church referred to as Catholic in the West and Orthodox in the East. Unfortunately, when the northern Franks were converted to Christianity, they sought to overthrow both the political and ecclesiological practice of the Roman Empire and adopted some unfortunate doctrinal interpretations of the blessed Augustine who developed his own peculiar theology. Since this new theology (or re-worked philosophy to be more precise) in terms of form and content was both outside of the patristic consensus and uninformed by the patristic therapeutic method, its conclusions were often both destructive and antithetical to the teachings of Christ.[3]

It is beyond the scope of this small study to explore the tragic changes that took place in the once

---

[3] E.g., his characterization of mankind as a "*massa damnata*" (damnable lump), his thoroughly abstract and non-personal characterization of the Trinity in general and the Holy Spirit in particular, and his assertion that God desires some to go to hell and others to heaven.

Orthodox Patriarchate of old Rome, its inward transformation from a medical to a legal institution, its loss of the understanding of the stages in the healing of the human heart (purification, illumination, and deification), and the consequent doctrinal abnormalities that sprang therefrom.[4] Similarly time and space do not permit us to discuss the further devastation wrought by the perhaps well-meaning, but certainly ill-fated, attempts of the Protestant reformers to correct a sick institution on the basis of their own unillumined reason, resulting in the rejection of the priesthood, the Mysteries, the veneration of the Mother of God and the Saints, the Tradition of the Church, and the Church Herself as a concrete, historical, and theanthropic reality. In passing, we simply note these mutations that would increasingly distance the Western Christian from the practice, life and belief of One Catholic and Apostolic Church. And this we note in order to indicate the therapeutically inadequate form of Christianity that was brought over from Western Europe to America.[5] It is worth stressing that the Pentecostals (and later charismatics) were among the first to recognize the deficiency or sickness in the Roman Catholic and Protestant churches and to propose the Pentecostal movement as their completion or cure.

What is perhaps insufficiently stressed, however, is another third alteration that took place in

---

[4] For more information, cf., Fr. John Romanides, *Franks, Romans, and Feudalism,* or on the internet: www.Romanity.org.

[5] In the upcoming chapter, we shall apologetically investigate the scriptural foundation for such positions.

Protestantism when it immigrated from Western Europe to North America: the shift in emphasis from confessional dogma to personal experience. In general, the Protestants who immigrated to America were weary of the bloody confessional wars that had plagued Western Europe and helped drive it to atheism. They viewed America as the New Promised Land where they, like a New Israel, could freely worship God as they pleased. It was understood that other groups might have the same desire, so a spirit of toleration with respect to those outside of their sect, replaced the doctrinal absolutism of their predecessors. Within each group, however, the importance of concrete beliefs continued to be emphasized.

Max Weber's famous sociological study *The Protestant Work Ethic and the Spirit of Capitalism*, masterfully chronicles how the Calvinist understanding of prosperity as a sign of election (= legalistic salvation) contributed to the rise of capitalism in the West. This peculiar prosperity gospel so contrary to the Christian virtues of poverty and non-acquisitiveness[6] is the result of incorrect theological opinions. It nevertheless still runs through the many Protestant circles including most Pentecostal and charismatic ones. As the sole proof of salvation, however, most Protestants could see the severe limitations of the "prosperity test" in practice. In partially rejecting this principle, the descendants of the Puri-

---

[6] "And when Jesus saw that he was very sorrowful, He said, How hardly shall they that have riches enter into the kingdom of God!" *Luke* 18:24.

tans likewise rejected the theological institutions that provided them with it. The only solution which seemed to answer the problem that the Protestant of a Calvinist background faced (am I one of the elect predestined to go to heaven, or one of the damned predestined to go to hell?) was experience, an experience of salvation. And with this "solution," a new type of Protestantism was born that would be able to father the antagonistic siblings of the evangelical/fundamentalist and Pentecostal movements.

On the anti-Calvinist side of the fence, John Wesley, an Anglican priest who was disenchanted with the lack of fervor in his fellow Anglicans and inspired by Moldavian Protestantism, initiated his "holiness club" which would later coalesce into the Methodist church. Wesley taught his followers that holiness consists in an *experience* and "grace" separate from one's initial conversion to Christ, known as a "second blessing." From the late colonial period, traveling Methodist preachers (circuit riders) would tour the Eastern Coast of North America rousing their audiences with fiery sermons and emotionally charged worship services. As with their Calvinist (and Baptist) rivals, experience would again be placed at the center of the Christian life rather than a precise confession of faith.

During the eighteenth century, both movements spawned a series of revivals in which an emotionally charged conversion experience of accepting Christ as one's personal Savior would be equated with salvation (being saved) in which both church and creed played a decisively secondary role. Signifi-

cantly, with these revivals, a new type of enthusiastic emotionalism verging on the ecstatic enters into
Christian worship. This enthusiasm would leave little room for any sense of the sacred that could be
found even in conventional Protestant piety. At the
same time, an important, yet, subtle shift in emphasis in their worship took place: the culmination of
Christian worship is not the offering of praise and
thanksgiving to God, nor man's union with God
through Holy Communion, but the altar call in which
sinners come forward to confess their sinfulness, to
accept Christ and to vow to lead a new life. Thus, the
sinner aware of his need for God and his conversion
experience become the new center of Protestant worship.

Meanwhile in the political sphere following the
American Revolution, the "founding fathers" forged
the American Constitution on the basis of the latest
humanist thought of the day expressing the rights of
man and other French democratic ideals. Although
such figures as George Washington, Benjamin
Franklin, and Thomas Jefferson would become the
"saints" of the American civil religion which they in
fact helped establish, it must be stressed that their
religion was far more deistic (or Masonic to be more
precise) than Christian. And although scriptural imagery might be invoked to portray the American people as the new chosen people of God, although many
Americans would look back to the Puritans as their
most noble forefathers, commemorating them yearly
on the American feast of Thanksgiving, the god in-

170

voked would always remain nebulously un-named.
Thus while American currency would be printed with
the words "in God we trust," no identification whatsoever would be made between that god and the Lord
Jesus of the Christian faith. Thus in another subtle
way, the importance of a concrete creed would be de-
creased in the consciousness (or subconscious) of
most American Christians only to be replaced by the
humanistic creed of "life, liberty, and the pursuit of
happiness," in other words, the creed of human experience.

· In time the seemingly innocuous "pursuit of
happiness" would be translated in practical terms
into the "pursuit of security, pleasure, and wealth."
"The American dream" simply expressed the desire
for a this-worldly security. Vaudeville, Broadway,
and Hollywood would help legitimize "the pursuit of
pleasure" on the one hand while fast food would ide-
alize instant gratification on the other. And "the almighty dollar" and an almost manic consumerism
would simply feed the desire for wealth. In this way,
the very moorings of American society would shift
from the moral severity of the Puritans to "an impassioned mindless friendship with the body."[7] With the

---

[7] "Self-love is an impassioned, mindless love for one's body.
Its opposite is love and self-control." St. Maximus the Confessor,
"Third Century on Love," *Philokalia* v. ii, page 84. A more nu-
anced translation would be *"friendship* with self (φιλαυτία) is the
passionate and irrational friendship (φιλία) with the body. It's
opposite is love (ἀγάπη) and abstinence." Christian love (ἀγάπη),
the name of God and fruit of deification can never be viewed as
a vice, friendship (φιλία) and romantic desire (ἔρωτα), however,
most certainly can.

justification of such selfish relations with the world and one's fellow man, a selfish relationship with God would not lag far behind. The security, pleasure, and power sought so avidly in the secular realm would soon be translated into the religious sphere in the form of a narcissistic spirituality that brings instant results. Again for those lacking in self-control and unselfish love, experience would be the most immediate answer to these now spiritualized carnal demands.

In such an environment, there would be nothing extraordinary whatsoever for a new Christian movement to develop based on a powerful and pleasurable experience which offers security in the spiritual life. Furthermore, there would be no reason for members of this new Christianity even to question the use of experience as a criterion especially when recourse is made to Scripture in typical Protestant fashion. As we have seen in our previous chapter, the pursuit of experience that does not contribute to the faith of the heart is a serious error that opens the door to a host of traps set to destroy the believer's soul. Unfortunately, there were few who could recognize such a danger and so strangely enough for the "people of the book" the sand of subjective experience would replace the foundation stone of divine revelation.

2. Touch and Tongues: the Discovery of the First American Pentecostals

Historically, the Pentecostal movement stands on palpably shaky ground. To justify their position, on the one hand they would try to link their own enthusiastic experiences with the grace-filled experiences on the day of Pentecost.[8] On the other hand, they would adopt a modified theory of the radical reformation asserting that the Church was in apostasy until their own group was formed, even though this very theory clearly contradicts Holy Scripture's witness that the Church exists throughout the ages and that the gates of hell will not prevail against it. Individuals may apostasize,[9] but not the Church, the Uncreated Body of Christ. Furthermore, the question is raised: how did the Truth leap over the centuries to reach them?[10]

Although Pentecostals may try to show continuity with the past and how their movement predates the twentieth century by referring to a series of bizarre and highly questionable heretical sects from the Montanists and Gnostics to the Swiss Anabaptists,[11] this new form of Christianity in fact began to

---

[8] Dimitrios Th. Kokoris *Pentecostalism: Heresy and Deception* (Dimitrios Kokoris: Athens, 1997), page 42 (in Greek).

[9] cf.,. *1Timothy* 4:1-13; *2 Thessalonians* 3-4.

[10] Ibid., pages 75 and 166 (in Greek).

[11] John Warren Morris, *The Charismatic Movement: An Orthodox Evaluation,* page 5. For example, Eusebius of Ceasarea in his Ecclesiastical History (5:14-16:1) notes that the heretical Montanists fell into a state of ecstasy and delusion, were

be formed in the womb of some of the more unusual revival movements at the close of the nineteenth century and the threshold of the twentieth. It is a strange tale of well-meaning, but misguided seekers, who would begin with the reasonable, but conclude with the ridiculous. Almost all of the pre-Pentecostal and Pentecostal leaders desired absolute fidelity to Holy Scripture, which can hardly be blamed, but strict adherence to the letter is of little use to those who hardly know how to read.

John Alexander Dowie (1847-1907) who inspired the Father of American Pentecost (Charles Parham) began his healing ministry proclaiming, "Christ the same, yesterday, today and forever" and desiring to organize his church on Apostolic principles. By the end of his life, however, he had believed a "voice" which said, "Elijah must come, and who but you is doing the work of Elijah." His dying words were "the millennium has come, I will be back for a thousand years."[12] So ended in madness the life of the immediate forefather of Pentecostalism whom the Pentecostals themselves claim as their own.

In a similar vein, Maria Woodworth Etter (1844-1924), the so-called "grandmother of the Pentecostal movement," likewise began her ministry with the close study of Scripture. In her revival meetings, phenomena that would be common in later Pentecos-

guided by the devil, slandered the Church, and became schizophrenic. (Kokoris, page 44 (in Greek)).

[12] Roberts Liardon, *God's Generals,* pages 28, 34, 38, and 42.

174

tal communities were manifested for the first time. For example, many would fall down as though they were dead while other would go into trances. Although this "trance evangelism," where being "slain in the Spirit" (falling down), pre-dated the appearance of the "gift of tongues," when that "gift" did appear, Etter was "the only leading evangelist of the holiness movement who embraced the Pentecostal experience of speaking in tongues" as legitimate.[13]

The phenomenon of speaking in tongues that would later become the trademark of Pentecostalism in all its forms first appeared "New Year's Day 1901 at Bethel Bible College in Topeka Kansas" as a result of the biblical research and spiritual experimentation of the holiness preacher Charles F. Parham (1875-1929), the "father of Pentecost." Like Dowie and Etter before him, he "studied God's word and took it literally"[14] preaching a similar "healing Gospel." On the one hand, Parham "refused to submit to the authority of the Methodist Church and left that denomination."[15] On the other hand, he sought to discover both "the marks of the 'second blessing' taught by Wesley"[16] and "the secret of the power of apostolic Christianity."[17] In others words, he was seeking some higher spiritual experience and spiritual power.

[13] Ibid., pages 53 and 61.

[14] Ibid., pages 110-111.

[15] Ibid., pages 115 and 113 respectively.

[16] John Morris, *The Charismatic Movement: An Orthodox Evaluation*, page 6.

[17] Fr. Seraphim Rose, *Orthodoxy and the Religion of the Future*, page 116.

Being ignorant of the means by which the heart can be purified and illumined, Parham and his pupils latched on to the most external sign of Pentecost that startled both the pious and impious alike, the comprehensibility of the Apostles' words to those who spoke other languages, which Parham confused with the gift of tongues. Not only did he misinterpret speaking in tongues in the most external manner as literally speaking in foreign languages, but strangely enough he even shifted the emphasis away from comprehensibility to those present to the incomprehensibility to everyone present! The goal was simply to speak in the "unknown tongues" of the KJV mistranslation of *Corinthians* loosely connected with the supposed foreign languages of Pentecost, which the Apostles most likely did not speak. Unaware of the practice of inner prayer of the heart, all of Saint Paul's injunctions on silent prayer in the Holy Spirit would be construed into the Holy Spirit making strange sounds with the human mouth and in this most ridiculous and blasphemous way "the Spirit also helpeth our infirmities: for we know not what we should pray for as we ought: but the Spirit itself maketh intercession for us with groanings which cannot be uttered." It never occurred to Parham that unspoken sighs (στεναγμοῖς ἀλαλήτοις) are literally not made out loud and that the Spirit helps us by reminding us to pray inwardly when we forget to do so.[18]

[18] Cf., Saint Hesychios the Priest, "On Watchfulness and Holiness," and Saint Diadochos of Photiki, "On Spiritual Knowl-

Based on this rather peculiar and erroneous interpretation of Holy Scripture, Parham and his students spent New Year's Eve trying to compel the Sovereign Spirit to give them the gift of tongues *as they understood it.* Despite their insistence, their efforts were unfruitful until they decided that the missing ingredient must be the "laying on of hands" or the human touch.[19] With this factor added, "Agnes Ottman began to make strange sounds,"[20] and the new Pentecostal movement, based on this "baptism in the Holy Spirit" and "speaking in tongues," was born. Parham describes this event as follows,

> I had scarcely repeated three dozen sentences when glory fell upon her, a halo seemed to surround her head and face, and she began speaking in the Chinese language and was unable to speak English for three days.[21]

There is no question that Parham seized upon an important principle in the rôle of touch or physical contact in the spiritual realm. After all, Christ and

edge," *The Philokalia,* v. 1, page 164 and page 271 respectively, "A Discourse on Abba Philemon," *The Philokalia,* v. 2, page 354, Saint Gregory of Sinai, "On the Signs of Grace and Delusion," *The Philokalia,* v. 4, page 260.

[19] Fr. Seraphim Rose, *Orthodoxy and the Religion of the Future,* page 117.

[20] John Warren Morris, *The Charismatic Movement: An Orthodox Evaluation,* page 6.

[21] Liardon, *God's Generals,* page 119.

the Apostles healed by touch.[22] Ordination to the
Priesthood and Diaconate would also take place by
touch.[23] There are even Scriptural examples of healings taking place solely by contact with objects that
had touched the Saints or their relics.[24] But most importantly for Parham, there are examples in *Acts* of
those receiving the gift of the Holy Spirit by the laying on of hands.[25] He no doubt thought, "Why should
not the same be able to take place today?"

What Parham chose to ignore, however, is that
not every believer was able to transmit the grace of
the Holy Spirit in this way. In fact, those who have
not first been properly purified, illumined and glorified by grace and unworthily desire to do such not

---

[22] "And the whole multitude sought to touch him: for there
went virtue out of him, and healed them all." *Luke* 6:19 as one
example among many.

[23] "Lay hands suddenly on no man" *1 Timothy* 5:22 as well
as *Acts* 6:6 and 13:2.

[24] In the Old Testament, "And it came to pass, as they were
burying a man, that, behold, they spied a band of men; and they
cast the man into the sepulchre of Elisha: and when the man
was let down, and touched the bones of Elisha, he revived, and
stood up on his feet." *2 Kings* 13:21. In the New Testament,
"And God wrought special miracles by the hands of Paul: So
that from his body were brought unto the sick handkerchiefs or
aprons, and the diseases departed from them, and the evil spirits went out of them." *Acts* 19:11-12.

[25] "Then laid they their hands on them, and they received
the Holy Ghost." *Acts* 8:17

"And when Paul had laid his hands upon them, the Holy
Ghost came on them; and they spake with tongues, and prophesied." *Acts* 19:6

178

only do not transmit the grace of the Holy Spirit, but receive the Apostle's curse as well. For directly following the reception of the Holy Spirit by the laying on of the Apostle's hands in *Acts* 8:17, Simon the sorcerer unworthily sought the ability to grant others the Holy Spirit through the laying on of hands and was cursed.[26] What separates Simon from the Apostles is a selfish desire for spiritual power on the one hand and the spiritual state in which he found himself on the other. Saint Luke writes that Simon the sorcerer both believed and was baptized, but it is clear that he was still very much in the arena of purification from the passions, whereas the humble Apostles were already purified and illumined seers of God. A purified, illumined, and glorified heart through a burning love for Christ and obedience to the will of God together with a special gift given to them by Christ Himself (which is the apostolic gift)[27] is what separated the touch of the Apostles and their successors from that of other believers. The only observable difference between Parham and Simon the sorcerer's mechanical, magical, and superstitious understand-

[26] "And when Simon saw that through laying on of the apostles' hands the Holy Ghost was given, he offered them money, Saying, Give me also this power, that on whomsoever I lay hands, he may receive the Holy Ghost. But Peter said unto him, Thy money perish with thee, because thou hast thought that the gift of God may be purchased with money. Thou hast neither part nor lot in this matter: for thy heart is not right in the sight of God." *Acts* 8:19-21.

[27] "Verily I say unto you, Whatsoever ye shall bind on earth shall be bound in heaven: and whatsoever ye shall loose on earth shall be loosed in heaven." *Matthew* 18:18.

ing of spiritual gifts and their quest for spiritual power via the "laying on of hands" is that Simon at least asked the Apostles, whereas Parham and his students forged ahead being subject to none and asking no one at all.

Touch, however, is a sword that cuts two ways. There is also an entire negative spectrum of touch ranging from the clearly demonic (as in the case of voodoo and witchcraft) to the many cleanliness injunctions of the Levitical law. Furthermore, while generally "each of the bodily senses directs, feeds, and directly influences specific passions," the sense of touch in particular can incite the grosser passions of the flesh.[28] Saint John Climacus teaches that "touch alone is sufficient for bodily defilement, for nothing is so dangerous as this sense."[29] Saint Nikitas further writes, "our sense of touch is not partial in the sense that its activity is not restricted to one part of the body, as is that of the other senses; it is a general all-over sense belonging to the whole body. Thus if while still addicted to the lubricity of things, we touch some object unnecessarily, passion charged thoughts disturb the intellect."[30] In other words, the touch of the passionate will neither help themselves in prayer,

---

[28] Anesti Kessolopoulos, *The Passions and the Virtues*, (Domos: Athens, 1990) pages 35-36 (in Greek).

[29] Saint John Climacus, *The Ladder of Divine Ascent*, trans. by Holy Transfiguration Monastery (Holy Transfiguration Monastery: Brookline, 1991) 15:51, page 111.

[30] Saint Nikitas Stithatos, "On the Practice of the Virtues," *The Philokalia*, v. 4, page 84.

nor those whom they touch, but can even defile the prayer offered.

In any event, through the common desire for tongues and spiritual power and through the common touch of those present, others soon began to utter strange and incomprehensible sounds. And although those thus "speaking in tongues" and those listening to them may not have understood what they were saying, all present understood that they had entered a new spiritual realm and embraced this phenomenon as the apostolic gift itself. In this way a new type of prayer which the Lord Christ never taught His Disciples by word or by example was hailed as the most perfect prayer necessary for all Christians. What is most strange is that this "speaking in tongues" could be called prayer at all, for if prayer is one's intimate conversation with God, how can there be a conversation if the person speaking does not even understand what he is saying.

One can rightly say with the birth of the Pentecostal movement a new type of "Christianity" was born as well, differing not only from the more staid forms of conventional Protestantism, but also from the experientially based Protestantism of the nineteenth century American revivals. "Speaking in tongues" for some Pentecostals became "the 'answer' with respect to the 'certainty' of salvation. Glossolalia was considered proof of 'baptism of the Holy Spirit,' that certainly derived 'from above' and could no longer be doubted."[31]In this new movement, the sense of repentance and sin that was central in the "salvation experience" of the revivals is replaced with a certain hazy, yet definitely pleasurable and sensual experience of "speaking in tongues."[32] Meanwhile, the distinction between worship and entertainment continues to be blurred in these communities. Following Dowie's example, Parham would wear "holy land garments" as a publicity stunt. In passing, we note that the "father of Pentecost" was also a supporter of the Ku Klux Klan.[33]

3. The First Pentecostal Communities: A Diversity of Tongues; A Diversity of Churches

In the next few years, Pentecostalism began to spread within the holiness movement gaining national publicity in Los Angeles at the Azusa Street Mission where what became known as "the Second Pentecost" took place under the catalyzing influence of one of Parham's former Bible students, William J.

[31] Alevizopoulos, *Handbook of Heresies and Para-Christian Groups,* page 158 (in Greek).

[32] Fr. Seraphim Rose, *Orthodoxy and the Religion of the Future,* page 128.

[33] Roberts Liardon, *God's Generals,* pages 125 and 133. This fact is significant in so far as the Apostles after Pentecost filled with divine love went forth to bring the good tidings of salvation to all nations and races. To support an organization based on racial hatred is surely indicative of a quite different Pentecost.

182

Seymour (1870-1922). For the Pentecostals, 312 Azusa Street was their upper room of Pentecost; thousands from across the nation rushed to the small building to gain the gift of speaking in tongues and see the "workings of the Spirit." One Pentecostal historian writes, "probably everyone in the Pentecostal movement can attribute their (sic.) roots in some way to Azusa."[34] The differences, however, between "the Pentecost" that transpired there and in Jerusalem are staggering indeed.[35] Seymour himself perceived the presence of another spirit besides the Holy Spirit, at this "Pentecost." One of the Azusa street leaders wrote, "we dared not call the attention of the people too much to the workings of the evil. Fear would result." Seymour, in any case, wrote to Parham to come and help discern the spirits. The "Father of Pentecost" came, whose comments we cite below:

> I hurried to Los Angeles, and to my utter surprise and astonishment I found conditions even worse than I had anticipated... manifestations of the flesh, spiritualistic controls (sic.) saw people practicing hypnotism at the altar over candidates seeking baptism, though many were receiving the real baptism of the Holy Ghost...

[34] Ibid., pages 143 and 163.

[35] John Warren Morris, *The Charismatic Movement: An Orthodox Evaluation,* page 7. Cf., our previous discussion of Pentecost itself. One is hard-pressed to find a single common thread between the two in terms of prophecy, preparation, place, those involved, sobriety, comprehensibility, or unity.

Let me speak plainly with regard to the
work as I have found it here. I found hyp-
notic influences, familiar spirit influences,
spiritualistic influences, mesomeric influences, all kinds of spells, spasms, falling
trances, etc... No such thing is known
among our workers as the suggestion of
certain words or sounds, the working of the
chin, or massage of the throat. There are
many in Los Angeles who sing, pray, and
talk wonderfully in tongues, as the Spirit
gives utterance, and there is jabbering here
that is not tongues at all.[36]

While Parham was honest enough to recognize
the presence of the fraudulent and demonic, it remains a mystery how he could distinguish between
spiritual and non-spiritual jabbering. For his honesty, Parham was pad-locked out of the meetings and
with him the teaching that one can receive a spirit
other than the Holy Spirit was padlocked out of the
Pentecostal movement.

Within a short time, the "Pentecostal fire" at
Azusa was extinguished due to internal intrigues and
Seymour's teaching that through sin, one can lose the
Holy Spirit and salvation. With such a teaching, the
thousands who once mobbed Azusa Street dwindled
to twenty people.[37] Understandably, the early Pente-

---

[36] As quoted in Roberts Liardon's *God's Generals,* pages
157-158.

[37] Ibid., pages 159-162.

184

costals rejected Seymour's teaching and maintained that one can "be saved," "have the Holy Spirit," and *not live* a holy life!

The two "truths" from Azusa that strangely lingered in Pentecostalism were an openness to all spirits and the complete independence of holiness and tongues. Even though both teachings contradict the very spirit of the Gospel, Pentecostal "theologians" claim that these "comforting doctrines" are the result of a literal reading of Holy Scripture. Thus, in spite of the spiritual aberrations described at Azusa and which continues to this day in some Pentecostal gatherings, contemporary Pentecostal teachers assert that "if a person is a child of God, he is not going to receive an evil spirit," on the basis of *Luke* 11:11-13 ("If a son shall ask bread of any of you that is a father, will he give him a stone").[38] In similar fashion, because the Apostles were "endued with power on high" at Pentecost, they teach that "the fruits of the Spirit are for holiness, but the gift of the Holy Spirit is for power."[39] Thus Christ's injunctions for watchfulness and holiness are brought to no effect.

Theologically, Pentecostals would later interpret their "second Pentecost" as the evening rain of *Joel* 2:23, despite the fact that this phrase is never employed chronologically or prophetically, but always descriptively and qualitatively to indicate simply the

[38] Kenneth Hagin, *Concerning Spiritual Gifts,* (Rhema Bible Church: Tulsa Oklahoma, 1985) page 46.

[39] Ibid., page 22.

bounty of God's blessings.[40] Despite the shady pedigree of the forefathers of Pentecostalism, despite the "father of Pentecost's own reservations about the "American Pentecost" of Azusa Street, despite the fact that the holiness movement itself was the first to condemn the practice and teaching of the Pentecostals as "the heresy of the third grace," the powerfully real experience of "baptism in the Holy Spirit" attracted the naïve and the unquestioning by droves. It is certainly no exaggeration to call Pentecostalism a new Christianity, for the entire Christian world rejected their practices and with no uncertainty confessed that the "speaking in tongues" of the Pentecostals had little to do even with the supposed foreign languages of *Acts* or the practice of the Church in Corinth.

This "persecution," however, did not stop the Pentecostals from spreading their new gospel, but further convinced them that they were living in the last times. By 1911, they began to form new churches and communities such as "The Pentecostal Church of Holiness."[41] Although these communities were united by a common experience, they quickly splintered and fragmented into a large number of competing sects all with their own particular emphasis and teachings. For example, in 1907 the Church of God of A. T.

[40] Kokoris, page 91 (in Greek). Cf., *Deuteronomy* 11:13-14, *Jeremiah* 5:24, *James* 5:7, *Leviticus* 26:4, *Deuteronomy* 28:2, *Zachariah* 1:1, and *Hosea* 6:3.

[41] Alevizopoulos, *Handbook of Heresies and Para-Christian Groups,* page 157 (in Greek).

Tomlinson was founded, followed in 1909 by the Church of God of Cleveland Tennessee, in 1917 by the Primitive Church of God, in 1930 by the Tent of Faith, the Church of Jesus, the Remnant of the Church of God, *ad inifinitum* until the present day.[42] Far from bringing unity, this new spirit only brought discord and confusion.

For the next fifty years, the Pentecostal sects remained isolated and scorned by the entire Protestant world which labeled them as "holy rollers"[43] on the basis of some of the bizarre displays manifested in their worship services. And while conventional Protestants continued to keep their distance from Pentecostal gatherings, their attitudes towards Pentecostal experiences began to change in response to certain inner changes within the Protestant world and American society at large. This in turn opened the way for the second wave of Pentecostalism, the so-called "charismatic movement."

4. New Wine in Old Wine Skins: The Charismatic Movement

During the twentieth century, the pace of American society continued to accelerate. Alienated from themselves and those around them, Americans increasingly began to seek comfort through the im-

---

[42] Kokoris, page 20.

[43] John Warren Morris, *The Charismatic Movement: An Orthodox Evaluation,* page 7.

mediate gratification of their various desires. Many would turn to the products of the developing film and television industries for diversion and escape; others would turn to alcohol and drugs; others still would turn towards ecstatic experiences. The hippie movement and back to nature movement both reflected a reaction to the falseness of an increasingly plastic and hollow society. While attempting to remain aloof from such movements, the Protestant world felt the same anguish that plagued the rest of society.

More specifically in the Protestant world, liberal theology and biblical criticism began to make inroads into the mainline Protestant denominations, undermining the very foundation of Protestantism, belief in Holy Scripture and Christ as portrayed in Holy Scripture. A large sector of the American Protestant world rejected these new theories as a denial of Christianity itself and became known as the fundamentalists. Significantly, these Protestants who held scripture in the highest regard were to remain the fiercest opponents of Pentecostalism in all of its forms (the Pentecostal, Charismatic and the non-denominational born-again Christian movements). Meanwhile in the liberal Protestant sector, the former scriptural and credal emphasis was replaced by the "social gospel." Although this new emphasis on social justice would sound so very reasonable, contemporary, and humane, this further turning of the attention outward left the souls of its adherents even drier still. Many of these Protestants felt that their religion was "dry, over-rational, merely external, lacking in fervency or power,"[44] yet hesitated to leave the confession into which they were born. No longer thoroughly grounded in Scripture, hungry for any real experience of religion and weary of political and social issues, these disenchanted Protestants were fertile soil for the new form of Pentecostalism, the charismatic movement.

John Sherrill's vastly popular and carefully crafted *They Speak With Other Tongues* would offer the "mainline" Protestant world with a revised and palatable history of Pentecostalism without the disturbing details that the Pentecostals themselves would take no pains to hide. More significantly, however, this work would introduce its Protestant readers to the "human face" of sunny Pentecostalism and the then burgeoning charismatic movement. The sincerity, the kindness, and the vibrancy of the people whom Sherrill describes, rather than any reasonable argumentation,[45] are the positive tools that Sherrill employs to make his case. Negatively, Sherrill relies on the fact that most mainline Protestants no longer seriously accepted the Church's teaching on deception and the reality of the fierce spiritual warfare be-

[44] Fr. Seraphim Rose, *Orthodoxy and the Religion of the Future,* page 118.

[45] In fact, there are cases of clear *non sequitur* in his work. Notably on page 82, he claims that Pentecostal tongues did not disappear from the Christian Church, although among the highly questionable and sporadic cases of supposed Pentecostal tongues that he lists there is a gap of one thousand years. Cf., John L Sherrill, *They Speak with Other Tongues* (Chosen Books: Grand Rapids, 2000), pages 82-84.

tween God and Satan. Without this teaching, there would be little to discourage the modern Protestant from exploring this lively world.

The chief characteristic of the charismatic movement is that its partisans do not cut themselves off from the churches to which they belong, but remain within them and aim to regenerate them thereby.[46] At the same time, they accept the basic beliefs and practices of the Pentecostals as the heart of a more spiritual Christianity.[47] Since they view their experiences as the sure signs of a living faith, the credal boundaries separating the various confessions become less important thus making the charismatic movement *ipso facto* highly ecumenical.

Historically, Pentecostalism began to penetrate the older Protestant bodies through the lay movements such as "the full gospel businessman's fellowship" on the one hand, and television evangelist-healers such as Kathryn Khulman and Oral Roberts on the other.[48] In 1959, the Episcopalian priest of Saint Mark's Church in Van Nuys, California, Dennis J. Bennett heard a married couple "speaking in tongues" (making inarticulate sounds) and was "baptized in the Holy Spirit" by them and also began to "speak in strange tongues." Rev. Bennett then de-

---

[46] Alevizopoulos, *Handbook of Heresies and Para-Christian Groups,* page 261 (in Greek).

[47] John Warren Morris, *The Charismatic Movement: An Orthodox Evaluation,* page 7.

[48] John Warren Morris, *The Charismatic Movement: An Orthodox Evaluation,* pages 7-8.

voted himself to spreading the charismatic movement while remaining within the Episcopal Church. Soon Methodists, Lutherans, Presbyterians and members of other denominations began to have similar experiences, and so the movement spread like fire through the dry straw of rationalistic Protestantism.[49]

Meanwhile in the Roman Catholic world, the confusing signals from the Second Vatican Council were interpreted by many American Catholics as license for a wide array of innovation and experimentation. Catholics felt quite free to seek inspiration from many sources that but a few years before would have been strictly forbidden.[50] Given the new reevaluation of the Protestant Reformation and openness to the "wisdom" of Eastern Religions, it is not in the least bit surprising that they would be open to the charismatic spirit now pulsing with "new life" in the withered Protestant ecclesiastical bodies. It is worth noting that just as Protestants who adhered most vehemently to Holy Scripture rejected the charismatic movement as fraudulent, likewise those Roman Catholics who were most devoted to a more traditional Catholic piety also rejected the movement. Despite fundamentalist or revival overtones, the charismatic movement is in essence a liberal one.[51]

---

[49] Ibid., page 8 and Alevizopoulos, *Handbook of Heresies and Para-Christian Groups,* page 261.

[50] Ibid., page 8.

[51] Of course, Pentecostals, like their fundamentalist stepbrothers, claim to be following the literal interpretation of Scripture and would be quick to assert that they are "conservative."

In 1967, Ralph Keifer, an instructor in theology at Dusquesne University in Pittsburgh, became intrigued with the charismatic movement after reading John Sherrill's *They Speak With Other Tongues*. When the Episcopalian priest William Lewis admitted Kiefer to a charismatic prayer group, Kiefer soon also began to "speak in tongues" (make nonsense sounds).[52] In a short while, other faculty members began to babble as well. Kiefer, in turn, introduced Kevin Ranaghan, a member of the faculty of Notre Dame University, to the movement. Through Ranaghan's efforts and a series of charismatic summer seminars that were attended by Catholics from across the country, the charismatic movement spread throughout the Catholic world.[53]

The charismatic movement was generally less successful in infiltrating the Orthodox Churches in America. Nevertheless, on account of the weak monastic presence in America, some Orthodox Christians misunderstood the purpose of asceticism in the Christian life since they lacked living examples of the genuine spiritual life and were generally unaware of the most basic stages in the spiritual life (purification, illumination, and deification). This, in conjunction with the understandable desire of many immigrants to fit into American culture in every way

[52] John Warren Morris, *The Charismatic Movement: An Orthodox Evaluation,* page 9.

[53] Fr. Seraphim Rose, *Orthodoxy and the Religion of the Future* , page 120.

possible[54] (short of apostasy) and to adopt an American perspective on life, made it possible for the misguided priest Eusebius Stephanou both to be enticed by the charismatic movement, and after receiving the "gift of speaking in tongues" (the ability to mouth strange and incomprehensible sounds) in 1972 to be the major advocate of Neo-pentecostalism in the Orthodox Church.[55] Nevertheless, while the modern Roman hierarchy and main-line Protestant authorities latently accepted the charismatic movement, the Orthodox hierarchy universally rejected it as heretical, prideful, and damaging to the soul.[56]

5. The Tele-Church: Christians of the Third Wave

In the 1980's, a third Pentecostal wave began to sweep the country with its adherents known as "neo-pentecostals," "Pentecostals of the third wave," or more generally non-denominational Christians. These neo-pentecostals sought to convert the world through the mass media (radio and television) and the organization of mass gatherings in which tens of

[54] The use of pews and organs is a prime example in the liturgical sphere.

[55] John Warren Morris, *The Charismatic Movement: An Orthodox Evaluation,* page 10.

[56] "The Church of Greece labeled the movement as heretical as early as 1976. Recently (sic.), the Synod of Bishops of the Greek Orthodox Archdiocese of North and South America and the Sobor of the Ukrainian Orthodox Church of Canada have also condemned the movement." Ibid., page 38 (printed in 1984).

thousands participate.[57] In this way, Christianity is construed as a purely personal affair of the isolated individual.

An important forerunner for these Christians of the third wave was Aimee Semple McPherson (1890-1944). Although McPherson was among the original Pentecostals who predated the television era, she believed that religion should be entertaining, for "the world's love for entertainment brought them encouragement, joy, and laughter."[58] Both her Pentecostalsim and her life kept in step with Hollywood. In her "Angelus Temple," she resorted to everything from brass bands to animal acts while in private life, she was married three times, in litigation forty-five times, and died from an overdose of sedatives. Nevertheless, this woman, beloved of the KKK and founder of the four square Gospel Church, was according to one Pentecostal historian "the spiritual pioneer who paved the way for the rest of us and largely responsible for the way we demonstrate Christianity today."[59]

While the original Pentecostals and their charismatic, inter-denominational children may be the spiritual precursors of the non-denominational Christians of the third wave, their immediate history is entangled in the development of religious radio and television stations independent of any ecclesias-

---

[57] Alevizopoulos, *Handbook of Heresies and Para-Christian Groups,* page 289 (in Greek).

[58] Roberts Liardon, *God's Generals,* page 253.

[59] Ibid., page 229.

tical authority beginning in the 1940's.[60] In this form of Pentecostalism, the televangelist as a "spiritual super-star" would take on an importance in the life of believers beyond that of their local pastor, even though they would have no personal relationship with the televangelist. The believers would trust the televangelists, because nearly all of the televangelists would claim to have "direct communication with heaven" and the ability to work all kinds of signs and wonders. Of course, they would be dependent on their television audience (television believers) to send in money to support their ministries. Although not a few of these televangelists have been publicly proved to be fraudulent, there seems to be little waning in their popularity. In a culture addicted to entertainment, a "religious show" focusing more on miracles than the gospel of Christ entertains without placing any of the difficult demands of the gospel on the believer. It has been noted that "the tele-church movement has destructive consequences for the religious and political substance of the US. The local community in which the spiritual and political life develops is literally destroyed and a new religious ethos is created."[61] The internet will no doubt continue this process.

[60] Ibid., page 290.
[61] Ibid., page 298.

5. The Pentecostal Answer

In our brief outline of the history and development of the Pentecostal movement, we should point out that there is not so much the transformation of one group into another group, but a spreading of Pentecostalism into previously uninhabited domains. All three Pentecostal groups coexist and continue to grow. All three groups share certain Pentecostal teachings on tongues and the gifts of the spirit; all share the same Pentecostal practices. We do note, however, with each new appearance of Pentecostalism, there is an increasing individualism and decreasing acceptance of even the notion of the Church as a tangible reality. And while all Pentecostals sincerely believe that they are the most "biblical" of Christians, their interpretations are diverse and contradictory. The same Holy Spirit can hardly be inspiring them all.

In each stage in the history of modern Pentecostalism, we also mark the relative ease and speed with which the gifts (especially that of "tongues," making inarticulate sounds) are received in obvious opposition to the normal laws of the spiritual life. Generally, great labor and time are required for man to humble himself (purify himself) in order to fulfill the commandments of Christ and obtain the gift of undistracted prayer of the heart (the genuine gift of tongues) and other gifts of the Spirit. In the Pentecostal movements, however, the gifts seem to be dispersed according to some new dispensation in which spiritual holiness and spiritual power are kept strangely apart.

At every step in the history of Pentecostalism, we find that these new phenomena, which must not be questioned, are not manifested in those who remain obedient to their ecclesiastical authorities nor in those who are devoted to Christianity in any of its pre-Pentecostal forms, but to those who are independent, self-guided, impatiently seeking spiritual power, and easily moved by the theatrical. In many ways, it is a religion tailored for contemporary American society. A very limited amount of time and effort yields seemingly great and supernatural gifts. Although the origins of Pentecostalism are spiritually dubious, we question neither the sincerity of its founders, nor the authenticity of their miracles. We simply ask the reader to compare what has been described in this chapter with the previous patristic exposition of *Acts*.

In a world where easy experience is coveted and true knowledge acquired through labor is scorned, the movement in any of its forms seems to offer the perfect answer. But the question remains... is that answer truly Christian?

The Dogmas of the Non-dogmatic

1. Dogma, Heresy, and the Church

In the previous chapter, we discussed the general background, history and development of the experience-based, American Pentecostal movement. We indicated that according to their own confession a concrete creed based on the fruits of divine revelation[1] is of less importance than the spiritual experience of the individual, irrespective of his spiritual maturity (i.e., degree of purification or illumination). Such is, however, only partially true. In reality, the Pentecostals have inherited some very precise dogmatic beliefs and naturally have constructed their own new dogmas on the basis of their Pentecostal experiences.

Their inherited dogmatic structure is based on the negative Protestantism of the radical reformers and can be summarized as the rejection of all the traditional channels of grace that Christ sanctioned in order to heal and sanctify man: the mysteries of Holy Baptism, Holy Communion, and Confession. This is most significant, for in the absence of these traditional channels of grace, the need to discover a *new way* to enter the spiritual realm became much

---

[1] I.e., Scripture and Tradition; cf., relevant discussion in chapter one.

more pressing. On the other hand, based on their own experience, they developed a new theory of salvation and embraced a peculiar interpretation of the end-times consistent with their own views on the spiritual life. Both the negative and positive poles of the Pentecostal's dogmatic world must be examined in order to more fully appreciate the great spiritual thirst of those who turned to the movement as well as to evaluate the movement as a whole.

From the onset, the task of sketching the dogmatic world of Pentecostalism is made quite formidable by the great fluidity in dogmatic positions held by those who align themselves with Pentecostalism in any of its forms. Naturally, those in the charismatic movement who still remain in their native confession will maintain many of the beliefs intrinsic to that confession. The Roman Catholic charismatic will by no means deny the importance of the sacramental life, even though his understanding of it will be somewhat skewed by his adherence to the charismatic movement. The various Protestant charismatics (Episcopalians, Lutherans, Presbyterians...) will still don the theological garb of their particular denomination (predestination, salvation by faith...), but will just as easily shed it whenever the "higher revelation" of tongues and of the gifts of the Spirit moves them to do so. Even in the variety of strictly Pentecostal groups, beliefs on key doctrines of the faith (such as the Holy Trinity, Baptism...) will vary greatly. This in itself is a commentary on the "spirit" that should be leading them to *all Truth*. Nevertheless, there is a general contour of beliefs that can be discerned in most Pentecostal circles and that affects, to a greater or lesser extent, all those who align themselves with the Pentecostal movement in any form.

Interestingly enough, one of their main dogmas is that they are non-dogmatic: "no Creed but Christ" they proudly exclaim. This strange dogma is expressed in a number of ways. On the one hand, the strict "non-dogmaticists," often Pentecostals of the original variety, refuse to admit the very existence of dogmas (and hence their necessity for man's salvation). On the other hand, the "moderates," who are comprised of more "progressive" Pentecostals and most charismatics, believe that salvation is not a matter of dogma, that salvation exists in all confessions, and that everyone can express himself dogmatically as he wishes. These "moderates" may admit the existence of dogma, but they overlook it because they believe that it plays no rôle in man's salvation.[2] What dogmatically (!) unites the more "conservative" Pentecostal with his more "liberal" charismatic cousin is the underlying presupposition that dogma does not contribute to salvation. Although dogma is not an end in itself as all Pentecostals correctly intuit (the end being the purification, illumination, and perfection of man's soul), their position "against" dogma takes them to another extreme that is both unreasonable and unscriptural.

---

[2] Kokoris, page 93. In fact, their most basic dogma is that one must belong to their church to be saved. (Ibid., page 153 (in Greek)).

THE DOGMAS OF THE NON-DOGMATIC

The most strident anti-dogmatic Christian group in practice accepts a small number of beliefs (dogmas) as serious and essential while it rejects the rest as unimportant and inessential. Many "non-dogmatic" Pentecostals will reject churches that believe differently from them, but "if dogmas have no bearing on salvation, how can they reject those who have a different faith or other dogmas?"[3] In other words, their claim to being "non-dogmatic" has no basis in reality, but is simply a means of maligning the more conventional confessions as rigid, overly complicated, and lacking in the Spirit. In the absence of a positive historical foundation, they build upon this negative one of being anti-dogmatic. It is truly amazing that so few of their adherents realize that the very *belief* that one can be *non-dogmatic* is itself self-contradictory.

The "anti-dogmatic Christian's" practice of accepting some dogmas as important, while rejecting others as unimportant (refusing to "major in minors" as they will put it) is in sharp contrast with the practice of the early Church.[4] The early Church taught that all revealed dogma was necessary and had to be believed and accepted even as the medical establishment requires the acceptance of all practices that contribute to good health. The rejection of but one

[3] Ibid., page 146.

[4] The adjective "early" is inserted for the sake of those readers who may accept the "early Church" as authoritative even while they reject the Church which is in unbroken continuity with those earliest Christian communities. In reality, the "early Church" and the Orthodox Church are one and the same.

201

dogma as insignificant or not fundamental was considered to be deviation from revealed Truth and consequently heresy. We observe this not only in the canons of the early Councils, but even in Holy Scripture, which the Pentecostals claim to accept. Saint Paul in his *First Epistle to Timothy*[5] speaks out against those who condemn certain foods as ethically defiling man. In a similar situation (e.g., fasting) the anti-dogmatic would no doubt consider diet not to be a fundamental dogma, but one which could easily be rejected as having no bearing on man's salvation. Saint Paul, however, calls such a faith apostasy inspired by "deceiving spirits and demonic teaching."[6] In other words, the very stance of being "anti-dogmatic" is both unscriptural and heretical.

In today's world of religious tolerance and doctrinal relativity, the term "heresy" has become taboo for many progressive Christians well aware of the horrors of the Inquisition committed by the no longer

---

[5] "Now the Spirit speaketh expressly, that in the latter times some shall depart from the faith, giving heed to seducing spirits, and doctrines of devils (ἀποστήσονταί τινες τῆς πίστεως προσέχοντες πνεύμασιν πλάνοις καὶ διδασκαλίαις δαιμονίων: literally, apostasizing from the faith, paying attention to deceiving spirits and teachings of demons). Speaking lies in hypocrisy; having their conscience seared with a hot iron; Forbidding to marry, and commanding to abstain from meats, which God hath created to be received with thanksgiving of them which believe and know the truth. For every creature of God is good, and nothing to be refused, if it be received with thanksgiving: For it is sanctified by the word of God and prayer." *1 Timothy* 4:1-5.

[6] Ibid., page 147.

Orthodox Church in the West. Even contemporary Orthodox, however, will employ the word "heterodox" to avoid this insulting and scandalous word. The word "heresy," however, refers to a mortal sickness in the Christian world that the Holy Fathers out of great love for man refused to overlook because heresy stands in the way of man's purification, illumination, and perfection.[7] From a therapeutic perspective, it is akin to an unsound and harmful medical procedure that any competent medical society would be obliged to condemn. Any other stance would be no less than criminal. To take this analogy a bit further, dogma and even the liturgical life are not exalted as transcendental ends venerated for their own sake, but rather they are like the sterility and medical apparatus that a hospital must possess in order to heal its patients with ease and success. They are neither the healing process nor health, but the prerequisites for the healing process (purification and illumination) to take place and health (unceasing prayer, unselfish love, and the vision of the glory of Christ) to be attained.

Although all heresy employs the Bible to justify itself, heresy is by its very nature unbiblical because its ultimate basis is not the vision of Christ in His Uncreated Divine Glory seen by the Prophets, Apostles, and Saints, but a philosophy constructed on the basis of human reflection and the laws of reason.[8]

---

[7] Cf., *2 Peter* 2:1-2, *1 Timothy* 1:19-20, and *2 John* 7 (Kokoris, page 17 (in Greek)).

[8] Romanides, *Dogmatic and Symbolic Theology of the Orthodox Catholic Church,* page 14 (in Greek).

With such a radically different basis, heresy as a teaching quite naturally deviates from what is commonly received. Among the four fatal diseases that plague the Christian world—sin, schism, deception, and heresy—heresy is the most deadly and difficult to cure. "Sin consists in the transgression of God's commandments. Schism divides the Body of Christ into warring factions. Deception leads the believer to false choices, but heresy insults the person of God."[9] This is why Saint John the Theologian in no uncertain terms calls heretics deceivers and antichrists.[10] Elsewhere, heresy is referred to as the overturning of the faith, as gangrene, blasphemy and atheism.[11] If "the way of reverence to God consists in pious doctrines and good practices" as Saint Cyril of Alexandria teaches, there can be no greater threat to man's spiritual healing than impious doctrines and wrong practices.[12]

The Truth and the Life that God has revealed to His Saints for man's salvation must be embraced and lived with great precision even as the sick are required to take the correct medicine and proper dosage to be healed. The devil ultimately uses heresy to counterfeit the saving Truth, so that it will not be

---

[9] Kokoris, pages 17-18.

[10] "For many deceivers are entered into the world, who confess not that Jesus Christ is come in the flesh. This is a deceiver and an antichrist." *2 John* 7.

[11] Cf., *Matthew* 12:31-32, *1 Timothy* 6:20-21, *2 Peter* 2:1-2, 3:1 (Kokoris, page 16).

[12] Catechetical Homily 4:2 (Ibid., page 6 (in Greek)).

applied with the requisite exactness, so that man will be left unhealed and enslaved to him.[13]

Of course, every heretical group will claim to possess the Truth, though in fact they camouflage a lie with a semblance of the truth. If evil "must live like a parasite on the body of the good," then heresy lives as a parasite on the body of the Truth. Like evil, "it strives to present it positive aspect as a jewel so precious that all means are justified to attain it."[14] Truth, however, mixed with falsehood is sapped of its saving power and no longer true, for Truth or falsehood are not restricted to the mind's ivory tower, but are incarnated in the sweat and tears of man's daily life. For example, "it is not enough to believe in the Blood of Christ, one must also receive It. It is not enough to repent and recognize one's guilt, one must also confess one's sins."[15]

Heretical groups will naturally claim to be the Church, "the pillar and ground of the truth,"[16] but they lack the following prerequisites of the Church of Christ:

> 1. Historical continuity with the upper room of Pentecost that is objectively demonstrated through the apostolic succession of the shepherds of the flocks via ordination (cf., *Acts* 14:23; *1 Timothy* 4:14, 2:6).

[13] Kokoris, page 305.

[14] Archimandrite Sophrony (Sakharov), *Saint Silouan the Athonite,* page 117.

[15] Kokoris, page 6.

[16] *1 Timothy* 3:15.

2. Spiritual continuity with the first Church established on Pentecost that is characterized by the same life of ascetic struggle nourished by the deifying Mysteries of Christ: Baptism, Chrismation, Divine Eucharist, Ordination, Confession... and that is capable of purifying, illumining and deifying the believer.

3. Freedom from heresy or wrong opinions.

4. The confession of all the dogmas great or small given by Christ and the Apostles in word or writing together with the Nine Ecumenical Councils.[17]

Without a trace of triumphalism,[18] only the Orthodox Church fulfills all of the above requirements. The Pentecostals, on the other hand, will be hard pressed to demonstrate that they can fulfill even one of them. The absence of apostolic succession in the Pentecostal "churches" is evident to all. Our previous discussion of Pentecost and the history of the Pentecostal movement indicate the lack of spiritual continuity and complete ignorance of the process

[17] Based on Kokoris, page 178 with point 2 modified according to Fr. J. Romanides, *Dogmatic and Symbolic Theology of the Orthodox Catholic Church,* page 18 (both in Greek).

[18] The centrality of the teaching on humility in the Orthodox Church does not permit the believer to be triumphant in an arrogant way. He loves the purity and holiness of Orthodoxy, but ever confesses that he is a sinner, a prostitute and a tax-collector upon whom Christ has ineffably had mercy and just as ineffably continues to do so.

of purification, illumination, and deification. A brief examination of the dogmatic positions of the Pentecostals will in turn indicate their failure to meet the last two criteria as well.

2. Salvation and the Start of the Christian Life: Belief, Baptism, and Spiritual Gifts

Like other Protestants, the Pentecostals teach justification by faith alone. Salvation for them is realized through the following process: man hears about Christ; he believes in Him, in His Redeeming Blood, and in His Saving Work; he recognizes his own sinfulness; he accepts Christ as His personal Savior; he is baptized; and (in distinction to other Protestant bodies) the Holy Spirit descends on him bearing witness (through "tongues" {making inarticulate sounds} and other gifts) that he is a member of the Church and will later be raptured away when Christ comes again.[19] Salvation is thus automatically and quickly effected on man's side by the rational processes of the brain and emotional reactions of the heart. In this process, Holy Baptism has a decidedly marginal rôle emptied of its saving content.[20] For the Pentecostals, Baptism does not grant remission of sins, but merely confirms the faith of the believer.

In contrast with this quick fix for the plight of sinful man, "salvation" or "being born again" in the

---

[19] Kokoris, pages 38, 63, and 164-165.
[20] Ibid., page 305.

Church is akin to the natural process of maturation. It slowly, but surely unfolds like a blossom,[21] for "the kingdom of God cometh not with observation."[22] While man's spiritual healing involves the gradual process of purification, illumination and deification through which the Apostles themselves passed,[23] the *sine qua non* of the whole process is Holy Baptism, through which man is given "the pre-requisites needed to become a perfect man and the potential for spiritual growth through struggle, participation in the Mysteries of the Church, by prayer, repentance and obedience to the law of God."[24] Baptism is not a simple "rite of dedication to God," but is the initial means by which the believer is given the potential to be united with Christ and incorporated into His Body. In Holy Baptism, the believer not only "puts on Christ,"[25] but according to Christ's words, the Holy Spirit as well.[26] During Baptism, Divine Purifying Grace invisibly descends, blots out sin, regenerates,

---

[21] Ibid., page 65-66.

[22] *Luke* 17:20.

[23] Father J. Romanides writes, "The Apostles passed through these stages having the Incarnate Word as their spiritual Father Who by casting out demons (purification) initiated them into the mystery of the rule (kingdom) of God (illumination) and the three apostles into the vision of the rule (kingdom) of God at the transfiguration, ...and all the Apostles at Pentecost." *Dogmatic and Symbolic Theology of the Orthodox Catholic Church,* page 87 (in Greek).

[24] Kokoris, page 65.

[25] *Galatians* 3:27.

[26] *Luke* 24:49. Kokoris, page 311.

and sanctifies the baptized.[27] In terms of catechesis, this means "pre-baptismal instruction on the energies of God and the energies of demons, on the struggle to participate in the first and repel the second, and afterwards on purification in Baptism. Following Baptism and the Chrismation of illumination by the seal of the gift of the Holy Spirit, the new-Christian is guided by the elders towards deification and friendship with God."[28] This whole process is a great Mystery, though not in the sense of being "mystical" or "hidden," but ontologically in the sense of being beyond the mind of man.[29] The process transcends man's mind and reason quite simply because man is healed through the Uncreated grace (or energies) of the Holy Spirit. Since this grace is *uncreated*, there are **no** *created* categories of thought or feeling that can comprehend it, much less explain it.[30]

While some Pentecostals correctly intuit that Baptism is the door and not the chamber of the King, rationalism and emotionalism pushes them to extreme positions. When they present the process of salvation with the categories of created rational thought and reject Baptism as a Mystery, they dem-

[27] Ibid., page 308.

[28] Romanides, *Dogmatic and Symbolic Theology of the Orthodox Catholic Church,* page 87.

[29] Kokoris, page 272. Cf., *1 Timothy* 3:16.

[30] Romanides, *Dogmatic and Symbolic Theology of the Orthodox Catholic Church,* page 80. In precisely this sense the mysteries are referred to as such. Cf., our discussion on revelation in the introduction and the "meaning of 'as'" in the chapter on Pentecost.

onstrate a deep ignorance of the meaning of the faith
and the working of divine grace. According to the
teaching of the Ancient Church, the grace of the Holy
Spirit overshadows the believer in all the Mysteries
beginning with Baptism.[31] Of course, their contention
that salvation requires the union of the faith of man
and the grace of the Holy Spirit[32] is outwardly quite
true, but this is inaugurated in a concrete way with
the Mystery of Baptism in the waters that have been
sanctified by the prayers of the Church and it continues in the struggle of the believer after Baptism.[33]

According to the words of Christ Himself, salvation without Baptism in water and in the Spirit
does not exist.[34] The Pentecostals are basically correct in *not* identifying Baptism in water with Baptism in the Spirit on the basis of *Acts* 10:44-47 and
19:5-6 in which Baptism in water and Baptism in the
Spirit with "speaking in tongues" (the Spirit praying
silently in the believer's heart) took place at distinct
and different periods of time.[35] This is in fact the central teaching of Saint Symeon the New Theologian
(misinterpreted by "orthodox" charismatics) who
writes:

> The Holy Spirit is called the key because
> by Him and in Him we are first illumined

[31] Kokoris, page 307.

[32] *Ephesians* 2:8.

[33] Kokoris, pages 64-65. Cf., *Collosians* 2: 11-14.

[34] *John* 3:3-6, *Mark* 16:16, and *Ephesians* 5:25-28.

[35] Fr. J. Romanides, "Jesus Christ: the Life of the World,"
pages 326-327.

in our *nous* and being purified we are enlightened with the light of knowledge, we
are *baptized from on high and reborn* and
become children of God as Paul says, "the
Spirit itself maketh intercession for us
with unspoken sighs" (*Romans* 8:26). And
again, "God hath given His Spirit in our
hearts, crying, Abba, Father" (*Galatians*
4:6).[36]

In other words, for Saint Symeon the New
Theologian, Baptism in the Holy Spirit takes place
when the Spirit begins to pray in the heart. The gift
of tongues (the silent prayer of the heart) in turn illumines the soul (the *nous*) with the light of divine
knowledge. The Pentecostals err, however, first of all,
in not perceiving the real activity of the Holy Spirit
by which the baptized soul is cleansed of her sins;
second in ignoring the distinction between the *purifying grace* (energy) of the Holy Spirit in Baptism and
the *illumining grace* of the Holy Spirit active in the
prayer of the heart; and third and most significantly
in interpreting tongues (baptism in the Holy Spirit)
as making strange sounds with the mouth rather
than the Holy Spirit praying silently in the heart.
When Pentecostals refuse to consider Baptism with
water in the name of the Holy Trinity to be a Mystery by which all man's previous sins are forgiven,
when they refuse to accept triple immersion as a type
of the three day burial of Christ, when they deny the

[36] Saint Symeon the New Theologian, "Discourse 33, On
Participation in the Holy Spirit," page 468 (in Greek).

presence and activity of the Holy Spirit sanctifying and purifying the believer,[37] they place themselves completely outside of the experience of the Church and at odds with the witness of Holy Scripture.

As a consequence of the Pentecostal's rationalistic misunderstanding of Baptism in particular and salvation in general, they also hold the position that only mature individuals capable of understanding, of believing and of confessing should be baptized.[38] Despite their abhorrence for the papacy and tendency towards the emotional extreme, this belief in exclusively adult baptism show that they are no less free from the iron grip of medieval scholasticism with all its latent Gnostic and Neoplatonic underpinnings than their Roman Catholic cousins who in similar fashion refuse to commune baptized infants.[39]

---

[37] Kokoris, pages 305-306 and 313. Cf., *Romans* 6:3-4 and *Collosians* 2:12. We also note in passing a few of the many statements offered by the most early of the Church Fathers on Baptism: Justin Martyr (110-165 AD) called Baptism "the bath of regeneration for the remission of sins," Theophilus of Antioch (169 AD) spoke about the fount of baptism in terms of rebirth, and Origen referred to Baptism as a mystery that grants salvation and through which the believer is reborn. (Ibid., page 68).

[38] Ibid., page 315.

[39] For both the Gnostics and the Neoplatonists, salvation was realized through the acquisition of esoteric knowledge. Saint Augustine in the West (like Origen in the East) resorted at times to this facile quasi-philosophical approach instead of the more difficult path of purification, illumination and deification. In making Augustine *the* exclusively authoritative father of the Church, the Scholastics outdid Plotinus in their penchant for constructing intellectual labyrinths. Unfortunately, contem-

This is in sharp contrast with the example of Christ who did not require the children brought to Him to be capable of understanding in order to be blessed.[40] Furthermore, the early practice of the Church as witnessed in the New Testament and early Church documents was to baptize irrespective of age.[41]

Although we will discuss in the next chapter the modern Pentecostal experience of "baptism in the Holy Spirit" and the "spiritual gifts" that spring therefrom, we should consider at this point the related dogmatic assertion that "speaking in tongues" (making inarticulate sounds with the mouth), "prophesying," or even "working wonders" indicates that one is "a vessel of the Holy Spirit" and "saved." On the one hand, it *is true* that the indwelling of the Holy Spirit in the believer's heart manifested by the genuine gift of tongues (the prayer of the heart) indicates that the believer is truly a member of the Body of Christ.[42] On the other hand, outward signs and wonders *are not* sure indications of inward purification and illumination by themselves. The Pentecostals' error is not in seeking the tangible presence of the Holy Spirit in their lives, but in their identifica-

porary Roman Catholicism continues to understand theology as the prerogative of a philosophically trained intelligentsia that undoubtedly would have excluded the uneducated, but divinely-wise fishermen of Galilee.

[40] Ibid., page 316.

[41] Ibid., page 321. Cf., *Acts* 16:15; 16:33; 18:8; *1 Corinthians* 1:16.

[42] Fr. J. Romanides, "Jesus Christ: the Life of the World," page 328.

tion of "tongues" with the ecstatic experience of freely making unfamiliar sounds with the mouth. The binding decrees of the Councils of 1341, 1347, and 1351 in Constantinople set a dogmatic and ecumenical seal on the central rôle of the prayer of the heart in the spiritual healing of *every* believer. Unfortunately today even in the Orthodox world, there are many who mistakenly believe that salvation is a matter of venerable dogma, splendid liturgics, and irreproachable ethical conduct. Such "Orthodox" influenced by a Protestant mindset will be no more able to respond to the seeking Pentecostal or charismatic than their "equally conservative" Roman Catholic and Protestant non-charismatic cousins. "Tongues" (the prayer of the heart) are indeed necessary, but they are preceded by the believer's inward purification so that the Holy Spirit can enter the heart and pray therein.

In developing a theology for their strange utterances, the Pentecostals believe that they are being absolutely biblical. One Pentecostal theologian writes, "I don't care what I feel or don't feel. I know I've received Him because I have spoken with other tongues. I have the Bible evidence."[43] Their biblical exegesis, however, is inevitably outward, superficial, and literal to the point of being ludicrous. Hence, it is not surprising that they maintain that outward and audible sounds were necessary for the Apostle Philip (in *Acts* 8:14) to realize that the Samaritans had re-

---

[43] Hagin, page 15.

ceived the Holy Spirit.[44] The Saints, however, recognize the grace present in others by the same grace present in their hearts and are in no need for a buzzer to sound in order to discern the spiritual. The Pentecostals further claim that tongues are "a supernatural way of communication" with God,[45] but they are hard pressed to explain precisely what is *supernatural* about making sounds that one does not understand. Infants quite *naturally* do the same, while adults *unnaturally* do so. In reading Pentecostal tracts, one is given the impression that they are grasping for straws in order to justify their practices. For example, the above-cited theologian writes "praying in tongues keeps selfishness out of our prayers,"[46] without realizing that the issue at hand is to keep selfishness out of our hearts.

As for the Pentecostals' use of outward gifts as a means of assessing the believer's inner state (whether he has the Holy Spirit), Holy Scripture offers some colorful examples that belie such a premise. If outward gifts and miracles were the sure "sign of salvation," then we would be compelled to include Barlaam's ass, who audibly spoke in another tongue and saw an angel, in the company of the born-again and the saved. Moreover apart from the example of the many false prophets who would cry out, "thus saith the Lord" without having heard the Lord's voice, there are examples of those who were neither

---

[44] Ibid., page 5.
[45] Ibid., pages 21 and 32.
[46] Ibid., page 33.

believers nor virtuous, yet uttered true prophecies such as Barlaam and Pharaoh. Nebuchadnezzar was a complete transgressor but saw what would take place in the distant future. In the New Testament, Caïaphas who would call for Christ's crucifixion prophesied truly as high priest, and Judas, the deceitful betrayer, received the gift to cast out demons.[47] In none of these cases can anyone maintain that the presence of an outward supernatural gift was an indication of being "filled with the Holy Spirit" or of "salvation." For this reason, Christ Himself warns us "Beware of false prophets, which come to you in sheep's clothing, but inwardly they are ravening wolves," and tells us that "Ye shall know them by their fruits"[48] which He Himself lists in the beatitudes and that Saint Paul refers to in his *Epistle to the Galatians.*[49] And lest there be any doubt that outward charismatic gifts are no sure sign of salvation, the Giver of all good gifts exclaims, "many will say to Me in that day, Lord, Lord, have we not prophesied in Thy name? and in Thy name have cast out devils? and in Thy name done many wonderful works? And then will I profess unto them, I never knew you: depart from Me, ye that work iniquity."[50]

[47] Kokoris, pages 82-83, 88. Cf., *Jeremiah* 13:16-17; 14:14-15; *John* 11: 49-52.

[48] *Matthew* 15:16-17.

[49] "But the fruit of the Spirit is love, joy, peace, long-suffering, gentleness, goodness, faith, meekness, temperance" *Galatians* 5:22-23. Cf. also, *Matthew* 5: 3-11 and *Luke* 6:21-22.

[50] *Matthew* 7:22-23.

3. Dogmas of Denial:
a. Holy Communion

In Saint John's Gospel, the Lord Christ explicitly teaches that in order for man to enter into the Kingdom of Heaven or inherit eternal life, it is necessary not only to be born of water and the Spirit (be baptized and have the Holy Spirit praying in the heart), but also eat His Flesh (receive Holy Communion).[51] Holy Writ compels the Pentecostals to admit that Holy Communion is divinely instituted, but in contrast with the ancient Church they refuse to consider it to be a Mystery.[52] For the Pentecostals, what is performed on the Holy Altar is not a sacrifice, but a representation of the sacrifice of the Cross and a commemoration of Christ's Passion.[53] They offer, however, no explanation why Holy Communion cannot be *both* a commemoration *and* a sacrifice. The divinely instituted celebration of Passover in the Old Testament involved both the commemoration of Israel's exodus from the Land of Egypt *and* the sacrifice of a real (not merely symbolic) paschal lamb.

---

[51] "Jesus answered, Verily, verily, I say unto thee, Except a man be born of water and of the Spirit, he cannot enter into the kingdom of God" (*John* 3:5). and "Then Jesus said unto them, Verily, verily, I say unto you, Except ye eat the Flesh of the Son of man, and drink His Blood, ye have no life in you. Whoso eateth My Flesh, and drinketh My Blood, hath eternal life; and I will raise him up at the last day" (*John* 6:53-54).

[52] Kokoris, page 335.

[53] Ibid., page 339.

Why then should the celebration of the new Passover be solely a commemoration and not also a sacrifice since a real Lamb is present here as well?[54] Saint Paul, moreover, makes it clear that "we have an altar,"[55] that we "proclaim (by celebrating the sacrament rather than with words) the Lord's death,"[56] and in general that the celebration of the Holy Eucharist is indeed a sacrifice in contrast with the idolaters' blasphemous sacrifices to demons and the earlier Judaic sacrifices to God under the law.[57] Above all, the Holy Eucharist is a sacrifice, because through it the believer partakes of the Body and Blood of Christ. The Pentecostals who view the Bread and the Wine as symbols of the Lord's Body and Blood place themselves at odds with Christ's very words. Christ does not say "this is *like* my Body," but "this **is** my Body." There is no reason to interpret His use of the verb "is" metaphorically, especially since the Evangelists make a clear distinction between parable and historical fact.[58] Furthermore, not only did all the early Church Fathers understand Christ's

[54] Ibid., pages 346-347. Cf., *Exodus* 12: 14, 25-26.

[55] *Hebrews* 13:10.

[56] *I Corinthians* 11:26 based on the definition of καταγγέλλω in William Arndt and F. Wilbur Gingrich' *A Greek-English Lexicon of the New Testament and Other Early Christian Literature From Walter Bauer's Fifth Edition,* (University of Chicago Press: Chicago, 1979), page 409.

[57] *1 Corinthians* 10:14-21. Cf., Kokoris, pages 342-343 (in Greek).

[58] Cf., *Matthew* 26: 26-28; *Mark* 14: 22-24; *Luke* 22:19-20. Kokoris, page 347.

words literally, but even Christ Jewish listeners did so and were scandalized. Most significantly, Christ did not seek to correct their opinion.[59]

It is indeed a tragic but not surprising twist of fate that the Pentecostals, who are so intent on acquiring the gifts of the Spirit, in rejecting the Church also reject the only Mystery that could bestow upon them not simply the gifts, but the Giver Himself.[60] It is indeed ironic that these coveters of the spiritually tangible reject the only mystery by which they could become "flesh of His flesh and bone of His bone." Holy Communion offers to those members of the Church who have confessed their sins and have been properly prepared (i.e., are in a state of purification), the means for the healing of their souls. They feel the grace of the Holy Spirit according to their spiritual state—"soul mingled with soul, body with body, blood with blood," so that their mind could be strengthened by the divine mind, their will made firm by the blessed will, their clay enlivened by the heavenly fire if they are suitably purified and prepared.[61] In rejecting this most crucial medicine for man's spiritual malady,[62] they also reject the possibility of full health

---

[59] Cf., *John* 6:53-56. Kokoris, page 348-350 (in Greek).

[60] Nicholas Cabasilas, *On the Divine Liturgy and Life in Christ*, 22 Philokalia of Neptic and Ascetic Fathers, text, trans. (into modern Greek), and comments by Panagiotis Christos, (Gregory Palamas Patristic Publications, Thessalonika, 1979), page 414 (in Greek): "for we partake not of His, but of Him."

[61] Ibid., page 416.

[62] Ibid., page 430.

and the fulfillment of their most cherished desire: to become truly spiritual and spirit-bearing.

•

b. The Priesthood.

The Mysteries of Holy Eucharist and Holy Baptism,[63] in turn, presuppose another Mystery without which no baptism could be performed, nor Eucharist celebrated, the mystery of Holy Orders. Although there is clear indication in the New Testament that the special priesthood exists, the Pentecostals maintain that there is no priestly order, but that every Christian is a priest. Truly, the people of God are a priestly people, but this does not mean that everyone can perform the Holy Mysteries.[64] Even under the Law, the children of Abraham were a royal and priestly nation, but only those who belonged to the Levitical Priesthood had the right to perform sacrifices, whole burnt offerings, propitiate sins, and all the other functions of the priestly order. Those without the priesthood who dared to usurp the rights of the priests were duly punished.[65] Likewise under the law of Grace, Christ established His Own special Priestly Order higher than the Levitical priesthood, in order to perform sacrifices, offerings,

---

[63] We note that according to the apostolic canons 49 and 50 only Orthodox Bishops and Priests are permitted to baptize (Kokoris, page 308).

[64] Kokoris, pages 277-279.

[65] Cf., the cases of Korah, Dathan (*Numbers* 16:1-32), and King Saul (*1 Samuel* 13:9-14).

220

and the mysteries.[66] As priests under the Old Covenant participated in the high priesthood of Aaron, so priests under the New Covenant participate in the high priesthood of Christ, the only eternal High Priest.[67] During the Mystical Supper, Christ entrusted His Apostles and by extension their successors the Bishops and Priests with the sacrifice of His Body. Only the twelve were present because only they were entrusted with the sacrifice of the Mystical Supper as Priests.[68] Christ quite clearly exclaimed in the Gospel that He bestowed all authority given Him by the Father upon His Apostles. Even as He was sent by the Father as a Prophet, Priest, and King, so also did He send His Apostles. Among the priestly gifts that Christ granted His disciples and their successors was that of remission of sins.[69] As early as the late second century Origen, in his treatise on prayer, speaks about the priesthood, priests and the authority to remit sins.[70] Even more significantly, canons 2, 3, and 5 of the First Ecumenical Council, whose Creed even the Pentecostals accept, but do not understand, refer in detail to Bishops, Priests, Deacons and their ordinations. The Pentecostals offer no rationale for why they accept the Creed as expressing the faith and reject the canons as concrete guides for living the faith.[71]

---

[66] Kokoris, page 284.
[67] Cf., *Hebrews* 5:1-10.
[68] Kokoris, page 290.
[69] Ibid., page 284. Cf., *Leviticus* 5:10 and *John* 20: 21-23.
[70] Ibid., page 294.
[71] Ibid., page 297.

Having sapped the most fundamental mysteries of the Eucharist and Baptism of their transforming power, it is not surprising that the Pentecostals would reject the priesthood whose *raison d'être* is the performance of the mysteries. Having ruined their medical equipment, it is no wonder that they also dismiss the staff. This all follows naturally, since they have rejected the Church, the Hospital itself.

c. Holy Confession.

In accord with the Pentecostal's rejection of the Church, they likewise reject the mystery of repentance and confession, and in its stead they advise direct recourse to God. Here the Pentecostals present a dangerous "half truth," for indeed it is right for the sinner to cry out to God for forgiveness when he sins and truly God alone can remit sins. These two facts, however, do not prevent God from employing instruments that He Himself established for that very purpose, viz., father confessors.[72] To bolster their position, the Pentecostals first of all claim that King David provides an example of direct confession of sin to God in *Psalm* 32:5 where he says, "I acknowledged my sin unto Thee, and mine iniquity have I not hid. I said, I will confess my transgressions unto the Lord; and Thou forgavest the iniquity of my sin," and in *Psalm* 51:3-4 where he exclaims, "For I acknowledge my transgressions: and my sin is ever before me. Against Thee, Thee only, have I sinned, and done

---

[72] Ibid., page 355.

this evil in Thy sight." What the Pentecostals fail to point out, however, is the context of his sin with Bathsheba and the fact that his confession took place before the Prophet Nathan as the very title to *Psalm 51* indicates, "A Psalm of David, *when Nathan the prophet came unto him,* after he had gone in to Bath-sheba." In fact the account in *Second Samuel* is quite clear: David confessed his sin against the Lord to Na-than and Nathan granted David absolution: "and David said unto Nathan, I have sinned against the Lord. And Nathan said unto David, The Lord also hath put away thy sin; thou shalt not die."[73] The Pre-incarnate Word, of course, was the One Who forgave David's sin, but this forgiveness was realized through David's confession to the prophet.[74]

In the New Testament, the Pentecostals make their case by bringing forth the words "forgive us our trespasses" from the Lord's prayer as an example of direct confession to God without the intervention of a priest, but according to such "logic" the words "give us this day our daily bread" must be interpreted as seeking bread directly from heaven without the in-tervention of the entire process by which wheat is made into bread. Secondly, they bring forth that sec-tion of *Hebrews* in which Saint Paul compares Moses and Christ in order to show the superiority of Christ to Moses and of the Gospel to the Law:

> Seeing then that we have a great high
> priest, that is passed into the heavens, Je-

[73] *2 Samuel* 12:13.
[74] Ibid., page 356.

sus the Son of God, let us hold fast our pro-
fession. For we have not an high priest
which cannot be touched with the feeling of
our infirmities; but was in all points
tempted like as we are, yet without sin. Let
us therefore come boldly unto the throne of
grace, that we may obtain mercy, and find
grace to help in time of need.[75]

This passage, however, does not exclude coming before the throne of grace via the Church by
means of Father Confessors. The very fact that Saint
Paul calls Christ the Great High Priest in this passage means that the priesthood is necessary to approach the throne of grace and receive mercy.[76]
Christ the Word is God Who revealed the will of the
Father in the Holy Spirit *both* in the Old Testament
and the New.[77] When He gave Moses the Law, He established the Levitical priesthood assigning them
specific duties and granting them specific authority,
among which was the absolution of sins. Likewise
when His Apostles were well instructed in the law of

[75] *Hebrews* 4:14-16.

[76] Ibid., pages 357-358.

[77] Even the Pentecostals would reject the antithetical and
blasphemous position of the heretical Gnostics and Manicheans
who held that the God of the Old Testament was a lower and
evil deity whereas the God of the New Testament was a good
and higher one. This position led these heretics to conclude that
the prophets were deluded and that the Old Testament should
be rejected. Cf., J. Romanides, *Dogmatic and Symbolic Theology
of the Orthodox Catholic Church,* pages 162-163 (in Greek).

grace, He made them priests who would share in His own High-priesthood. Under the law, sinners would have to pay in the form of offerings for sacrifice. Under the Gospel, the price was paid once and for all by Christ's own Precious Blood.[78]

In the Gospel account, we note that Saint John the Baptist readied the soil for both the mysteries of Confession and Baptism, since the Jews who came to him "were all *baptized* of him in the river of Jordan, *confessing their sins.*"[79] Christ made it clear to the Jews who would ask "who can forgive sins but God only?" that He as God has "the power on earth to forgive sins" by showing them the authority of His all creating word, which could strengthen paralyzed limbs.[80] This same "power to forgive sins" He gave to His Apostles and their successors (bishops and priests) at various points in the Gospel. He first granted the power to bind (not forgive) and loose (forgive) to Peter upon his confession of Christ's di-

---

[78] Kokoris, pages 360-361. Cf., *Leviticus* 4:20; 4:22-26; 5:1-18; 16:21; *Numbers* 15:25. E.g., "And it shall be, when he shall be guilty in one of these things, that he shall confess that he hath sinned in that thing: And he shall bring his trespass offering unto the Lord for his sin which he hath sinned, a female from the flock, a lamb or a kid of the goats, for a sin offering; and the priest shall make an atonement for him concerning his sin. And he shall offer the second for a burnt offering, according to the manner: and the priest shall make an atonement for him for his sin which he hath sinned, and it shall be forgiven him" (*Leviticus* 5:5-6,10).

[79] Ibid., page 368. Cf., *Matthew* 3:6 and *Mark* 1:5.

[80] *Matthew* 9:2-6 and *Mark* 2:7-10.

vinity,[81] and later to all the Apostles both before[82] and after His Resurrection.[83] Thus, the Apostles and their successors would hear men's confessions, weigh their intentions, their sincere repentance, and either forgive them (loose) or place them under a penance (bind), thus opening or shutting the gates of paradise according to the Lord's word.[84] This we see manifested in *Acts* 19:18 where Saint Luke records, "and many that believed came, and *confessed*, and showed their deeds." Obviously, the believers did not come and confess because the Apostles needed to learn of any impropriety on the believer's part, but because the believers needed to receive remission of sins and forgiveness through the priestly grace and authority of the Apostles.[85] This in turn became the practice of the Church.

Pentecostals may object that this confession in *Acts* and early Church was public, while confession before the priest is private. Private confession before a priest however is also an ancient practice as Origen (A.D. 187-254) in his second homily on Psalm 37 bears witness.[86] Moreover, as Christ accepted Nicodemos who for fear and shame did not come before Him publicly, so the Church also allows sinners to come privately before a priest. In fact, since the con-

[81] *Matthew* 16:19.
[82] *Matthew* 18:18.
[83] *John* 20:23.
[84] Kokoris, page 366.
[85] Ibid., page 368.
[86] Ibid., page 373-374.

fession of marital infidelity and fleshly sins could create other problems among the faithful, by A.D. 250 the most common practice was private confession before a priest.[87]

In rejecting the healing balm and purifying medicine of Holy Confession, the Pentecostal deprives himself of the opportunity that he would have, were he a member of the Church, to break out of the gloomy isolation in which the passions can develop, to expose his wounds to the Light that prevents the demons from acting in secret,[88] and to receive practical counsels that would aid him to fight against his sickly tendencies and passions and to acquire healthy habits and permanent virtues. Above all, he deprives himself of the purifying grace of absolution that alone can loose the bonds of sin, restore him to his former purity, and set him on the hopeful path towards his ultimate cure granting him peace and joy.[89]

d. The Saints and the Holy Icons

Having rejected the Priesthood and Confession and having emptied Baptism and Holy Communion of all salvific content, it should not be surprising that the Pentecostals also reject the Saints, their relics, their intercessions, their miracles, and the Holy Icons.[90] Extremist Pentecostals will senselessly condemn the Orthodox for a "cult of the Saints" and

[87] Ibid., page 372.
[88] Larchet, page 359 (in French).
[89] Ibid., page 364.
[90] Kokoris, pages 39-41.

idolatry, while moderates will simply claim that such "externals" are not necessary and that Christ is sufficient. What none of them realize is that this position is the clearest indication of the rupture of apostolic succession, that theirs is not the Church of the Prophets, the Apostles and the Saints.[91]

While the Pentecostals may admit the existence of Saints, they deny their intercessions beyond the grave, their miracles, and the miraculous properties of their relics. They believe that the Saints in heaven are found close to God, but that they are inactive, irresolute, and at rest, in a kind of holy coma or blissful nirvana.[92] Again, their position is both unscriptural and ahistorical. When Christ says "there is joy in the presence of the angels of God over one sinner that repenteth,"[93] it stands to reason that those who are joyful in the angels' presence includes the entire heavenly world of angels and holy men.[94] *The Book of Revelation* further shows that the Saints in heaven are quite alive and active,[95] serving before the throne of God by day and by night.[96] They not

---

[91] Romanides, *Dogmatic and Symbolic Theology of the Orthodox Catholic Church,* page 153 (in Greek).

[92] Kokoris, page 386.

[93] *Luke* 15:10.

[94] Ibid., page 397.

[95] "Four and twenty elders fell down before the Lamb, having every one of them harps, and golden vials full of odours, which are the prayers of saints" *Revelation* 5:8.

[96] "And one of the elders answered, saying unto me, What are these which are arrayed in white robes? And whence came they? And I said unto him, Sir, thou knowest. And he said to

only have a lively interest in the lives of those on earth, but also intervene through their intercessions before the Lamb[97] that accompany the angelic offering of incense upon the golden heavenly altar.[98] Throughout the history of the Church in response to the invocations of the faithful, the Saints in heaven have intervened innumerable times according to individual, family and national needs. Both their relics and objects that have touched them[99] are rightfully

---

me, These are they which came out of great tribulation, and have washed their robes, and made them white in the blood of the Lamb. Therefore are they before the throne of God, and serve him day and night in his temple: and he that sitteth on the throne shall dwell among them" *Revelation* 7:13-15.

[97] "And when he had opened the fifth seal, I saw under the altar the souls of them that were slain for the word of God, and for the testimony which they held: And they cried with a loud voice, saying, How long, O Lord, holy and true, dost thou not judge and avenge our blood on them that dwell on the earth?" *Revelation* 6:9-10.

[98] "And another angel came and stood at the altar, having a golden censer; and there was given unto him much incense, that he should offer it with the prayers of all saints upon the golden altar which was before the throne. And the smoke of the incense, which came with the prayers of the saints, ascended up before God out of the angel's hand" *Revelation* 8:3-4.

[99] "And he took the mantle of Elijah that fell from him, and smote the waters, and said, Where is the Lord God of Elijah? and when he also had smitten the waters, they parted hither and thither: and Elisha went over." *2 Kings* 2:14 "Came behind him, and touched the border of his garment: and immediately her issue of blood stanched." *Luke* 8:44 "So that from his body were brought unto the sick handkerchiefs or aprons, and the diseases departed from them, and the evil spirits went out of them" *Acts* 19:12.

honored,[100] fragrant and wonder-working[101] as Holy Scripture and the experience of the faithful to the present day bear witness.

To justify their rejection of the friends of God, the Pentecostals will often cite *1 Timothy* 2:5, "For there is one God, and one mediator between God and men, the man Christ Jesus." Such an interpretation, however, is completely unreasonable, for if "one mediator" excludes the Saints in heaven, it also excludes all believers. If it excludes all believers, how then did Peter and Paul intercede and mediate, not to mention Abraham, Moses, and the host of Prophets? If "one mediator" is interpreted absolutely excluding all others, than "one God" should also be interpreted absolutely as referring to the Father and thus blasphemously excluding the Son and the Holy Spirit. A correct interpretation of this verse is that Christ is the *unique* Mediator, not as the only one who relays messages between God and man like Moses and the other Saints, but as the only One Who united in His Person humanity and divinity. This fact by no means

---

[100] "And Moses took the bones of Joseph with him: for he had straitly sworn the children of Israel, saying, God will surely visit you; and ye shall carry up my bones away hence with you." *Exodus* 13:19 "And his disciples came, and took up the body, and buried it, and went and told Jesus" *Matthew* 14:12.

[101] "And it came to pass, as they were burying a man, that, behold, they spied a band of men; and they cast the man into the sepulchre of Elisha: and when the man was let down, and touched the bones of Elisha, he revived, and stood up on his feet" *2 Kings* 13:21.

230

excludes the existence of the Prophets, Apostles and Saints as relative mediators.[102]

It is worth stressing that with each of these unfortunate dogmatic errors the Pentecostal ultimately harms himself. In rejecting the Saints, he rejects those most willing friends who with perfected love are ready to guide and comfort their struggling brethren on earth. These holy companions are in fact the truly qualified physicians of the soul and body, healing the faithful by divine grace and offering the spiritually infirm the living proof that spiritual health (selfless love) does exist. Rejecting the Mother of God and their Mother, rejecting the Holy Angels, rejecting the hosts of Saints, the Pentecostals isolate and estrange themselves from those who have gained in truth the most sacred desire of their heart.[103]

As a natural consequence of their rejection of the Saints, the Pentecostals also reject the holy icons as unnecessary or even as "idol worship" by citing verses such as *Leviticus* 26:1: "Ye shall make you no idols nor graven image, neither rear you up a standing image, neither shall ye set up any image of stone in your land, to bow down unto it: for I am the Lord your God."[104] They completely ignore, however, other verses where the Pre-incarnate Word not only allows

---

[102] Kokoris, pages 394-395.

[103] Hieromonk Makarios, *The Synaxarion: The Lives of the Saints of the Orthodox Church,* trans. by Christopher Hookway, vol. 1, (Holy Convent of the Annunciation of Our Lady, Ormilia: 1998), pages xiii-xiv.

[104] Kokoris, page 408. Cf. also, *Deuteronomy* 4:16, 19 and 7:26.

for the use of articles that facilitate worship, but even commands the use of them, allowing man to distinguish between Creator and creation.[105] In the earliest years of the Christian Church, in the Catacombs, one can find sacred vessels painted or engraved with symbols of the faith, the Cross, the Good Shepherd, the face of Christ, the face of the martyrs. Obviously, this was permitted without the slightest suggestion that such was idolatrous.[106] The rejection of icons is no small detail, for as Fr. Romanides writes,

> Without them, it is impossible for one to ascend to the level of perfection, since the basis of man's salvation is unceasing memory of God, His Will and Activity through Christ in the lives and teachings of the Prophets, Apostles and Saints. The Holy Icons and Relics of the Saints call forth continuous love, veneration and honor towards the imaged models and their veneration, love, and dedication to Christ, the Father and the Holy Spirit. They also instill in the souls of the faithful a Christ-like

[105] Ibid., pages 412-413. Cf., *Exodus* 25:1-8,22, 17; *Numbers* 7:8-9; *Exodus* 25:32, 26:1, 26:31. E.g., *Exodus* 25:18 "And **thou shalt make** two cherubims of gold, of beaten work shalt thou make them, in the two ends of the mercy seat."

[106] Ibid., pages 414-415.

piety by the ceaseless memory of Him, His Holy Mother, and the Saints."[107]

The ultimate criterion for the shape of the worship in the Church (iconography, hymnography, liturgies, liturgical vessels, and vestments, etc.) is again therapeutic: whether or not it will help and encourage the believer to struggle to ascend through the stages of purification, illumination, and deification. This is why icons, hymnography, and liturgies in the Orthodox Church have "an ascetic and heroic orientation." That which leads to the believer's perfection is thus welcome and accepted, whereas that "that which leads to spiritual stagnation, attachment to physical pleasure or sensuality, worldly sentimentality, ecstasy, or demonic states" is rejected.[108]

4. Christianity without the Cross: the Pentecostal "Church" of the End-Times

The Pentecostals maintain that their mission is to form the "church of the end times" that the Lord will receive before the reign of the anti-Christ.[109] They link misfortunes with "the end times" described in Holy Scripture, and with utter Calvinistic determinism proclaim that man is powerless to act or re-

---

[107] Romanides, *Dogmatic and Symbolic Theology of the Orthodox Catholic Church,* page 156 (in Greek).

[108] Ibid., page 154.

[109] Alevizopoulos, *Handbook of Heresies and Para-Christian Groups,* page 166 (in Greek).

spond in any way other than by placing himself in the "church of the saved" that will be raptured away.[110] They paint a terrifying landscape of the present reality embellished with Biblical imagery in order to create in their partisans a feeling of great insecurity and impending doom.[111] These methods not only help to keep their believers bound to the group, but are sometimes used in order to extort money from the believers on the basis of supposed impending economic catastrophes that can be avoided by purchasing gold or other precious commodities. The false teachings and misinterpretations of the *Book of Revelation* are so many and diverse that it is beyond the scope of this small study to list them in detail. As an example, we will simply consider the most commonplace teaching on the "rapture."

According to the Pentecostals, Christ will descend from heaven to rapture His own to heaven, resurrecting those who were truly in the Church, selecting those who were born again and leaving behind those who were not. This rapture takes place so that the elect will not have to suffer the great tribulations that will come upon the rest of the humanity under the rule of the Anti-Christ. After those seven years, Christ will descend to earth again and establish an earthly kingdom for 1,000 years with those raptured. Afterwards Christ will resurrect the rest of

[110] Ibid., page 172.
[111] Kokoris, page 187.

the dead and judge the whole world.[112] The true
Church of Christ, on the other hand, has always
taught that following a series of signs,[113] Christ will
come to earth accompanied by the Holy Angels and
Saints. Those who died in Christ will rise first to
greet Him and then the rest of mankind. When He
descends to earth, He will judge all according to their
deeds separating the just from the unjust. This is
then followed by the wedding of the Lamb.[114]

The Pentecostal's teaching on the rapture is in
fact an extension of their teaching that they are enti-
tled to privileged treatment from God Who is obliged
to protect them from sickness, worries and difficulties
by miraculous interventions. Thus, the "rapture of
the Church" must take place, so that the believers
will not have to suffer what everyone else will under
the anti-Christ.[115]

It is astonishing that a belief so absolutely
contrary to Scripture could be held by the "simple
people of the book." What then is the meaning of
Christ's "blessed are ye, when man shall revile you
and persecute you" if the believers are to be exempt

[112] Ibid., page 193.

[113] E.g., the appearance of false prophets and false Christs
(*Matthew* 24:4-28), apostasy from the correct faith (*1 Timothy*
4:1), the appearance of the Anti-Christ (*2 Thessalonians* 2:1-10),
the proclamation of the Gospel throughout the entire world
(*Matthew* 24:14), the appearance of two prophets (*Revelation*
11:3-4, *Malachi* 4:4-6), the return of the Jews to Christ (*Luke*
21:24), the Battle of Armageddon (*Revelation* 16:14-16). Ibid.,
page 194.

[114] Ibid., page 195.

[115] Ibid., page 199.

from tribulation? What is the meaning of His prophecy "then shall they deliver you up to be afflicted, and shall kill you"? Why does He assure His elect Apostles "in the world ye shall have tribulation"? Why was James the brother of John killed with the sword? Why did Saint Paul have to go through such trials on every side "in stripes above measure, in prisons more frequent, in deaths oft"? Why did he teach the Christians "that we must through much tribulation enter into the kingdom of God"?[116] But above all, what becomes of the symbol and trophy of our faith, the life-giving Cross of the Savior? Have not those who hold that they will be raptured away from tribulation become "enemies of the cross of Christ" who have made "the cross of Christ of no effect"?[117]

Of course, the Pentecostals do try to find support for their peculiar doctrine in Sacred Scripture. They claim that *Matthew* 24:40-41 refers clearly to the rapture of the just, "Then shall two be in the field; the one shall be taken, and the other left. Two women shall be grinding at the mill; the one shall be taken, and the other left." The entire passage, however, refers to Christ's Second Coming, where He will judge in the living and the dead and separate the just from the unjust. The one taken is the one who will participate in Christ's uncreated glory, while the one

---

[116] Ibid., page 200. Cf., *Matthew* 5:4; 5:10; 5:11; 10:16-18; 10:21-22; 24:9; 24:20-22; *Luke* 24:26; *John* 16:33; *Acts* 9:15-16; 12:1-2; 14:22; *2 Corinthians* 4:8-10; 11:23-27; *Philippians* 2:6-11; *Revelation* 7:13-15.

[117] *Philippians* 3:18 and *1 Corinthians* 1:17.

left will not participate in it, but the same light will be for him fire and darkness.[118]

The Pentecostals likewise see the rapture in Saint Peter's words, "But the day of the Lord will come as a thief in the night." They fail, however, to cite the full verse which is not to their advantage, for Saint Peter continues, "in the which the heavens shall pass away with a great noise, and the elements shall melt with fervent heat, the earth also and the works that are therein shall be burned up." In other words, the passage refers to the Day of Judgment, and not to some seven-year rapture of the faithful.[119]

Christ words are so very clear, "But in those days, **after that tribulation**, the sun shall be darkened, and the moon shall not give her light, And the stars of heaven shall fall, and the powers that are in heaven shall be shake. And then shall they see the Son of man coming in the clouds with great power and glory. And then **shall he send his angels, and shall gather together his elect** from the four winds, from the uttermost part of the earth to the uttermost part of heaven."[120]

---

[118] Kokoris, pages 210-211.

[119] Ibid., page 218. Cf., *2 Peter* 3:10.

[120] *Mark* 13:24-27. Saint Paul's words to Timothy are worth noting: "Perverse disputings of men of corrupt minds, and destitute of the truth, *supposing that gain is godliness:* from such withdraw thyself" *1 Timothy* 6:5.

237

5. The Spiritual Vacuum of the Unscriptural and Nonsacramental Life

In this brief survey of the general dogmatic positions of the Pentecostal "churches," we have not even begun to test the deep and luminous waters of the patristic writings. Through their writings, the Holy Fathers would unanimously reject the rather naïve Pentecostal beliefs, not simply because their reasoning is rather lame and their exegesis flat-footed, but primarily because their beliefs are therapeutically unsound. Instead of healing man's arrogant mind and selfish heart, the merely bandage the wound with the unsterile gauze of deception.

Since the Pentecostals would *a priori* exclude the Fathers from consideration, we have restricted ourselves to Holy Scripture, which they claim to follow limiting ourselves to but a few practical observations on the effects of their positions. This very brief examination makes it painfully obvious that Pentecostalism as a movement is neither conservative, nor traditional, nor scriptural. Having rejected all the divinely-revealed means for purifying and illumining the human soul, a spiritual vacuum was quite naturally created only to be filled by new experiences of the "spirit."

When, however, they reject the Mysteries, they reject union and communion with Christ and set off on another road foreign to that upon which the Prophets, Apostles, and Saints tread. It is not surprising that Christ becomes less prominent both in

238

their spirituality and teaching. In rejecting the Mysteries, they reject the Truth about God, the Truth about man and the Truth about man's ultimate goal: glorification with Christ. According to Christ's own words, the Apostles were "sanctified through the Truth"[121] and thus prepared to behold His Uncreated Pre-eternal Glory on Holy Pentecost.

What can those poor "non-dogmatic" souls who are indifferent to the Truth, however, hope to see? What spiritual gifts can be found among those whose souls are not purified by Baptism, cleansed again by the Mystery of Repentance followed by Confession, and united with Christ in Holy Communion? With what measure can those who have cut themselves off from the Saints and do not keep their examples before their minds possibly judge? What "tongues" will be spoken by those who have never heard of, much less experienced, the prayer of the heart? What can be the basis for their new gospel about the rapture and prosperity that is so antithetical to trials and tribulations that mark the narrow way of the Prophets, Apostle Saints, and ultimately Christ Himself? These questions we shall finally answer in the upcoming chapter.

[121] *John* 17:19.

The Ecstatic[1]

"Have you ever put your finger in a light socket and remained still? ...When the power of God comes upon you, you will enjoy it. And when you enjoy something you show it."

— William Seymour[2]

1. Religious Ecstasy in the Non-Christian World

In the preceding pages, we have spoken in depth about the characteristics of genuine experiences of grace. We noted that on Pentecost, speaking in tongues (the prayer of the heart) was not employed as a means of entering an ecstatic spiritual state, but that together with the vision of the glorified Christ it brought a clarity and spiritual power to the Apostles' prophetic utterance that by the grace of the Holy Spirit was comprehensible to all irrespective of their native language. We noted that the Apostles were already purified and partially illumined vessels well prepared for receiving the grace of the Holy Spirit and that both their words and actions were marked by peace, sobriety, and unity. In general, we noted

[1] The Pentecostal teacher K. Hagin outwardly describes the reception of the Holy Spirit as "an experience or feeling of ecstasy" (page 39).

[2] Liardon, *God's Generals*, page 54.

240

that genuine spiritual experiences are experiences of the glorified Christ in the Holy Spirit. They are characterized by good order, clarity, and peace welling forth with unselfish love, humility, joy, meekness, and abstinence.

False spiritual experiences, on the other hand, are marked by disorder, agitation, and confusion spewing forth mindless joy, presumption, sterile levity and a certain sensual sweetness. In our exposition on the gifts of grace, we noted the presence of an intimate relationship between man's own inherent strengths and qualities and the respective gifts that are given. We especially underscored the fact that "God's grace *does not* suspend man's natural powers."[3] In fact an ecstasy in which one is not free to speak or does not know what one says characterizes not the experience of the sober and watchful prophets, but the oracles of the pagan world.

Any spirituality, mysticism, or worship that is based on or culminates in an ecstasy in any of its forms is foreign to the divinely revealed path of the Prophets, Apostles and Saints as recorded in Holy Scripture and Sacred Tradition.[4] Non-Orthodox "divine manifestations" are often characterized by a "spiritual ecstasy" in which man's psychosomatic activities are repressed and in which hallucinations appear accompanied by a light having shape and form. Such experiences arise from the created nature

[3] Saint Maximus the Confessor, Fourth Century, *The Philokalia,* v. II, page 238.

[4] Fr. John Romanides, *The Dogmatic and Symbolic Theology of the Orthodox Catholic Church,* page 150 (in Greek).

of man often under demonic influence. Saint Gregory Palamas writes quite vividly on this subject: "To extract the intellect (*nous*) not from a materialistic manner of thought, but from the body itself, in the hope that there, outside the body, it may attain noetic visions, is the worst of profane delusions, the root and source of every heresy, an invention of demons, a doctrine engendering folly and itself the result of dementedness. It is for this reason that those who speak by the inspiration of the demons are out of their wits and do not even comprehend what they say. But we, on the contrary, install our intellect (*nous*) not only within the body and the heart, but also within itself."[5]

Genuine "divine manifestations," on the other hand, are manifestations of the uncreated glory of the Father in the Holy Spirit by means of the Word under the influence of divine grace.[6] The Fathers may employ the word "ecstasy" when the believer "suffers" this manifestation of the Divine Light for the first time, and for that reason loses his orientation. When, however, the experience of this radiance, in which the entire man participates, is repeated, it is no longer called "ecstasy," but vision that becomes more perfect and long lasting. In any event this patristic "ecstasy" bears no similarity whatsoever with

[5] Saint Gregory Palamas, "On Behalf of Those Who Practice a Life of Stillness," *The Philokalia*, v. IV, page 335.
[6] Romanides, *The Dogmatic and Symbolic Theology of the Orthodox Catholic Church*, pages 84-85.

the experience of "ecstasy" in the non-Orthodox religious world at large[7]

When considering the "ecstasy" experienced in non-Christian religions or fringe Christian sects, one is confronted with a phenomenon that is both psychological and psychic arising from the natural capabilities of the human soul and the effect of evil spirits on the soul that has opened itself up to them. In dealing with these phenomena, it is useful to define a few basic terms. Ecstasy can be defined as a state of over-excitation (to the point of standing outside of oneself as the term etymologically indicates) in which other-worldly visions appear. Enthusiasm is a state of religious frenzy accompanied by a frantic, yet joyful, exaltation. Self-suggestion is the suggestion to oneself by a person or state of an idea that is outside of reality.

In concrete terms, religious rites that provoke ecstasy, enthusiasm, and self-suggestion all follow a predictable pattern. Music often in the form of evocative hymns, speech often in the form of emotional exhortations, and motion often in the form of dance are employed in a progressively intense fashion. Characteristically, the music, speech, and motion is slow-paced, calm, and quiet in the beginning, but con-

---

[7] Ibid., page 264. Cf. *2 Corinthians* 12:2-4: "I knew a man in Christ above fourteen years ago, (whether in the body, I cannot tell; or whether out of the body, I cannot tell: God knoweth;) such an one caught up to the third heaven. And I knew such a man, (whether in the body, or out of the body, I cannot tell: God knoweth;) How that he was caught up into paradise, and heard unspeakable words, which it is not lawful for a man to utter."

cludes with a feverish pace, agitation, and heightened volume. Correspondingly, those present feel a kind of well-being, calmness, and a tendency towards the divine world at the onset until they eventually reach a manic and frenzied state in which their breathing becomes more rapid, their eyes become glassy, and their bodies automatically begin to sway rhythmically. In such a state, they will often clap their hands, let out cries, and then make inarticulate sounds.[8]

This pattern is observed frequently in the non-Christian religious world. In Greek antiquity, such an ecstasy combined with prophecy was the characteristic trait of the worship of the goddess Cybelis,[9] the god Dionysius and other pagan deities.[10] In the contemporary non-Christian world, ecstasy combined with the uttering of incomprehensible sounds (the Pentecostal misinterpretation of "speaking in tongues") can be encountered in Eskimo Shamanism, in the Spirit worship of Caddoan Indians, and in the rites of Lamanist Buddhism, Dervish Islam, and several Japanese cults.[11] In the "Christian" world, this same ecstasy combined with inarticulate cries was also observed sporadically among the heretical Mon-

---

[8] Kokoris, page 126.

[9] Ibid., page 52-53. It is noteworthy that the ancient heretic Montanist (whom Pentecostals view as one of their forerunners in the early Church) was formerly a priest of that god.

[10] Ibid., pages 126-127.

[11] John Warren Morris, *The Charismatic Movement: An Orthodox Evaluation,* page 25.

tanists, Huguenots, Jansenists, Quakers, and Mormons.[12] Ecstasy in general is likewise found in the animistic worship of Africa and in the polytheistic Hindu rituals of India.

In all the above non-Christian examples, precise techniques are employed for entering into an ecstatic state in which preternatural phenomena become common-place. The shamanism of primitive religions is a particular form of ecstatic religious experience especially worthy of examination since the phenomenon of Pentecostal "speaking in tongues" (making inarticulate sounds) is also observed. In shamanism, the witch-doctor follows "a regular technique for going into a trance and then gives a message to or from 'a god' in a language he has not learned."[13] The more general term for this type of ecstatic experience is "mediumism." Fr. Seraphim Rose defines a medium as "a person with a certain psychic sensitivity which enables him to be the vehicle or means for the manifestation of unseen beings."[14] In particular, the attitudes or techniques necessary for mediumism (as observed in the spiritist seance) are:

1. Intellectual and physical openness or passivity to the invading spirit.

---

[12] Alevizopoulos, *Handbook of Heresies and Para-Christian Groups,* page 175 (in Greek).

[13] Fr. Seraphim Rose, *Orthodoxy and the Religion of the Future,* pages 127-128.

[14] Ibid., page 129.

2. Solidarity of faith expressed by a sympathetic attitude.

3. A magnetic circle formed by the joining of hands.

4. A spiritist atmosphere induced by hymns.[15]

It is noted that when one of these elements is missing, the mediumistic experience fails to be a success.

2. Pentecostal Worship and Religious Experience

We have already noted that the Pentecostals maintain that their worship with their form of "speaking in tongues" is a repetition of the Apostles' experience in the upper room on the day of Pentecost,[16] and as such an experience to be coveted. For them, the reception of "tongues" (the ability to make strange sounds uninhibitedly) and subsequently other gifts are the proof that they are "born-again" saints, honorable vessels and freed from sin.[17] Those new-comers who believe that the "tongues" (inarticulate cries) and "supernatural phenomena" observed in the Pentecostal worship are indeed equivalent to the very manifestations recorded in

[15] Ibid., pages 131-132.
[16] Alevizopoulos, *Handbook of Heresies and Para-Christian Groups,* page 176.
[17] Kokoris, page 78.

Acts will gradually be made to feel inferior to those who can "speak in tongues" (freely make inarticulate sounds) and uncertain about their own salvation or at least "the fullness of their Christian walk." Simultaneously in the free atmosphere of Pentecostal worship where almost any kind of behavior is permitted, they are left completely free to experiment with themselves and with their imagination or to mimic the behavior of those who are "born-again."

The Pentecostals believe that the "liturgical" forerunner to their form of worship is the tamer revival meeting of the nineteenth century. Among the standard elements are a sermon about the "workings of the spirit" or the "end-times," evocative hymns, an altar call to receive the gifts of the Spirit, and then a state of mass enthusiasm in which "speaking in tongues" (freely making inarticulate sounds) and other manifestations of the "spirit" are observed.[18] In the course of the Pentecostal meeting, a friendly atmosphere becomes increasingly intense and electrified until all are seized by a spirit of great religious exaltation.[19] This is the "high point" of the service when the Pentecostals begin to "speak in tongues" (freely make inarticulate sounds) which they consider to be the initial sign of "Baptism in the Holy Spirit" and the continuing indication of His presence in their lives.[20] These "tongues" are composed of "incoherent,

[18] Alevizopoulos, *Handbook of Heresies and Para-Christian Groups,* pages 172 and 263.

[19] Kokoris, page 127.

[20] Fr. Seraphim Rose, *Orthodoxy and the Religion of the Future,* page 124.

strange and incomprehensible sounds without the formation of words or normal speech." The one "speaking in tongues" speaks uninterruptedly without any concern for the meaning of his unintelligible speech that he considers to be the fruit of the Holy Spirit supernaturally praying within him.[21] In fact, the Pentecostals assert that the proof that the tongue is spiritual lies in the fact that it acts independently of the mind (known as the "autonomy of the tongue").[22] They also claim that these "unknown tongues" are either the "personal prayer language" of the believer or "messages" for the faithful to be interpreted by those with the gift of prophecy.[23] The prophecies, "thus saith the Lord," are "invariably monotonous, vague, dreamy trance-like utterances that are nearly always consoling."[24]

In order to receive their "gift of tongues," the candidate is mentally prepared by being told to expect "the Holy Spirit to move on his vocal organs and to put supernatural words on his lips" and to "not fear receiving something false."[25] He is instructed to say in his heart "now I am receiving the Holy Spirit," to open his mouth widely, and to be careful not to utter a single word in his native language. With this

[21] Kokoris, pages 92-93.

[22] Alevizopoulos, *Handbook of Heresies and Para-Christian Groups,* pages 163.

[23] John Warren Morris, *The Charismatic Movement: An Orthodox Evaluation,* page 22.

[24] Fr. Seraphim Rose, *Orthodoxy and the Religion of the Future,* page 161.

[25] Hagin, pages 45 and 46.

preparation in place and in the presence of others who are to be softly praying in tongues (not in English), the Pentecostal pastor lays his hands on the candidate, tells him to receive the Holy Spirit, and commands him to speak. At this point, the candidate will usually begin to make strange sounds, albeit awkwardly at first. With time, he will become accustomed to such an experience and by it know that he has received the Holy Spirit.[26]

Although there are reported cases of healings and other gifts in their meetings, prophecy and tongues (which cannot be checked) are the only "gifts" that one can be sure to encounter.[27] It is worth stressing that "tongues" (freely making inarticulate sounds) are also practiced privately for individual edification.[28] Believers are even taught that the frequency of other manifestations of the Spirit (visions, lightning, revelations, and miracles) is directly proportional to the amount of time they devote to "speaking in tongues.[29] "Tongues" are, however, not the only outward religious expression encountered in Pentecostal worship. Some begin to laugh ("laughter in the spirit") again without knowing or examining why they are laughing. Others begin to weep, to tremble, to dance about, and to fall to the floor again

[26] Ibid., page 48.

[27] Kokoris, page 76.

[28] Alevizopoulos, *Handbook of Heresies and Para-Christian Groups,* pages 163.

[29] Hagin, page 15 and Fr. Seraphim Rose, *Orthodoxy and the Religion of the Future,* page 124-125.

without consciousness or understanding.[30] All these religious expressions are considered Christian because they are "in the Spirit." The more subdued and "moderate" Charismatic may well object that his "speaking in tongues" has been purified of earlier Pentecostal excesses and has become a quiet devotional that brings the good fruits of peace, joy and love. To such objections, we note that Zen Buddhism may well differ experientially and theoretically from the coarser spirit worship of the Tibetan plain, but they both occupy the same spiritual universe. The same is true of Charismatics and Pentecostals. Buddhist meditation also brings tranquility and compassion, but that hardly makes it Christian.

3. "This is an hard saying; who can hear it?"

In *the Gospel of Saint John* (8:32), the Lord Christ called out to the Jews, "and ye shall know the truth, and the truth shall make you free." This saving Truth revealed by Christ and preserved in His Church encompasses every aspect of man's life: how he believes, how he prays, and how he relates to God and his fellow man. It is the Way that can purify and illumine fallen man. When Christ exclaims that those scribes who "for a show make long prayers" "shall receive greater damnation,"[31] when He tells the Sadducees who do no believe in the resurrection

---

[30] Ibid., page 154.
[31] *Luke* 20:47.

that they "do greatly err,"[32] when He teaches the multitudes that "whosoever shall say, Thou fool, shall be in danger of hell fire,"[33] He makes it perfectly clear that any deviation from this therapeutic way is a deviation from Truth and Life. Dogma, worship, and the ethical life are in this sense as much a matter of spiritual life and death as sterility, proper medical equipment, and diet are for the physically infirm.

Earlier, we noted that a good medical association is not only concerned with the practice of good medicine, but also with the discontinuation of unsound and harmful medical practices that tarnish the reputation of the entire field of medicine. In this spirit, the Apostle Paul instructs us, "Brethren, if a man be overtaken in a fault, ye which are spiritual, restore such an one in the spirit of meekness; considering thyself, lest Thou also be tempted."[34] Although we by no means claim to be spiritual, we have attempted in the first part of this work to sketch out the teachings of those who certainly were. It is against this sacred standard that Christian love now compels us to examine the claims of the Pentecostal and charismatic communities.

The chief claim of the Pentecostals is that their worship is a repetition of Holy Pentecost. We noted that having passed through the stage of purification and entered the stage of illumination, the Apostles were prepared to receive the gift of the Holy

[32] *Mark* 12:27.
[33] *Matthew* 5:22.
[34] *Galatians* 6:1.

Spirit at Pentecost by their virtuous life of utter obedience to all of Christ's commandments. We have seen that on Holy Pentecost, the Apostles first received the gift of tongues (silent prayer of the heart), then they prophesied and simultaneously in response to a concrete need their proclamation was understood by the entire multi-lingual crowd present, bringing those from different nations into unity and leading many to repentance. We highlighted the fact that the accusation of drunkenness was no more based on the Apostles' words, actions, or behavior than the accusation of demon possession could be founded on Christ's miracles. On the contrary, the Apostles' words and actions were sober, wise, and able to touch the very depths of the human heart.

In sharp contrast with the above, we note that in Pentecostal worship the gifts of the Spirit are received quickly and easily with little or no previous preparation.[35] Not only are the inward prayer of the heart and the stages of purification and illumination completely unknown, but even the foundational emphasis on observing Christ's commandments is absent. Not only are the "languages" spoken not understood by those present, but there is also no concrete need for the believers to pray in different languages since all present presumably speak the same language. For the Pentecostal, holiness and power are separate concepts. And while they confess that it

---

[35] D. Kokoris notes a case in which someone began to speak in an incomprehensible tongue within 20 minutes from the moment that he stepped into a Pentecostal auditorium (page).

is best to have both, they ignore the fact that spiritual power without holiness is *ipso facto* demonic spiritual power. The fact that the Pentecostal sects continuously split off into smaller camps together with the inner strife that characterized the Azusa street Pentecost indicates that their experience leads not to the unity of Pentecost, but to the disunity of Babel. In Pentecostal worship, there is little sense of repentance (the ultimate goal of the Apostles' words), but rather a strong desire for or intense pleasure in "supernatural experiences." Unsober actions not recorded in *Acts* such as trembling, senseless laughing, weeping, the waving of hands, falling trances, and leaping up and down are also commonly observed in Pentecostal worship. We also observed Parham, the Father of Pentecost detected the presence of the demonic in the Azusa street revival, "the upper room" of the American Pentecost.

These major dissimilarities make it impossible to conclude that Pentecostal worship has any relationship whatsoever with what took place in the upper room on Holy Pentecost. Furthermore, the text of *Acts* quite readily allows for the interpretation that the Apostles were speaking in Hebrew, but through the grace of the Holy Spirit everyone present heard and understand their proclamation in their own language, in which case, the Pentecostal insistence that by speaking foreign languages (making foreign sounds) they have the gift of Pentecost and are repeating Pentecost is without foundation.

In our examination of Saint Paul's discourse on spiritual gifts, we noted the cooperation between

253

God and man in the gifts given to the believer in order to fulfill the commandments. We noted that unlike the pagan soothsayers, whose speech was controlled by a demon in a state of ecstasy, the prophets were not in a state of ecstasy and were completely free to speak or not to speak.

The most serious interpretation of Saint Paul's discourse indicates that "speaking in tongues" is neither a matter of foreign languages, nor incomprehensible sounds, but of the gift of silent prayer activated by the Holy Spirit in the heart. Such silent prayer in the Holy Spirit is truly worth pursuing, but the ultimate goal is the vision of the glorified Christ that grants the highest gift of perfect love. The use of "tongues" in the divine services was discouraged because it excluded those who did not have this gift of prayer and could hence not hear anything and be properly instructed. "Else when thou shalt bless with the spirit, how shall he that occupieth the room of the unlearned say Amen at thy giving of thanks, seeing he heareth not what thou sayest? For thou verily givest thanks well, but the other is not edified."[36]

The Pentecostals, on the other hand, not only reject the importance of synergy and the connection between the commandments and the gifts, but they even fail to notice the real presence of freedom in spiritual gifts. Their own understanding of prophecy and tongues has much more in common with the idolaters than with the tradition of the Prophets,

[36] *1 Corinthians* 14:16-17.

Apostles and Saints. Their wooden interpretation of the passage is moreover based on an English mistranslation of this text. Since the "speaking in tongues" of *Acts* and *Corinthians* is the prayer of the heart, the Pentecostal "speaking in tongues" (freely making inarticulate sounds) is again found to be without precedent in Holy Scripture, not to mention previous and subsequent Holy Tradition.

In our discussion on spiritual experiences, we noted that in addition to the genuine experiences of grace that most believers encounter in the sacramental life of the Church, there are experiences that may seem to be of God, but are in fact deceptive experiences produced by the devil who can pose as an angel of light. Godly spiritual experiences are characterized by good order, clarity and peace. They bring clarity of thought, freedom from the passions, humility, and love that seeks not its own interest. Spurious spiritual experiences, on the other hand, are characterized by chaos, disorder, disturbance and confusion. They bring "mindless joy and a muggy sense of pleasure," self-satisfaction, sensuality and vanity. Given the chaos, disorder, yet real pleasure ("a high" as they will call it employing the very jargon of the drug culture) present in Pentecostal worship together with the spiritual elitism that it produces (vanity), it seems reasonable to conclude that the Pentecostal experiences belong to the latter category rather than to the former.

The entire attitude of going to Church in order "to get a charge" or "a high" stands in sharp contrast with attending divine services in order to repent, to glorify Christ, to pray, and thus prepare oneself for Holy Eucharist. The "charismatic" attitude reflects an essentially selfish "relationship with God" Who is loved not for His own sake and for all that He has given us, but for the spiritual pleasure He can give us now. Thus, their very worship stands directly in the way of the ultimate goal of the Christian life, the acquisition of unselfish love and becomes a means of deception.

We have already noted that historically the Pentecostal movement is the fruit of the spiritual experimentation of the power seeking and self-guided C. Parham. It is also a historical fact that those Roman Catholics most devoted to Tradition as well as those Protestants most dedicated to Holy Scripture instinctively rejected the charismatic movement. Significantly, the very Protestant world in which Pentecostalism was born was the first to reject the worship of the Pentecostals as foreign to their experience of Christian worship and to declare it to be heretical. In contrast to the fear of God and awe that characterized true worship of the Prophets, Apostles, and Saints as described in the Old and New Testament and still lived in the Orthodox Church,[37] informality, license, and familiarity that derive from the absence of such a sense of the sacred are prevalent in Pentecostal worship.

One of the most important indicators of the presence of the Holy Spirit is the presence of the

---

[37] Cf. ibid., page 150.

Truth, as the Lord Christ Himself said to His Holy Disciples, "when the Comforter is come, whom I will send unto you from the Father, even the Spirit of Truth, which proceedeth from the Father, He shall testify of Me."[38] This Truth about Christ expressed in the dogmas of the faith and the life of the Church remains "the same yesterday, and to day, and for ever."[39] When the Pentecostals understand the Church as a whole as well as Baptism and Holy Communion in particular in a way different from the teaching of Christ and His Apostles, when they reject the Priesthood that Christ established, Confession, and the Saints, when they present a "gospel" that does not require the believer to take up his own cross, they not only reject the natural divinely established channels of divine grace, they not only demonstrate that their movement is not scriptural, but they also reveal that they are not led by the same Holy Spirit who illumined and inspired the Prophets, Apostles, and Saints.

If the significant weight of the above evidence indicates that Pentecostal claim that their worship is a repetition of Pentecost is without foundation, it is not difficult to demonstrate that the Pentecostals are in a state of intense enthusiasm if not religious ecstasy during their worship. The structure of their worship services follows quite closely the previously described outline for ecstasy inducing rites (the increasingly intensifying use of music and speech until

[38] *John* 15:26.
[39] *Hebrews* 13:8.

all begin to be moved by the "spirit:" some "speak in tongues" (freely make inarticulate sounds), others weep, others laugh, other tremble... Although the terms "prophecy" and "speaking in tongues" are referred to in Scripture, their presence in the pagan world (in both a different form and context) indicates that on their own they are not evidence that a person is even a Christian, much less "filled with the Holy Spirit."[40]

In this ecstatic atmosphere, however, the borders are completely removed that separate states derived from the activity of the Holy Spirit, those derived from psychological suggestion, and those derived from evil spirits.[41] What is most dangerous, even to question the source of the behavior observed in Pentecostal worship is considered to be the unforgivable "blasphemy against the Holy Spirit."[42] Although the Pentecostals may label all the behavior observed in their worship as being "in the Spirit," although they consider themselves to be Bible Christians *par excellence*, there is nothing Christian or Biblical whatsoever about "laughing in the Spirit," "trembling in the Spirit," or "being slain in the

[40] John Warren Morris, *The Charismatic Movement: An Orthodox Evaluation*, page 25.

[41] Alevizopoulos, *Handbook of Heresies and Para-Christian Groups*, pages 173-174.

[42] Fr. Seraphim Rose, *Orthodoxy and the Religion of the Future*, page 119.

Spirit."[43] Christ nowhere blesses those who laugh now, but on the contrary those who weep for their sins.[44] Falling down and trembling are no where signs of the presence of grace, but in the very Gospels they are sure signs of demon possession.[45] Such phenomena do not indicate the presence of the peaceful Spirit of God,[46] but rather pagan religious ecstasy, a state of delirium, or even demon possession.

Fr. Seraphim Rose's presentation of mediumism seems especially apt as a model for describing Pentecostal/Charismatic worship. Every characteristic of mediumism we cited earlier is present in Pentecostal experience of baptism in the Holy Spirit that results in "tongues", namely:

> 1. Passivity to the spirit by a "letting go" that is in sharp contrast to the watchfulness that is cultivated in Orthodoxy.

[43] There are other more extreme and bizarre manifestations such as barking, snorting, and crawling on the ground that are shameful even to mention. No comment is necessary.

[44] *Luke* 6:25: "Woe unto you that laugh now! For ye shall mourn and weep."

[45] Cf., *Luke* 4:35: "And Jesus rebuked him, saying, Hold thy peace, and come out of him. And when *the devil had thrown him in the midst*, he came out of him, and hurt him not." *Luke* 8:28: "When he saw Jesus, he cried out, and *fell down* before him, and with a loud voice said, What have I to do with thee, Jesus, thou Son of God most high? I beseech thee, torment me not." *Luke* 9:42: "And as he was yet a coming, *the devil threw him down*, and tare him."

[46] Archimandrite George Capsanis, *Experiences of the Grace of God,* page 30.

2. Solidarity in faith through a common desire for charismatic phenomena.

3. The laying on of hands in place of hands joined together to form a magnetic circle.

4. A spiritist atmosphere through suggestive hymns.[47]

Fr. Seraphim concludes "'charismatic' speaking in tongues is not a 'gift' at all but a *technique,* itself acquired by other techniques and in turn triggering still other 'gifts of the Spirit' *if one continues to practice and cultivate it....* The modern Pentecostal movement has discovered a new mediumistic technique for entering into and preserving a psychic state wherein miraculous 'gifts' become commonplace."[48]

Fr. Seraphim's conclusion that the Pentecostal religious experiences are "pagan religious experiences" corresponding to the mediumist initiation experience of spirit possession[49] may seem far-fetched to some and unduly severe to others. After all, many Pentecostals and charismatics very openly confess their love for Christ and devotion to Holy Scripture. While there is no reason to doubt their sincerity, love for Christ is proved and evaluated by obedience to and the practice of His commandments, and not by one's opinion about oneself or one's feelings. The fact

[47] Fr. Seraphim Rose, *Orthodoxy and the Religion of the Future,* pages 133-134.
[48] Ibid., page 136.
[49] Ibid., page 156.

that they understand themselves as Christians and interpret their experiences as Christian should not be confused with the issue of whether or not their experience and their attitudes springing therefrom are in fact Christian.[50] The lack of repentance, the undeniable presence of extreme ecstatic elements, and striking similarities with non-Christian religious phenomena all point to the fact that charismatic/Pentecostal experiences are not Christian at all.

Some well-meaning but misinformed souls who deny any demonic influence may still try to defend Pentecostal worship as an emotional religion suited for emotional people. The position that some are in need of an "intellectual faith" and others of an "emotional one," however, reveals a serious misunderstanding of the Church and deep ignorance of the anatomy of the human soul. God is known directly neither through the reasoning brain, nor through the emotions, but through the compunction of the spiritual heart or *nous*. Any prayer that does not eventually lead the reason to the heart is consequently not one that leads to union with God.

Precisely because the "Kingdom of God is within," ecstatic "speaking in tongues" (making strange sounds with the mouth) leads in the opposite direction. Orthodox Christians who have become involved with the Pentecostal movement as well as Pentecostals who have tried to approach Orthodoxy both report a significant occurrence at prayer. When

[50] Ibid., pages 153 and 172.

they try to say the Jesus Prayer, "Lord Jesus Christ, Son of God, have mercy on me," they find themselves compelled to start "speaking in tongues:"[51] "ka se ma ka ka, la do, ba ba, ga lo, la, da, da se mou ka ka..." or whatever the "spirit" happens to "inspire."[52] This inability consciously to call out to Christ and thus confess Him at the time of prayer when the believer should be united most closely to Him is perhaps the most vivid sign (and empirical symptom) that the "spirit" inspiring this type of "worship" is not of God, for Saint John the Theologian clearly teaches that "every spirit that confesseth not that Jesus Christ is come in the flesh is not of God: and this is that spirit of antichrist."[53] For this reason together with all the above, the Holy Church exhorts those who seek Christ and have strayed upon the Pentecostal's broad and unmarked path of temporary spiritual pleasure to return to the strait and narrow path of the Prophets, Apostles and Saints, the only path that leads not only to the true acquisition of the gifts of the Holy Spirit, but to life Eternal as well.

---

[51] Archimandrite George Capsanis, *Experiences of the Grace of God,* page 27.

[52] Quite significantly, those who have delved into Eastern religions (be it Buddhist meditation or Hindu Yoga) encounter similar difficulties in practicing the Jesus Prayer.

[53] *1 John* 4:3.

Epilogue:
Yet I show I unto you
a more excellent way

1. "No Man can Serve Two Masters"

It is the property of angels not to fall, and
even, as some say, it is quite impossible for
them to fall. It is the property of men to fall
and to rise again as often as this may hap-
pen. But it is the property of devils and
devils alone, not to rise once they have
fallen.

> — Saint John Climacus,
> *The Ladder of Divine Ascent,* 4:31

In the history of man, there are but two responses to the Truth: it can be accepted and embraced with humble repentance or rejected and hated
with arrogant hard-heartedness; it can furnish the
humble soul with golden wings of hope or cast the
proud soul into the dark pit of despair. What son of
Adam has never been deceived? What daughter of
Eve has not seen "that the tree was good for food, and
that it was pleasant to the eyes, and a tree to be desired to make one wise, and taken of the fruit

thereof"?[1] Who has not been mistaken in spite of the desire to be correct? Who has not fallen short of the mark? "For all have sinned, and come short of the glory of God."[2]

The Pentecostal or Charismatic reader of this little study will no doubt find himself to be at a crossroads whose markings at first may not seem especially clear. He may well ask himself whether he was truly deceived in his Pentecostal experiences or whether the foregoing presentation was truly fair. We suggest, however, that he ask himself another question, "to what extent have I accustomed myself to walk upon the path of repentance?" This is in fact the crossroads set before him. On his left lies the broad way upon which Pharaoh, Saul, Herod, Pilate, Judas, and the unrepentant thief once walked; on his right, the narrow path upon which Moses, David, Nicodemos, Peter, and the repentant thief once tread. What separates these two ways is not that one group was deluded and impassioned while the other was not. It is not a matter of the virtuous versus the villain, but the presence or absence of a humble heart willing to repent.[3] Saint Isaac writes, "repentance is the door of mercy, opened to those who seek it. By

---

[1] *Genesis* 3:6. The Most Holy Theotokos through the good use of her own free will is a notable exception.

[2] *Romans* 3:23.

[3] "But that on the good ground are they, which in *an honest and good heart*, having heard the word, keep it, and bring forth fruit with patience" *Luke* 8:15.

way of this door we enter into the mercy of God, and apart from this entrance we shall not find mercy."[4]

The Orthodox Church does not address the Pentecostals with proud triumphalism, but with the honest knowledge that the path of humility and repentance has been received from the Prophets, Apostles, and Saints is the *only way* that leads to the Kingdom of Heaven, the vision of the glorified Christ. Instead, the Orthodox Church invites them to "come and see," and then honors their God-given freedom to choose to hear Christ's glad tidings of repentance or to turn a deaf ear. Even as Christ called the man who denied him thrice to feed His flock, even as He called the persecutor of the Church to be His Apostle to the Gentiles, so He calls each one of us wherever we may be. Of course, other voices will also be heard. The tempter may well murmur in the former Pentecostal's inward ear, "so was it all a mistake?" in order to lead the soul to despair or to reject the Truth.

In the Holy Orthodox Church, however, we do not judge ourselves solely on our mistakes, but also on the grace of God, that is on His love that we have received and that gently guides us to salvation. Recognizing both our sins of knowledge and of ignorance and God's great mercy, we simply repent and change our path. In the mystery of confession, the believer "is given the possibility to bring his falls and defeats, his defilement and blunders, in general the failure of his very existence to be what it was fashioned to be,

[4] Saint Isaac the Syrian, *The Ascetic Homilies*, page 223.

and 'in repentance' to place it all before the Church."[5] And when human freedom meets divine grace in the Mystery of Repentance, the sinner already begins to leave the land of sin, the deluded his world of delusion, and the heretic the sway of heresy. In other words, he becomes a "new creation"[6] in Christ living righteously, seeing clearly, and believing correctly. Like the Holy Apostle Paul, "forgetting those things which are behind, and reaching forth unto those things which are before, he presses toward the mark for the prize of the high calling of God in Christ Jesus."[7] Let no Pentecostal who desires to change merely lament the past, but especially let him place his sure hope in a new future, for if Joannicius the iconomachist (November 4) and Cyprian the magician (October 2) were able through repentance to become great Saints of the Orthodox Church, nothing apart from their own free will hinders the former Pentecostal or Charismatic from following their example and doing the same.

2. A Higher Goal, a Safer Way

"For as the heavens are higher than the earth, so are My ways higher than your ways, and My thoughts than your thoughts."

[5] Anesti Kessolopoulos, *The Passions and the Virtues,* page 110 (in Greek).
[6] *2 Corinthians* 5:17.
[7] *Phillipians* 3:13-14.

EPILOGUE

— Isaiah 55:9

And indeed in the Orthodox Church, the Pentecostal or Charismatic will find a goal infinitely higher and a way infinitely safer than what he previously experienced. The Pentecostal who seeks the experience of the Apostles will find the Church the Charismatic who seeks the gifts of the Spirit will find the fount of all spiritual gifts. They will find the most sacred desires of their heart if they but choose to walk along the path of the Prophets, Apostles and Saints, if they but choose to humble themselves, to crucify themselves to the world, to be baptized into Christ's death and Resurrection, and then to lead a life of repentance nourished by the Holy Mysteries and guided by obedience to a spiritual father. And if indeed they crucify themselves with Christ, they will also in time partake of His Resurrection and the true fruits of Holy Pentecost itself. In all honesty, however, we must inform the Pentecostal or Charismatic who is entering the Orthodox Church, that he will not encounter the "wide path" upon which he was accustomed to tread, but the "narrow path" of ascetic struggle in order to gain the health of his soul and consolation from the Holy Mysteries.

The goal is infinitely higher, for it is not simply to enjoy some kind of spiritual experience nor even to acquire some kind of spiritual power, but to achieve that real and ineffable union with Christ through the Holy Spirit in the heart, that union which in turn makes man Christ-like. "From this (union) comes foreknowledge of things future, under-

267

standing of mysteries, apprehension of things hidden, distribution of spiritual gifts, citizenship in heaven, the dance with the angels, unending joy, divine largesse, likeness to God, and the desire of all desires, to become god."[8] Thus, the most exalted goal, revealed by God and not by man, is no less than man's perfection through Christ, his glorification with Christ, his deification in Christ. This means "to be made new by the grace of the Holy Spirit and in all things to become like unto the Lord," "filled with love for Christ and Christ's humility."[9] And so, the humble soul is clothed with Christ's grace, the very wedding garment of the Lamb[10] and henceforth moved by a love that seeks not its own.

The way marked out by the purification of the passions on the one side and the observance of the commandments on the other is also infinitely safer, for it has not only been tested for millennia by those who have pleased God, it has also been revealed by the Only One capable of healing man's spiritual ills, God Himself. The way that purifies, illumines, and perfects the believer, the way that enables the faculties of the believer's soul to function properly, the way that cleanses the heart of all the thoughts so

[8] Saint Gregory Palamas, "Topics of Natural and Theological Science," *Philokalia,* IV, page 381.

[9] Archimandrite Sophrony, *Saint Silouan the Athonite,* page 389.

[10] "Humility is the raiment of the Godhead. The Word Who became man clothed Himself in it." Saint Isaac the Syrian, page 381.

that it can become pure and "see God"[11] is the *only* tested way that leads to tangible evidence of Christ's presence not only by the abundance of Christ-like virtues observed in the friends of God and pure in heart in this earthly life, but also by the relics of the deified which remain fragrant and work miracles after their repose.

Whatever was good and pure in the past of the Pentecostal or Charismatic will not be lost. "Whatsoever things are true, whatsoever things are honest, whatsoever things are just, whatsoever things are pure, whatsoever things are lovely, whatsoever things are of good report; if there be any virtue, and if there be any praise,"[12] these will be the bricks with which they can rebuild the house of their soul on the good and solid foundation of the teachings of Christ's Holy Church. The healing of man's soul entails neither the mortification of the soul's faculties, nor the mortification of the passionate aspect of the soul, but their redirection, transfiguration, and proper use. And when the image is thus restored to its native nobility and pristine beauty, then communion and union with the desired archetype Christ Himself follow as naturally as day follows night.

The Pentecostal or Charismatic who previously found much delight in studying Christ's Word will have the same Scriptures "opened to him"[13] anew if he chooses to be baptized into the Orthodox faith

[11] *Matthew* 5:8.
[12] *Phillipians* 4:8.
[13] *Luke* 24:32.

and to follow the way of the Fathers, for the same union with Christ experienced by the Prophets, Apostles and Saints recorded in Scripture will be possible for him. Then, the words of the Psalmist will become his own: "The unfolding of Thy words will give light and understanding unto babes."[14] His desire to "worship in Spirit and in Truth" will be fulfilled initially in the divine services of the Orthodox Church where he will be taught how to have humble thoughts, how to have repentant thoughts, how to glorify God and to rejoice spiritually in His Saints. If he is attentive to the divine services and lets them shape his heart, he will find himself led into the Tradition of the friends of Christ (Prophets, Apostles, and Saints).

The Pentecost and Descent of the Holy Spirit that he will have first beheld in his own Baptism, he will encounter again and live again in the other Mysteries of the Church, especially in Holy Communion to the extent that his heart is purified and the vessel of his soul is capable to receive Him.[15] And if like the Prophet David, "he will not give sleep to his eyes, or slumber to his eyelids, until he find out a place (in his heart) for the Lord, an habitation for the mighty God of Jacob;"[16] if like the Wise Solomon he adorns the temple of his soul with all manner of comely virtue, then he will surely "worship in Spirit and in Truth" entering the Holy of Holies, the depths of his

[14] *Psalm* 118:130.

[15] Archimandrite George Capsanis, *Experiences of the Grace of God,* pages 32-34.

[16] *Psalm* 132:4-5.

270

heart and offering up the incense of inner prayer to the Lord.

3. "Sing unto the Lord a new song"

Above all, the Pentecostal's or Charismatic's zeal for spiritual prayer misdirected by the counterfeit gift of "speaking in tongues" (making unintelligible sounds with his mouth) will find fulfillment in the genuine gift of tongues, the prayer of the heart. The genuine gift of tongues is a profound experience granted by the Holy Spirit Who descends upon the heart and prays therein with "unspeakable sighs." It is the most basic element of the Tradition of the Prophets of the Old Testament and the Apostles and Saints of the New. For if Pentecostal speaking in tongues is an irrational activity that enables the practitioner thereof to escape from rational thought processes and thereby gain entry to the "spiritual realm," the genuine gift of speaking in tongues involves the direction of the mind's attention not outward, but inward to the spiritual heart where the Holy Spirit prays within man without abolishing his freedom to think rationally and without leading him to an over-excited state.

Ultimately, the quest for this genuine gift of tongues is an invitation to discover the spiritual heart that Christ spoke about in parable after parable calling out as it were, "my son, give me thine heart."[17] The spiritual heart must be discovered because it no longer functions properly (or at all) in fallen man who is darkened by sin and stripped of the grace of God.[18] Most people do not even suspect its existence, because their heart has been so filled with *logismoi* (thoughts and imagination)[19] and thus

---

[17] *Proverbs* 23:26. E.g., "Again, the kingdom of heaven is like unto treasure hid in a field (the heart); the which when a man hath found, he hideth, and for joy thereof goeth and selleth all (his thoughts) that he hath, and buyeth that field (by the prayer of the heart)" *Matthew* 13:44. "But thou, when thou prayest, enter into thy closet (of the heart), and when thou hast shut thy door (shut out all the thoughts), pray to thy Father which is in secret" *Matthew* 6:6. "Behold, a sower went forth to sow (the words of prayer in the field of the heart); And when he sowed, some seeds fell by the way side..." (there follows a description of the various thoughts *logismoi:* demonic, of pain and of pleasure, that prevent the prayer from taking root in contrast with the good ground of a heart whose soil is cleared of all thoughts both good and bad). *Matthew* 13:3-8.

[18] Fr. J. Romanidis, "Dogmatic Introduction" in Gregory Palamas, *On Behalf of the Sacred Hesychasts Triad 1, The Works of Gregory Palamas,* vol. 1, *Roman Fathers of the Church,* edited by John S. Romanidis, text, trans. (into modern Greek) and comments by Despoina Kontostergios, (Pournara Publications: Thessalonica, 1984), page 146 (in Greek).

[19] "Logismos" is the technical term in ascetic literature for a thought combined with an image. According to Saint Maximus, a logismos can be simple (dispassionate) or composite (passion-charged: e.g., a memory combined with a passion). Cf. Bishop Hierotheos Vlachos, *Orthodox Psychotherapy: The Science of the Fathers,* trans. by Esther Williams (Birth of the Theotokos Monastery, Levadia: 1994), pages 215-216. According to Saint Isaac the Syrian, four causes generate *logismoi:* "Firstly, from the natural will of the flesh; secondly, from imagination of sensory objects in the world which a man hears and sees; thirdly, from

so distracted that the heart's primary function of the continuous remembrance of God is inhibited.[20] Only through the prayer of the heart (kinds of tongues) can this continuous remembrance be restored. We must stress, however, that the discovery of the spiritual heart takes place when the Holy Spirit comes and prays within the heart, when *He reveals* it. Afterwards, the prayer of the heart begins to become ceaseless (i.e., the Holy Spirit continuously prays within the heart) and the remembrance of God continuous.

The Fathers sometimes call this prayer "noetic" (νοερά to be precise) because it involves the use of the "*nous*," a faculty of the soul equally unknown to contemporary man. The "*nous*" is the spiritual heart that is revealed by the Holy Spirit when *He* activates it. Sometimes, the term "*nous*" refers to the soul's essence, the spiritual heart or a faculty of the

---

mental predispositions and aberrations of the soul; and fourthly, from the assaults of demons who wage war with us in all the passions..." (Ibid., page 218) Although the logismoi first appear on the horizon of the mind, they are immediately transmitted to the heart, so that we feel as though they arise from the heart (Ibid., page 221). The Lord Himself referred to this saying, "For out of the heart proceed evil thoughts, murders, adulteries, fornications, thefts, false witness, blasphemies" (*Matthew* 15:19) and "A good man out of the good treasure of the heart bringeth forth good things: and an evil man out of the evil treasure bringeth forth evil things" (*Matthew* 12:35).

[20] Bishop Hierotheos Vlachos, *Orthodox Psychotherapy*, pages 130-131.

soul that can be called the "eye of the soul."[21] At
other times, the *"nous"* refers to the soul's energy or
activity in the form of "a most refined attentiveness."[22] In the spiritually unhealthy, the *"nous'"*
natural movement is hindered or scattered outward
by the senses while its essence (the heart) is filled
with a motley array of *logismoi* (this is especially
evident in those who daydream or inwardly converse
with themselves). Spiritual health, on the other
hand, is quite simply achieved, when the *"nous"* is
emptied of all *logismoi* and energized by the grace of
the Holy Spirit, so that it can thus be united with
God.[23] In discovering this heart, the believer learns
the meaning of the Prophet David's words, "the heart
is deep"[24] and Saint Makarios of Egypt's exclamation,
"truly the heart is an immeasurable abyss."[25]

The terms used to describe this type of prayer
may seem foreign and abstract as things unknown
often do, but in fact for those with "eyes to see" this
practice of the prayer of the heart is quite natural,
concrete, and so extensively referred to in Holy Scripture that we refrain from wearying the reader with
endless citations. When the gift of the prayer of the

---

[21] Bishop Hierotheos Vlachos, *Orthodox Psychotherapy*,
page 126. Cf., also Luke 11:34: "the light of the body is the eye:
therefore when thine eye is single, thy whole body also is full of
light; but when thine eye is evil, thy body also is full of darkness."

[22] Ibid., page 124.

[23] Ibid., page 143.

[24] *Psalm* 64:6.

[25] Saint Makarios of Egypt, "The Raising of the Intellect,"
The Philokalia, v. iii, page 321.

heart or ceaseless prayer is acquired, than the prayer is repeated continuously in the heart, day, night, and even during sleep. In sharp contrast to ecstatic "prayer," the believer whose *nous* prays ceaselessly is in complete control of the movements of his body and his mind. He is able to analyze a problem with his reason, to look at an object with his eyes and to hear a sound with his ears, and all the while to pray with his *"nous"* within his heart. Once his *"nous"'* proper activity is set into motion by the grace of the Holy Spirit, the believer is able to repeat the words of a prayer (the Jesus Prayer or a Psalm verse) in unison with the prayer of the Spirit. This in turn opens and illumines his mind.[26]

Of course, even under the direction of a competent spiritual father the most basic maxim of the spiritual life holds true: "good things are acquired through toil and achieved though pain."[27] The *logismoi* that occupy the heart together with the various inward and outward passions all have a deceitful sweetness that makes their expulsion painful. The prerequisites watchfulness, fasting, and obedience to Christ's commandments are by nature self-emptying and thus most distasteful to the selfish self. But with persistence and insistence, in time a change takes place. By the grace of God, however this humanly difficult task is easily accomplished as Christ Himself

[26] Fr. J. Romanidis, "Dogmatic Introduction, *"On Behalf of the Sacred Hesychasts,* page 147 (in Greek).

[27] *Rubrics and Service of the Great and Angelic Monastic Schema* (Zealot Hagiorite Fathers: the Holy Mountain, 1983), page 21 (in Greek).

promised saying "my yoke is easy, and my burden is light."[28] When the Holy Spirit descends, the soul feels her own resurrection and beholds Christ in her own upper room. This is the very purpose of Pentecost.

Like the blind Bartimaeus, the son of Timaeus, the soul must "cry out, and say, Jesus, Thou son of David, have mercy on me." And when the *logismoi* "charge her that she should hold her peace," she must "cry the more a great deal, Thou son of David, have mercy on me."[29] Like the widow who troubled the unjust judge, she must "cry day and night unto God" that He come and abide in her through the prayer.[30] Then, she will observe,

> that the prayer (meaning the Jesus prayer) will bring all things, it contains all things, it encircles all things: requests, consolation, faith, confession, theology... Little by little, the prayer will bring peace, sweetness, joy, tears. Peace and sweetness will in turn bring more of the Jesus prayer. And the more of the Jesus prayer will bring peace and sweetness. The time will come, that if you stop saying the Jesus prayer, you will not feel well... So the prayer brings peace and sweetness, later it will bring tears. Tears are another rung on the ladder. First with the Jesus prayer you will find joy, peace, and sweetness. First you will feel

---

[28] *Matthew* 11:30.
[29] *Mark* 10:46-48.
[30] *Luke* 18:7.

these things, and then tears will come. Afterwards, if God so desires, you may taste other states as well.[31]

The Jesus Prayer can have such a powerful and transfiguring effect on the soul, that an anonymous hesychast calls out to the monk (and by extension to all Christians):

O monk, do you want to taste in your heart the Lord's nectar while you are still alive? Pray noetically and unceasingly to your Christ from the depths of your heart until it hurts.

O monk, do you want to see as in a mirror by divine revelation, the beauty and divine nobility of your soul? Pray noetically and unceasingly to your Christ from the depths of your heart until it hurts.

O monk, do you want the eyes of your mind to be illumined, or to put it better, do you want the eyes of your soul to be opened and thereby to see what eye has not seen? Pray noetically and unceasingly to your Christ from the depths of your heart until it hurts.[32]

These last words are but a sampling of the many offered by those who have reached a state of

[31] Elder Ephraim of Katounakia, "Unpublished Handwritten Letter" (in Greek).

[32] Anonymous Hesychast, *Neptic Theoria*, (Sacred Monastery of Xenophontos: Holy Mountain, 1996), page 236 (in Greek).

health to all of us who are still in need of healing. Having attained to that love which faileth not, having become all heart, Saint Paul's words become their own:

> "For I am in a strait betwixt two, having a desire to depart, and to be with Christ; which is far better: Nevertheless to abide in the flesh is more needful for you. And having this confidence, I know that I shall abide and continue with you all for your furtherance and joy of faith."[33]

Thus when they turn their blessed countenance towards us their struggling brethren, their one desire is to see us also ascend through the stages of purification and illumination until we reach Love and see no longer "through a glass, darkly, but face to face." Calmly yet earnestly, they call out to us: "ascend, brothers, ascend eagerly and be resolved *in your hearts to ascend and hear Him* Who says: "Come and let us go to the mountain of our God, Who makes our feet like hind's feet, and sets us upon high, *that we might be victors with His song,"*[34] And that ascent begins in Christ's Holy Orthodox Church with Her Hesychastic Tradition. It is an ascent that takes place not in some stagnant semi-conscious ecstasy, but in a dynamic watchful stillness powered by the ceaseless prayer of the heart. As if to stress this reality, the Church again and again reminds all of Her children

[33] *Phillipians* 1:23-25.
[34] Saint John Climacus, *The Ladder of Divine Ascent,* page 230.

at every stage of this sanctifying path, guiding and
comforting with this small, but sacred invitation:

In Peace
let us pray
to the Lord.
Amen.

Appendix

Every Man Heard Them Speak In His Own Language: God is Wonderful in His Saints

In our exegesis on Holy Pentecost, we noted the presence of three spiritual gifts: the prayer of the heart ("speaking in tongues"), prophecy ("utterance given by the Spirit"), and the comprehensibility of the word spoken to those of other languages. In the Orthodox Church, each of these gifts can be observed in the Lives of the Saints, the continuation of *The Acts of the Apostles*. The acquisition or reception of the prayer of the heart or noetic prayer ("speaking in tongues") is a most basic stage (illumination) through which all the Saints have passed.

The interested reader is especially directed towards the monastic tradition where teaching on this subject is preserved as its most precious treasure. Ascetic Fathers from the time of Saint Anthony the Great up until the present day have much experience with this gift of prayer.[1] The gift of prophecy is likewise observable in the many patristic commentaries on Scripture as well as in the lives of most

---

[1] Cf., the published lives and teachings of Saint Silouan the Athonite, the Elder Joseph the Hesychast, the Elder Paissius the Athonite, etc...

Saints, again especially the monastic ones. The gift of comprehensibility to those who speak another language, however, is far more rare, but by no means absent.

On account of the rareness of this latter gift, we offer the reader with extracts from the lives of Saints in which it was observed. Although these Saints served the Church in diverse ways (as martyrs, hierarchs, or monks) and lived in different historical settings, we observe in their lives the very same traits that characterized the manifestation of the gift of comprehensibility on Holy Pentecost. This particular gift is bestowed upon purified and virtuous souls because there is a pressing need to be understood by others. It is employed in order to speak with one's fellow man, rather than to pray to God. And the words uttered (the prophecy associated with the gift) are wise, peaceful, and sober.[2]

[2] Fr. George Maloney, S.J., in his introduction to St. Symeon the New Theologian's *Hymns of Divine Love*, calls St. Symeon a "charismatic reformer" (page 5), insinuating a connection between him and contemporary charismatic leaders. Although St. Symeon's clashes with ecclesiastical authorities and his "reference to tongues" in hymn no. 7, "that I speak in new languages by Your grace" (page 28), seem to bolster this hypothesis, a careful reading of his writings and life indicates that these seeming similarities are as external as the similarities between yoga and the hesychastic method of prayer. The similarities are in form, not content. For a thorough Orthodox treatment of St. Symeon's life and thought, see Archbishop Basil Krivocheine's *In the Light of Christ: St. Symeon the New Theologian* (Crestwood, NY: SVS Press, 1986).

1. The Holy and Glorious Greatmartyr Christopher († 249-251)

Saint Christopher was a giant with fierce features, but a gentle and compassionate heart. He lived during the reign of the Emperor Decius and belonged to a tribe of barbarians that were taken captive during a local war on the eastern border of the Roman Empire. Although he was not a baptized Christian at the time, he was a virtuous and sensible man. When he beheld how the idolaters tortured and killed the Christians, his sensitive heart felt much pain and his conscience prodded him to act in some way to help them. As a barbarian, however, Saint Christopher did not yet know the language of those who had captured him, so he could neither speak out against the crimes being committed nor reprove the idolaters. Moreover, there was no one present who could translate for him, so the Saint was unable to communicate his thoughts with anyone.

In such a state and with such a *pressing need* to speak, the Saint withdrew to a secluded spot, fell to the earth, and beseeched the Lord with tears to grant him the ability to be understood by the idolaters. With all his heart, he offered the following prayer: "O Lord God Almighty, hearken unto my humility and show Thy compassion to me the unworthy one. Open my lips and grant me to speak with the people here, so that I can reprove the tyrant." While he was still praying, a radiant youth appeared before him and said to him, "Reprobos (that was how he was

282

still called at the time), your supplication has been heard, arise and receive grace from the Lord."

When the blessed one arose, the radiant youth touched his lips and immediately as he breathed into his mouth, the Saint spoke freely in the new language. Able now to communicate with his brethren and the tyrant, the Saint went to the city and with heavenly wisdom reproved the idolaters and converted many to the Christian faith.[3]

In this small example, we note both the presence of humility, virtue, and love in the Saint and a real need to be understood by those around him. The gift is not in any way used to enter some nebulous spiritual state, nor as a means to pray to God, but as a way to proclaim the Gospel, in Christ's words "to be brought before rulers and kings for my sake, for a testimony against them."[4] We also note that his words were not simply comprehensible, they were also wise, wise enough to convert the soldiers sent to capture him, wise enough to convert the prostitutes who tried to seduce him.

2. Our Venerable and God-bearing Father Paisius the Great (b. 300)

Saint Paisius was one of the great luminaries of the Egyptian desert. He was the son of pious, vir-

---

[3] *The Great Synaxaristis of the Orthodox Church,* vol. V., Month of May (Matthew Laggis: Athens, 1985), page 224 (in Greek).

[4] *Mark* 13:9.

tuous, and wealthy parents and was especially selected by God to serve Him as a monk. Living in absolutely obedience to his elder, the Saint devoted himself to extreme fasting and all-night prayer. When his elder died, he doubled his efforts and went into the deep desert to be alone with God alone. On account of his great purity, his deep humility, and his fiery love for Christ, the Lord blessed him with numerous gifts and even appeared to him. Among these gifts was numbered the gift to be able to communicate in a foreign language that manifested itself in the following way.

While Paisius was laboring in the Egyptian desert, there was another great and virtuous struggler striving to please God in Syria. Once while this Syrian monk was praying, the thought came to him, "have I yet become like any of those who have pleased God?" While he was reflecting on these things, he heard a voice from on high say to him, "Go to the Egyptian desert and there you will find a struggler named Paisius who leads a life of humility and fervent love for God even as you do." Although the venerable elder was afraid to undertake such a lengthy journey, with trust in God, he set off for the land of Egypt.

When the Syrian elder reached the Mount of Nytras, he asked where he could find Paisius, and since the fame of Saint Paisius had spread far and wide, he quickly found the way leading to Paisius' dwelling. Meanwhile, Paisius also was informed from above of the elder's journey to him, so he went out to meet the elder. And thus on the way, they met each other and immediately recognized each other by the divine grace that abode in each of them. Together, they went to Paisius' cell, prayed, and sat down together.

The elder then began to speak to Paisius in Syrian, but since Paisius only knew the Egyptian language, he was not able to understand the elder's profitable words and this caused him great sorrow. With a contrite and humble heart, Paisius lifted up the eyes of his soul towards heaven, and prayed, "O Son and Word of God, grant Thy grace to me Thy servant that I might understand the power of the elder's words." As soon as he uttered his humble prayer, he was able both to speak and understand the Syrian language. Thus, the Lord Christ responded to the pressing need of the Saint to be understood. Without any fanfare or emotionalism, but in a most peaceful and natural way, He granted him the gift to understand and be understood, so that they could speak of "the wonderful works of God."[5]

And so, these two saintly men spoke together at length relating to one another the visions that they were accounted worthy to see, the holy fathers with whom they had spoken and lived, and the virtues with which these fathers were adorned. After having passed six days in such edifying conversation and full of spiritual joy, the elder prepared to return

[5] *Acts* 2:11.

to his homeland, Paissius had his disciples receive his blessing, and they bid the holy elder farewell.[6]

3. Our Father among the Saints Basil the Great (329-364)

Saint Basil the Great, the Archbishop of Ceasarea in Cappadocia, was one of the greatest theologians, apologists, ascetics, and hierarchs of the Church. In wisdom, in purity, in virtue, in divine gifts, he was unsurpassed in his day, and throughout the ages, the faithful have derived much sustenance from his divinely-inspired writings and heavenly intercessions. Among the many spiritual gifts that were given to the faithful through his powerful prayers, there is recorded one instance in which the ability to communicate in another language was given to the Venerable Ephraim the Syrian through Saint Basil's prayers.

When Saint Ephraim was leading a life of stillness in the Syrian desert, he often heard about Saint Basil's miracles and wondered precisely who this new Saint of the Church was. Having turned to God in prayer, Saint Ephraim then saw a pillar of fire that stretched up unto heaven and heard a voice saying, "Ephraim, behold this pillar of fire, for it resembles Basil the Great." After such a divine revelation, Saint Ephraim immediately decided to go to

[6] *The Great Synaxaristis of the Orthodox Church*, vol. 6., Month of June (Matthew Laggis: Athens, 1985) pages 265-266 (in Greek).

286

Caesarea bringing with him a translator who knew the Greek and the Syrian languages.

Saint Ephraim and his translator arrived at the Church in Ceasarea on the feast of Theopany. When Ephraim saw Saint Basil arrayed in lavish vestments and serving the Divine Liturgy with great boldness, he reproached himself for his decision to come to see the Saint and told his interpreter, "My brother, we have labored in vain, for anyone surrounded by such glory cannot be like the one I saw." The Holy Spirit, however, revealed Ephraim's thoughts to Saint Basil who immediately told his deacon, "Go to the Church's western door where you will see two monks: one without a beard, tall, and thin, and another with a black beard. Tell the beardless one, "Come into the Holy Altar, because your father the Archbishop is calling for you."

And so, the deacon went out and with effort made his way through the crowd to Saint Ephraim and told him Saint Basil's words. Saint Ephraim, however, answered through his interpreter, "You are mistaken, brother, for we are foreigners and unknown. How then does the Archbishop recognize us?" When the deacon returned and relayed Saint Ephraim's words to Saint Basil, Saint Basil again sent his deacon to Saint Ephraim with a new message, "Lord Ephraim, come into the Holy Altar, because the Archbishop is calling for you." Returning a second time, the deacon related Saint Basil's words, and Saint Ephraim in turn responded, "Truly Basil the Great is a pillar of fire. I only request that we be permitted to speak with him alone in the vestibule."

After the conclusion of the Divine Liturgy, Saint Basil called for Saint Ephraim, greeted him and spoke with him by means of his translator about various spiritual subjects. At the end of this conversation, Saint Basil asked Saint Ephraim if he had anything else hidden in his heart to tell him. To this, Ephraim responded through the interpreter, "I do have one favor to ask of you, Hierarch and servant of God." "Ask for whatever you desire," replied Saint Basil, "for I am greatly indebted to you for the labor you underwent for my lowliness." And so Saint Ephraim said, "I know, Holy Master, that if you ask God for something, it will be granted to you. I desire that you pray that I be able to speak in Greek, since I do not know your own language." The Saint answered, "Your request is beyond my strength, Holy Father and instructor of the desert. But since you seek it with such faith, let us both beseech God and it is possible for Him to fulfill your desire, for as the Prophet David says, 'He does the will of those who fear Him and hearkens unto their supplication and saves them.'" Having said that, Saint Basil and Saint Ephraim stood in prayer for quite some time, after which Saint Basil said with a loud voice, "May the Grace of the All-Holy Spirit be between you and me and enable you to speak Greek." As soon as Saint Basil had spoken, Saint Ephraim's mouth was opened and he spoke in Greek. Saint Ephraim remained with the Saint Basil for three days, benefiting much from his teaching. Saint Basil then ordained Saint Ephraim and then let him depart for the desert where he glorified and blessed God."[7]

As in the earlier examples, so here we see the ability to communicate was given to the pure and humble because of a concrete need. Again, it is not portrayed as a means of praying to God, but a way that enables one Christian brother to converse with another, to be understood, and to speak of "the wonderful works of God."

4. The Venerable Monk Martyr James the New (†1520)

Saint James the New belongs to the ranks of new-martyrs of the Turkish yoke. Born in Kastoria in Northern Greece, he went to Constantinople to gain his fortune by importing and selling sheep. Having made the acquaintance of Patriarch Niphon, he learned from him the ways of piety. With faith in God and love for his neighbor, he distributed his wealth and went to the Holy Mountain to venerate the monasteries and meet the ascetics. There, he became a monk in the Monastery of Docheiariou where he gave himself over to extreme asceticism with perfect obedience and great humility. Desiring a life of stillness, he settled in an abandoned cell in honor of the Forerunner near the Monastery of Iviron where he fur-

---

[7] *The Great Synaxaristis of the Orthodox Church,* vol. I., Month of January (Matthew Laggis: Athens, 1980) pages 44-46 (in Greek).

ther advanced in prayer, fasting, and vigil. Having reached great purity of heart, he was granted many spiritual gifts including the capability to communicate with those who speak another tongue.

Because of his ability to see deep into the hearts of men, many went to see the Saint for spiritual profit. In Iviron, there was a Georgian deacon who did not know Greek, but having heard so much about the venerable one, he went to his cell to see him and if possible to confess to him, even though he did not know how he would communicate with him. The venerable one felt sorry for the deacon and said to him: "Deacon, in the name of the Father and of the Son and of the Holy Spirit, say what you have to say." And immediately, the Deacon began to speak and confess to the venerable one who advised him and corrected him in Greek. The deacon departed greatly benefited and glorifying God."[8]

Again we note that as on the Day of Pentecost, the gift of comprehensibility is given to the pure and humble because of a concrete need. It is not privately employed in order to pray to God, but so that a believer (the Georgian deacon in this case) could be instructed and lead a more God-pleasing life.

[8] *The Great Synaxaristis of the Orthodox Church,* vol. XI., Month of November (Matthew Laggis: Athens, 1982) pages 28-41 (in Greek).

5. The Holy Elder Porphyrios († 1991)

The Elder Porphyrios was a clairvoyant elder and spiritual father from the Holy Mountain who lived for thirty years in Athens. Although rather uneducated, Elder Porphyrios was extremely wise and full of love. He spiritually transformed the lives of thousands who came in contact with him. Among the many miracles that took place around the Elder Porphyrios, there is one instance of receiving the ability to understand and be understood by one who spoke another language. What is so very precious about this particular case is that the Elder himself relates the miracle providing us with a description of this gift of comprehensibility that goes beneath the surface of outward events.

The Elder's cell was often filled with visitors seeking his counsels, his blessing, and his prayers. Once among these visitors, there was a young French woman around twenty-five years of age who desired to receive the Elder's blessing. The Elder had her brought into his cell and asked if there was anyone present who spoke French. As Mrs. Tasoula spoke French, she entered the Elder's cell as well. The Elder then told the translator to ask the French woman to tell him her name, what work she did and if she was married. The translator asked the woman the elder's questions, and the woman replied that her name was Anna, she was a professor, and unmarried. She had come her to Greece as a tourist The Elder then asked her via the translator if she believed in God. The young woman answered sobbing, "I am a nihilist. Nothing exists." At this point, the elder told the translator to leave despite the objections of others present who wondered how he would communicate with her. The Elder then held her head and the elder asked her if she lives with her mother. And the woman answered. The Elder then said, "My dear Anna, God loves you. He loves you. And God will speak to your little heart." The Elder continued to speak to her and the young woman understood completely. He talked alone with her for some time. When the French woman came out of his cell, she was quite enthusiastic exclaiming, "Who told you that the Elder does not know French? He told me everything! He told me everything" She was quite moved.

When the Elder was questioned about what took place, he explained that he spoke in Greek and "heard" the woman's responses in Greek, while she spoke in French and "heard" his advice in French.[9] As in the previous examples, there was a real need for communication, the gift was given through the prayers of the humble and virtuous elder, and his words were wise, sober, and deeply touched the woman's heart, to such an extent that she eventually became an Orthodox Christian and a monastic.

The above examples[10] demonstrate that the gift of comprehensibility *as described on the day of*

[9] Constantine Giannitsiotis, *Near the Elder Porphyrius*, pages 130-138 (in Greek).

[10] There are also other undocumented examples of this gift in which the same surrounding conditions and characteristics are present. For example, in more than one monastery on the

Pentecost has appeared in the Orthodox Church up to the present day. It should be stressed, however, that without the existence of the preconditions of humility, virtue, and need and without the characteristics of understandability an sobriety, this gift is not observed. Or to be more precise, without those preconditions and characteristics present, we are no longer dealing with this spiritual gift as portrayed in *The Acts of the Apostles*, but another counterfeit gift simply bearing the same name.

Holy Mountain, it has been observed that foreign monks with a limited knowledge of Greek may be unable to communicate well with their spiritual father outside of the mystery of confession, but within that mystery they both understand and are understood. It is also said that there was an instance of such a gift with the Elder Paissios the Athonite that in many ways resembled what took place with the Elder Poryphyrios.

Bibliography

Primary Sources Cited

Anonomous Hesychast, *Neptic Theoria,* Sacred Monastery of Xenophontos: Holy Mountain, 1996 (in Greek).

Igumen Chariton, *The Art of Prayer*, trans. by E. Kadloubovsky and E. Palmer, Faber and Faber: London, 1985.

Cyril of Alexandria, "In Epistolam I AD CORINTHIOS" The Extent Works, volume 7 PATROLOGIÆ CURSUS COMPLETUS, 74, ed. by J. P. Migne: Paris, 1859 (in Greek).

Dorotheos of Gaza, *Discourses and Sayings,* trans. by Eric Wheeler, Cistercian Publications: Kalamazoo, 1977.

Gregory of Nyssa, "Discourse on the Holy Spirit or On Pentecost" taken from *The Complete Works of Gregory of Nyssa, 11 Festal Discourses, Eucomiums, and Burial Orations* Greek Fathers of the Church,text, trans. (into modern Greek), and comments by Ignatios Sakalis, Gregory Palamas Patristic Publications, Thessalonika, 1991 (in Greek).

Gregory of Nyssa, "Polemic Against Eunomios," *The Complete Works of Gregory of Nyssa, 2 Dogmatic Works: Discourses Against Eunomius* Greek Fathers of the Church text, trans. (into modern

Greek), and comments by Ignatios Sakalis, Gregory Palamas Patristic Publications, Thessalonika, 1987 (in Greek).

Gregory Palamas, *On Behalf of the Sacred Hesychasts Triad 1, The Works of Gregory Palamas,* vol. 1, *Roman Fathers of the Church,* edited by John S. Romanidis, text, trans. (into modern Greek) and comments by Despoina Kontostergios, Pournara Publications, Thessalonica, 1984 (in Greek).

_____, "Homily 24 on Pentecost" taken from *The Complete Works of Gregory Palamas, 76: Homilies 21-52,* Greek Fathers of the Churchtext, trans. (into modern Greek), and comments by Panagiotos Christos, Gregory Palamas Patristic Publications, Thessalonika, 1985 (in Greek).

Gregory the Theologian, "Discourse 41 on Pentecost" *The Complete Works of Gregory the Theologian: Discourses 5,* Greek Fathers of the Church, text, trans. (into modern Greek), and comments by Nicholas Apostolakis, Gregory Palamas Patristic Publications, Thessalonika, 1977 (in Greek).

Hagin, Kenneth, *Concerning Spiritual Gifts,* Rhema Bible Church: Tulsa Oklahoma, 1985.

Isaac the Syrian, *The Ascetical Homilies,* trans. by Holy Transfiguration Monastery, Holy Transfiguration Monastery: Boston, 1984.

John Chrysostom, *Commentary on the Acts of the Apostles* taken from *The Complete Works of John*

Chrysostom 15, *Commentary on the Acts of the Apostles (Homilies 4-23)*, Greek Fathers of the Church, trans. (into modern Greek) and comments by Christos Krikonis, Gregory Palamas Patristic Publications, Thessalonika, 1983 (in Greek).

_____, *Commentary on the First Epistle to the Corinthians* taken from *The Complete Works of John Chrysostom* 18A, *Commentary on First Corinthians (Discourses 22-44)*, Greek Fathers of the Churchtext, trans. (into modern Greek), and comments by Ioannis Pelitis, Gregory Palamas Patristic Publications, Thessalonika, 1980 (in Greek).

_____, "Second Homily on the Holy Spirit" The Complete Extent Works, volume 4 *PATROLOGIÆ CURSUS COMPLETUS, 50,* ed. by J. P. Migne, Paris, 1859 (in Greek).

John Climacus, *The Ladder of Divine Ascent,* trans. by Holy Transfiguration Monastery (Holy Transfiguration Monastery: Brookline, 1991).

John of Damascus, *Commentary on Romans First Corinthians, and Second Corinthians, The Complete Works of John Damascus* 11 Greek Fathers of the Church text, trans. (into modern Greek), and comments by Eleutherios Meretakis, Gregory Palamas Patristic Publications, Thessalonika, 1993 (in Greek).

Laggis, Matthew ed., *The Great Synaxaristis of the Orthodox Church,* vol. I., Month of January, Matthew Laggis: Athens, 1980 (in Greek).

BIBLIOGRAPHY

_____, *The Great Synaxaristis of the Orthodox Church,* vol. V., Month of May Matthew Laggis: Athens, 1985 (in Greek).

_____, *The Great Synaxaristis of the Orthodox Church,* vol. VI., Month of June, Matthew Laggis: Athens, 1985 (in Greek).

_____, *The Great Synaxaristis of the Orthodox Church,* vol. XI., Month of November Matthew Laggis: Athens, 1982 (in Greek).

Hieromonk Makarios, *The Synaxarion: The Lives of the Saints of the Orthodox Church,* trans. by Christopher Hookway, vol. 1, (Holy Convent of the Annunciation of Our Lady, Ormilia: 1998).

Nicholas Cabasilas, *On the Divine Liturgy and Life in Christ,* 22 Philokalia of Neptic and Ascetic Fathers, text, trans. (into modern Greek), and comments by Panagiotis Christos, Gregory Palamas Patristic Publications, Thessalonika, 1979 (in Greek).

Nicodemos of the Holy Mountain, *Way of the Feasts.* 3, Orthodox Kipseli, Thessalonika, 1987 (in Greek).

_____, *The Fourteen Epistles of the Divine and Glorious Apostle Paul interpreted in Greek by Theophylact Archbishop of Bulgarius and translated in the more common dialect and commented on by Nicodemos of the Holy Mountain.* Book 1, Saint Nicodemos Press: Athens, 1971 (in Greek).

Nicodemos of the Holy Mountain and St. Makarios of Corinth, *The Philokalia: The Complete Text* trans. by G.E.H. Palmer,Philip Sherrard, and Kallistos Ware, 4 vols., Faber and Faber: London, 1979-1995.

Origen, "On Prayer," *Library of Greek Fathers andEcclesiastical Writers,* v. 10, part 2 Apostolic Diaconia of the Church of Greece: Athens, 1957 (in Greek).

_____, "On the Psalms," *Library of Greek Fathers and Ecclesiastical Writers,* v. 15, part 6, Apostolic Diaconia of the Church of Greece: Athens, 1957 (in Greek).

Prayer Book for Orthodox Christians, translated by Holy Transfiguration Monastery, Holy Transfiguration Monastery: Boston, 1995.

Rubrics and Service of the Great and Angelic Monastic Schema, Zealot Hagiorite Fathers: the Holy Mountain, 1983.

Symeon the New Theologian, *Catechetical Discourse* (8-34),*Philokalia of the Neptic and Ascetic Fathers,* 14D, text, trans. (into modern Greek), and comments by Demetrius Rizo and Katherine Goltsou, Gregory Palamas Patristic Publications, Thessalonika, 1989 (in Greek).

Writings from the Philokalia on Prayer od the Heart, trans. by E. Kadloubovsky and G.E. Palmer (London, Faber and Faber: 1992).

BIBLIOGRAPHY
Secondary Sources

Alevizopoulos, Fr. Anthony, *Handbook of Heresies and ParaChristian Groups*, Preveza: Sacred Metropoliate of Nikopolis and Prevsezis, 1991 (in Greek).

_____, *The Occult, Ghurus, and the New Age*, Anthony Alevizopoulos: Athens, 1990 (in Greek).

Capsanis, Archimandrite George, *Experiences of the Grace of God*, Holy Monastery of Saint Gregorios: Mount Athos, 1995 (in Greek).

Kessolopoulos, Anestis, *The Passions and the Virtues According to the Teaching of Saint Gregory Palamas*, Domos Publishers: Athens, 1990 (in Greek).

Kokoris, Dimitrios Th. *Pentecostalism: Heresy and Deception*, Dimitrius Kokoris: Athens, 1997 (in Greek).

Kontostergios, Despoinis, *The Ecumenical Councils*, Pournara: Thessalonica, 1997 (in Greek).

Larchet, Jean-Claude, *The Healing of Spiritual Diseases*, Les Editions de l'Ancre: Suresnes, 1993, (in French).

Liardon, Roberts, *God's Generals Why They Succeeded and Why Some Failed*, Aubury Publishing: Tulsa, Oklahoma, 1996.

Limouris, Gennadios ed., *Come, Holy Spirit Renew the Whole Creation*, Holy Cross Orthodox Press: Brookline, 1990.

Morris, John Warren, *The Charasmatic Movement: An Orthodox Evaluation,* Holy Cross Press: Boston, 1994.

Romanides, Fr. John, "Notes on the Palamite Controversy and Related Topics II", *Greek Orthodox Theological Review* 9:2, 1963-64.

_____, *The Dogmatic and Symbolic Theology of the Orthodox Catholic Church,* vol. 1, Pournara: Thessalonica, 1983).

_____, Fr. John, *The Ancesteral Sin,* Domos: Athens, 1992 (in Greek).

_____, "Criteria on the Application of Theology," (in Greek).

Rose, Fr. Seraphim, *God's Revelation to the Human Heart,* Saint Herman of Alaska Brotherhood, Platina: 1997.

_____, *Orthodoxy and the Religion of the Future*, Saint Herman of Alaska Brotherhood, Platina: 1996.

Sakharov, Archimandrite Sophrony, *Saint Silouan the Athonite,* trans. By Rosemary Edmons Stavropegic Monasttery of Saint John the Baptist: Essex, 1991.

Theotokis, Nicephoros, *Way of the Sundays,* ed. by Mathaios Laggis volume iv, Monastery of the

BIBLIOGRAPHY

Transfiguration of the Savior: Athens, 1976 (in Greek).

Velmirovicv, Bishop Nikolai, *Homilies,* vol I, trans. by Mother Maria Lazarica Press: Birmingham, 1996.

Vlachos, Hierotheos, *Orthodox Psychotherapy, The Science of the Fathers,* trans. by Esther Williams, Birth of the Theotokos Monastery, Levadia: 1994.

Yiannitsiotis, Constantine, *Near the Elder Porphyrius,* The Sacred Woman's Hesychastirion The Transfiguration of the Savior, Athens, 1995 (in Greek).

Zografos, Theodore, *Delighful Echoes of Glorious Greece: Way of the Sundays for the Book of the Epistles,* book 2, Literary Press of Athanasius Plataniptos: Volo, 1914 (in Greek).

THE FAITH

Understanding Orthodox Christianity, An Orthodox Catechism

By Clark Carlton

Editorial Committee: Metropolitan **ISAIAH** (GOA Denver) Archbishop **DMITRI** (OCA Dallas)
Bishop **BASIL** (Antiochian Archdiocese Wichita)

"An indispensable guide!"

Archbishop DMITRI (OCA Dallas)

"The best-written Orthodox catechism ever."

Metropolitan ISAIAH (GOA Denver)

"A joyous event in the life of the Church."

Bishop BASIL (Antiochian Archdiocese Wichita)

THE FAITH is the best Orthodox catechism in the English language. It is also the most widely used by English-speaking Orthodox all over the world. **THE FAITH** is a beautifully written book that fully answers the question, *"What is it you Orthodox believe?"*

THE FAITH includes: The foundation of Orthodox faith + The Holy Trinity + Creation + The fall of mankind + The promised Messiah + The Incarnation + The teachings of Christ + The birth and mission of the Church + The structure of the Church + Holy Baptism + The Holy Spirit + The Mystical Supper + The Church at prayer and fasting + The mystery of love + God and gender + Monasticism + The Lord's *return* + *more...*
$22.95 286 Pages   ISBN 0-9649141-1-5

THE WAY

What Every Protestant Should Know About the Orthodox Church

By Clark Carlton

"I recommend this book to seekers of truth, to Protestants or others trying to find their way to the Christian faith of the Apostles. Those Orthodox who wish to fully understand our faith should also read this book."
Archbishop **DMITRI**

"I wish I had read this book twenty years ago! It would have saved me years of spiritual wondering and brought me into the Orthodox church."

Frank Schaeffer

THE WAY is the highly praised and best-selling sequel to "The Faith." In a clear, well-written style Carlton introduces the Orthodox Church to the non-Orthodox in a way that has drawn many converts to the Church and deepened the faith of countless others. This is a great book for group study and the companion to "The Faith."

THE WAY includes: *Sola Scriptura*, the Protestant mistake + Proof-texts and the real teachings of the Church + The nature of tradition + The structure of worship in the Early church + The Protestant Reformation in the light of the Orthodox Church + A personal conversion story - from Southern Baptist to Orthodox and more...
$22.95 222 Pages ISBN 0-9649141-2-3

MORE FROM REGINA ORTHODOX PRESS
CHECK OR CREDIT CARD INFO A <u>MUST!</u>

BUY 5 ITEMS OR MORE *SAVE 40%* ON

BOOKS/BIBLES

#_____ THE TRUTH		$22.95
#_____ THE THIRD MILLENNIUM BIBLE		$45.00
#_____ THE NON ORTHODOX		$19.95
#_____ TWO PATHS		$22.95
#_____ THE SCANDAL OF GENDER		$22.95
#_____ ETERNAL DAY		$22.95
#_____ THE FAITH		$22.95
#_____ THE WAY		$22.95
#_____ DANCING ALONE		$20.00

CD ROM'S

#_____ HOLY WEEK		$45.00
#_____ PILGRIMAGE TO MT ATHOS		$45.00

VIDEO TAPES

#_____ THE DEFENSE OF ORTHODOXY		$59.85
#_____ ORTHODOX EVANGELISM		$29.95
#_____ PERSONAL JOURNEY - ORTHODOXY		$19.95
#_____ TRUE STATE OF THE UNION		$19.95

MUSIC CD'S

#_____ GATES OF REPENTANCE		$19.95
#_____ FIRST FRUITS		$19.95
Subtotal		$_____
MA residents add 5% sales tax		$_____

BUY 5 ITEMS OR MORE *SUBTRACT 40%* $_____

Add 10% for shipping (Non-USA 20%) $_____

GRAND TOTAL $_____

NAME _____

ADDRESS _____

CITY _____

STATE _____ ZIP _____

E-MAIL _____

PHONE _____

MC or VISA # _____ exp. _____

SIGNATURE _____

REGINA ORTHODOX PRESS PO BOX 5288 SALISBURY MA 01952 USA

TOLL FREE 800 636 2470 Fax 978 462 5079 non-USA 978 463 0730 \

QUESTIONS??? www.reginaorthodoxpress.com